6/15/50

The County Books Series

GENERAL EDITOR: BRIAN VESEY-FITZGERALD

CUMBERLAND AND WESTMORLAND

THE COUNTY BOOK SERIES

PLEASE WRITE TO THE PUBLISHERS
FOR FULL DESCRIPTIVE PROSPECTUS

CUMBERLAND AND WESTMORLAND

by

NORMAN NICHOLSON

LONDON
ROBERT HALE LIMITED
18 Bedford Square W.C.1

First published, 1949

THIS BOOK IS PRODUCED IN
COMPLETE CONFORMITY WITH THE
AUTHORIZED ECONOMY STANDARDS

Printed in Great Britain by
Billing and Sons Ltd., Guildford and Esher
F9560

To

WALTER WILSON, ESQ.

Schoolmaster
and
Friend

ACKNOWLEDGMENTS

My grateful acknowledgments are due to the many people who have helped me during my work on this book. I have found everywhere the most ready and generous response to my inquiries: recognised authorities and experts have been very willing to give me advice and criticism based on a lifetime's study.

In particular I would like to thank the following who have read part of the script: Mr. J. L. Hobbs, Mr. E. B. Hughes, Mr. J. Melville, the late Mr. T. W. Ogilvie, F.G.S., and Mr. and Mrs. G. Ward, all of the Barrow Naturalists' Field Club (and especially Mr. Hobbs, who has answered innumerable letters of inquiry); also Major W. D. Barrett, Mr. R. Davis, Mr. T. S. Durham, Miss M. C. Fair, Mr. A. W. McLaren, and Mr. W. Wilson.

Also to the following, who have given me information on particular matters: Mrs. Michael Roberts, Mr. J. R. Webb and the Stationmaster at Ravenglass. Also to the Librarians at Tullie House, Carlisle (with the magnificent collection of books of local interest in the Jackson Library), the Cumberland County Library and the Millom Public Library.

I must mention two works of reference which I have found continually useful: *The Victoria County History of Cumberland* and *The Transactions of the Cumberland and Westmorland Archæological Society*.

Finally, I wish to thank Miss Garnier, who has read and typed the longest and most illegible script I have ever written, and Mr. R. C. Morton and Mr. W. Wilson, who have gone to great trouble to get the photographs I wanted. In search of these photographs they have followed the principle laid down at the beginning of the book when I claim that, geographically, North Lonsdale belongs more with Cumberland and Westmorland than with Lancashire south of the Sands.

N. N.

CONTENTS

PART I

ILLUSTRATIONS

ACKNOWLEDGMENTS

*The illustrations above, numbered 10, 13, 30, 35, 36, 37, 38,
46 are reproduced from photographs by Mr. W. Wilson of Ulverston; 2, 5, 15, 20, 31 by Mr. Reece Winstone, A.R.P.S., of
Bristol. The remaining 36 are from photographs supplied by
Mr. R. C. Morton of Millom.*

PART I

CHAPTER I

THE LIE OF THE LAND

THE area with which we have to deal is that of Cumberland and Westmorland, together with Lancashire north of the Sands—the districts of Furness and Cartmel. This north-west part of Lancashire is detached from the main area of the county by the estuary of the river Kent and by a promontory of Westmorland. It contains two lakes (Coniston and Esthwaite) and borders on another (Windermere), and it includes the Coniston range of fells. Its geology, flora, people, dialect, place-names and customs belong to Cumberland and Westmorland rather than to Lancashire. It has an essential place in the main geographical system of the Lake Counties, a system of central mountains, radiating valleys and surrounding plains. There is every reason, therefore, why it should be included in this book. But Cumberland and Westmorland are large and rather sprawling counties which contain at least two outlying areas which do not belong to this central system. In the north, above the Roman Wall, there is an area which belongs to the Border. And to the east, running the whole length of the two counties, there is the Pennine Chain. Though these areas are both within the boundaries of the two counties, and though they may seem to have similar scenery and their inhabitants to have a similar way of life, they are really foreign to the Lake System.

The area which I call the Lake System is a large one, spreading a long way beyond the lakes. It is roughly an oval or ellipse standing on end. Its apexes are Carlisle in the north and Carnforth in the south; its borders are the coast on the west, and on the east the valleys of the Eden and the Lune, or perhaps a line a little nearer the Yorkshire border. Inside this area there is a great variety. In the centre there is the mountain dome, sliced with valleys, mostly rocky and half-barren, or fertile only along the riversides. North and south of the mountains are lowlands of good farming

I

land, with a few busy self-contained manufacturing towns, like Carlisle and Kendal. On the west, sweeping from tip to tip of the oval, is the coast, which varies from the immense sands of Morecambe Bay to the equally immense marshes of the Solway Firth. It includes estuaries and ports, limestone and sandstone rocks, and the long severe bulge of South Cumberland, where the mountains slant almost to the sea. Along the coast, too, and near it, are two important mining and industrial areas: the coalfield and iron ore of West Cumberland, and the iron ore of Furness, with the steel and shipbuilding towns of Workington, Whitehaven and Barrow.

But in spite of this great variety in scenery, in occupation, and in way of life, there is an astonishing unity. The country of Cumberland, Westmorland and North Lonsdale is one country; the people are one people. Whitehaven belongs to the same unit as Keswick (both owe their existence primarily to mining), and the shepherd of the High Street Fells is of the same stock as the shipbuilder of Barrow-in-Furness. A casual glance at the map seems to confirm this unity, for you see a huge cart-wheel pattern of lakes and valleys which focuses somewhere about Dunmail Raise or Fairfield in the Helvellyn range. But this physical unity has a dis-uniting effect. For the society of the district, the hub is not a focal point but a point of departure. Two people living twenty miles apart or less on opposite sides of the hub might be a hundred miles apart for social purposes. Each dale is divided from the next by high ridges. There are passes and roads, and the country offers no real obstacles to energetic people—we hear, for instance, of a young man who would climb a thousand feet and walk half a dozen miles each night, just to see the light burning in the bedroom of his girl in the next dale. But for practical and social purposes the life of the dales does not leap-frog from one to another over the ridges, but flows up and down the valley. Indeed, like the becks, it flows from the dale-head, gathering its tributaries from farms and hamlets till it reaches the lowlands. Here it usually finds a village or small town, which acts as a warehouse and post-office for the dale, or perhaps several dales. Such towns are Keswick, Cleator Moor, Gosforth, Broughton-in-Furness, Ambleside—some of which

2

have grown in size and importance for other reasons. These towns form a sort of inner ring round the mountains. Beyond this there is an outer ring of market towns, most of them rather larger than those already mentioned, where real contact is made between the dales and the lowlands. Such towns are Penrith, Appleby, Kendal, Ulverston, Whitehaven, Cockermouth, and (for the detached group of Caldbeck Fells in the north) Wigton. Some of these towns have become industrialised, but they still carry out their old function of market town for the surrounding district. To these should be added a few towns like Workington, Millom and Barrow-in-Furness, which are more purely industrial in origin, but whose position has made them useful for marketing. By now it is clear that the social life of the dales, packed close together at the centre, has diverged to the periphery of a huge circle. In most rural areas the life of the countryside flows naturally to one central town or group of towns—here the complete opposite is the case. The radiation cannot go on indefinitely, however, for to the west of this outer circle is the sea, and to the east the Pennines. In the northern lowlands the roads now converge on Carlisle, and in the southern on Lancaster, and these two ancient cities are the two main junctions through which the life of the dales, and indeed the whole of the counties, communicates with the rest of Great Britain.

How great is the diverging influence of the lie of the land can be seen by taking an example. There are two Seathwaites in Cumberland, both dale villages. From one to the other is less than ten miles as the raven flies. Men are not ravens, but even for men the route by Grain Ghyll, Esk Hause, Upper Eskdale and Mosedale is not much farther, though it is certainly rough. From the head of Grain Ghyll to the head of Mosedale (which, as regards this track, may be considered the daleheads of the two Seathwaite valleys) the distance is only three or four miles. One of the two villages is in Borrowdale, which runs due north, and the other in Dunnerdale, which runs south. The farmer's wife in Borrowdale does her shopping in Keswick: her neighbour in Dunnerdale goes down to Broughton, and beyond to Ulverston or Barrow. Barrow and Keswick are not widely separated to anyone with a private car, but private cars are not the dalesman's traditional means of transport. If, then, he tries to go from Barrow to Keswick by train he will be lucky to do the journey in four hours, even if he has the best of connections at Whitehaven and Workington. If he tries to go by bus, he will have a bewildering set of changes, and probably more than one bilious attack.

Yet, in spite of all these disuniting influences, and in spite of the great difficulties of communication, Cumberland, Westmorland and North Lonsdale form a whole, an entity, a small, separate and self-contained kingdom. This is partly due to the common Norse ancestry of the people, but more to the nature of the land, which imposes upon them a peculiar and uniform way of life. From the tenth century onward there grew up in the dales a group of small communities, poor, austere, largely self-subsistent, and always self-reliant. Even when the industrial revolution opened up new districts in West Cumberland and Furness, the same tradition peristed, for mining had been carried on in Cumberland for two thousand years, and the new towns found themselves in the nineteenth century almost as isolated as the lakes. The dalesman had always been on good terms with the miner of the lowlands. It is only since the development of a suburban class in the towns and the settlement in the dales of a race of resident tourists that there has arisen the snobbery which does not recognise the western industrial districts as part of the Lake District proper.

The Two Cartwheels

To tell of this unity will be one of the main aims of this book. For the moment we will discuss the means of communication which have been dictated by the shape and substance of the land. First, the central mountain dome.

The system of fells and dales has often been compared to a cartwheel, but a more careful look at the map shows that it falls into two cartwheel patterns, separated by the north and south fault along which lie Thirlmere, Grasmere, Rydal Water and Windermere. The hub of the western system is at Esk Hause; that of the eastern, at Helvellyn. Perhaps the most satisfactory image for the western system, however, is that of a lemon-squeezer, with the dales gouged out of the dome, and sloping radially. If, too, you imagine a crack along the right side of the lemon-squeezer, so that the bottom of the grooves are shortened, you get something of the effect of the Thirlmere-Windermere fault. The dales on that side of the dome are all short, and descend steeply to lake level from Bowfell, Langdale Pikes and the Coniston Fells. Easedale and the two Langdales turn south to Windermere; and the little valleys on the south-eastern slope of Wetherlam and Coniston Old Man turn into Yewdale and Coniston Water. Through the whole of the western semicircle from north to south the dales radiate in regular order: Borrowdale, the Buttermere-Crummock valley, Ennerdale, Wasdale, Eskdale and Dunnerdale, with smaller dales like Newlands, Miterdale, and the valleys of the Calder and the Bleng, to fill up the cracks, or rather to make minor grooves between the larger ones. The eastern cartwheel, which lies largely in Westmorland, is much less complete in pattern. It has two major dales, Patterdale and Mardale, both of which lie north-east. Westward there are only the ghylls which run to the Thirlmere-Windermere fault. To the south, the Troutbeck valley flows into Windermere about two miles above Bowness. South-east several valleys, of which those of the Kent and the Sprint are the largest, find their way eventually to Kendal.

The main lines of communication by road and railway enclose both these cartwheels in a rough bulging circle, of which the corners—for it is so odd a circle it has corners— are Whitehaven, Barrow, Kendal and Penrith. The route from Kendal to Penrith passes over Shap Fell, and a further out-fling along the valleys of the Lune and the Eden, via Kirkby Lonsdale, Tebay and Appleby, loops in the fells of eastern Westmorland. Across the diameter of this circle there is no railway, but there is a main road along the Thirlmere-Windermere fault, from Keswick to Ambleside and thence to the southern lowlands. Another main road from Penrith and up Patterdale, crosses Kirkstone Pass and joins the Windermere route by the Troutbeck valley.

The eastern cartwheel is divided by motor roads, but the western cannot be crossed except on foot. Whinlatter

Pass, Honister Pass, the Birker Moor road from Ulpha to Boot, and other minor roads, all cut off corners, but do not cross the circle. Nevertheless, the walker can visit each one of the dales of the western hub by hopping from one to another over the passes at the head of each. Starting in the north: from Borrowdale over Honister to Buttermere; from Buttermere over Scarf Gap to Ennerdale; from Ennerdale over Black Sail to Wasdale; from Wasdale by Burnmoor Tarn to mid-Eskdale, or by the Stye Head track, Sprinkling Tarn and Esk Hause to Upper Eskdale; from Eskdale over Hardknott to Dunnerdale; from Dunnerdale over Wrynose to Little Langdale; from Little Langdale by Blea Tarn to Great Langdale; and from Great Langdale up Mickleden, over Stake Pass, down Lang Strath into Borrowdale again. Stye Head Pass, from Borrowdale to Wasdale, is the chief route from north to south-west, and the two passes of Wrynose and Hardknott that from east to west. By means of these passes and Esk Hause, it is possible to walk from one dale to any other without a very great detour, though the path from north-west to south-east has many high obstacles.

The Cockermouth-Keswick-Penrith route skirts the northern rim of the dales, but beyond it is another large block of fells, with Skiddaw and Saddleback almost overhanging the route itself, and lower fells stretching farther north to Caldbeck.

The Shap Route

In the comparative lowlands north of the Caldbeck Fells and south of the Furness Fells there is the usual network of roads which is to be found in almost any part of rural England. But there are two main routes from Carlisle to Carnforth, around the outward edges of the oval, which need special notice. The first is the Shap route. This is the more familiar to people who live outside the two counties. It is of great historical importance, and is the main route from England to Scotland. Prince Charlie marched down by it in 1745, and shortly afterwards he was chased back by the Duke of Cumberland over the same way. It is by this route that most visitors approach the Lake District, branching off at Carnforth, or Kendal, or Penrith. Yet in many ways to

6

Kirkstone Pass from the Patterdale side

approach the district from this quarter gives a deceptive view, for it ignores the sea, which, next to the rock, has had the greatest formulative influence on the life and character of the two counties. Cumberland, as many people forget, is a maritime county. So is North Lonsdale. Westmorland only touches the coast at Arnside, but nevertheless its development has been influenced by the sea.

The Coastal Route

It is the second route, then, the long coastal route, which probably has had the greater importance in the lives of the people. It is a slow route. In the North Lonsdale section it is continually interrupted by estuaries, which send the road sweeping inwards in great scallops. In the long stretch from Millom to Whitehaven, where the mountains come down nearly to the sea, the road carefully avoids the level strip by the coast, and goes bumping over spurs and foothills, following what was once the line of cart-tracks from farm to farm. The railway, too, after being laid down rather later in the last century than in most parts of England, offers a slow journey, with magnificent views up the river-mouths, but with many stops. Along the rocky coast near St. Bees it is a single-line track, and the trains often wait in little coast-side stations for other trains to pass. For the commercial traveller, the lorry-driver, the man who wants to do the Lakes in a week-end, this route is a bugbear. Many of the people of West Cumberland prefer to travel to London by Carlisle, and the Furness people to approach Scotland by Carnforth. Yet for centuries the main stream of life in the two counties has flowed along the coast route. The Romans established a port at Ravenglass, possibly for the purpose of invading Ireland. Another invasion on the same coast, an *incoming* invasion, that of the Norsemen, decided the stock and the traditions of the people for a thousand years. The medieval packhorses passed up and down the coast, crossing the sands of Morecambe Bay and the Duddon Estuary at low tide. They continued long after the Middle Ages, indeed right up to the eighteenth and nineteenth centuries, and the tracks they used across the sand were marked by stakes or branches of broom known as Brogs, and guides were posted like pilots at

7 B

Foxfield Sands—evening

the estuarine towns. Later these tracks were used by private carriages, and by herds of sheep and cattle which were driven from Scotland, from Ireland and the Solway ports to the slaughter-houses of Lancashire. Even after the railways were built, carriers used to cross the sands, bringing goods and passengers of the poorer sort. Many, no doubt—sheep, cattle, horses and men—never got across. The quicksands are notorious, and not always in the same place. More treacherous, probably, is the incoming tide, for the water can rise in the channels, making curls and knots all round the traveller, and he unaware of it, because it is hidden in the steep-sided deep gulleys. Once the tide has poured over the kerb of the gulleys, however, it can cover acres of sand or marsh in a very short time. One minute the traveller is out in a huge plain, the flat wet sands all round, the coast far away and seemingly high above him. Even the low dunes or limestone rocks on the shore seem to make a high skyline, shutting him off from the world in a great hollow that is neither sea nor land. The tide rises six or nine inches and at once he is a mile or two out at sea, floundering about up to his ankles and looking like St. Peter walking on the waters. Then, unless he is a swimmer, he will find it hard to get back to the shore, for the gullies and the firm sand look very much alike under the water. Indeed, he might well be advised to stay quietly on his ridge of sand and trust that the tide will not rise above his head.

I have seen sheep follow the same policy. They are allowed to roam freely on most of the estuary marshes when the tides are low, but they are brought into the fields at times of high tides. These sheep—they were on the Duddon estuary— had been left on the marsh a day nearer spring tide than was really safe. They were feeding far out on the moss, on a turfy hump, when the tide outflanked them along the gulleys. For a while they remained on a little island, feeding quietly, taking no notice of the water. Then the tide flowed across the place where they were standing. Reluctantly they raised their heads from the grass, but otherwise they made no movement. The water rose a foot or two and still they were undisturbed. It was summer, and probably the water was fairly warm; at any rate, not till it rose to their necks were they alarmed. Then they started to baa, and a few plunged about, trying to find a ford. When their necks were stretched as far as they would go to keep above the water, the tide turned, and in a few minutes they were on nominally dry land again, and every sheep, without moving a step, put down its head and began to crop the grass.

To travellers with more imagination than sheep, however, the crossing of the sands of Morecambe has always been adventurous. Even now the railway, which runs along the edge of the marsh and crosses the rivers by viaducts, offers an exciting journey. And this route is not only attractive but of great commercial importance, for along it developed the two industrial areas of Furness and West Cumberland, and for a very large proportion of the inhabitants of the two counties these industrial areas are home.

CHAPTER II

ROCK BOTTOM

PERHAPS in no other part of England has the life and character of a district and its people been so controlled by the nature of the rock and by the forces which have acted upon it. In Cumberland and Westmorland the rock is indeed the land. The structure of the rock, together with the erosion of weather and ice, give the shape of the fells and dales, their character and vegetation. These dictated the agriculture and the development of small dale communities with a way of life which has persisted for centuries. Even when the industrial revolution came, it was the rock which laid down the form it was to take in the two counties, for it is coal and iron ore which have made modern Cumberland and Furness. The variety of landscape, the texture of a fell, the form of the buildings and even the appearance of the towns are all explained by the rock. To look at the scenery of Cumberland and Westmorland without trying to understand the rock is like listening to poetry in an unknown language—you hear the beauty of the sounds but you miss the meaning. For the meaning is in the rock.

But with even a little knowledge of the rock and the way it came into being the landscape is living and intelligible. It is even clearer to the eye, for differences of shape and texture become more apparent as you learn to distinguish the kinds of rock. Moreover, you get a greater respect for the land as it really is, and you lose the wish to treat it as a spectacle specially arranged to please you. Scafell, you realise, is Scafell—not just something to be looked at. It is certainly beautiful, but beauty is not its purpose. It has a function in the anatomy and machinery of the dales—the beauty is a by-product of the function.

The Old Geologists

Among the first people (apart from farmers and miners) to look at the Lake District *objectively* were the geologists. Jonathan Otley of Keswick brought a new type of observation to the dales—minute, exact and detached. He did not look at the landscape with a vision already fuzzy with adjectives.

The dales have been fortunate in producing many such men, and it is of them that we think most gratefully, rather than of the scholars, much as we owe to them, especially to Professor Sedgwick. Such a quiet and unpretentious student was John Bolton, whose *Geological Fragments*[1] is written in modest Victorian prose through which the kindly personality of the man glows like the sun through mist.

"Geology," he says, "has a peculiar tendency to induce the mind to reason upon long cycles of the past, forgetting the present and the future." And he tells how, when he was out on geologising expeditions, he would find that night would come before he was aware of its coming, and how he then would lie down under a rock and sleep till morning:

". . . to be caught up on a mountain by the approach of night is no great hardship to any man, but it belongs almost exclusively to the enthusiastic geologist to realise it. . . . These have been some of the pleasantest days of our life, and although we have seen seventy-nine birthdays, we are truly thankful to be blessed with health and strength for the work, even to this day, and we hope to have many more quiet and comfortable nights, free of cost at the 'Rock Hotel,' for there is a peculiar and awful solemnity in the thought of sleeping alone on the mountains, which the inexperienced cannot understand."

Wordsworth was not fond of geologists, and tackles them clumsily in some of his prosier passages,[2] but surely even he would have felt happy with old John Bolton. Wordsworth

[1] *Geological Fragments, Collected Principally from Rambles among the Rocks of Furness and Cartmel*: Atkinson, Ulverston, 1869.

[2] Here is what he says about the geologist in *The Excursion*, Book III:

> "He who with pocket-hammer smites the edge
> Of luckless rock or prominent stone, disguised
> In weather-stains or crusted o'er by Nature
> With her first growths, detaching by the stroke
> A chip or splinter—to resolve his doubts;
> And with that ready answer satisfied,
> The substance classes by some barbarous name,
> And hurries on; or from the fragments picks
> His specimen, if but haply interveined
> With sparkling mineral, or should crystal cube
> Lurk in its cells—and thinks himself enriched,
> Wealthier, and doubtless wiser, than before!"

presumably overcame some of this prejudice, since he incorporated Professor Sedgwick's Letters in his *Guide*. Professor Sedgwick refers to this passage in his first letter.

It is doubtful whether sleeping out on the mountains would have appealed greatly to Thomas Robinson, Rector of Ousby, yet he, too, deserves a place among the explorers of Lake District geology. In 1709 he published *An Essay towards a Natural History of Westmoreland and Cumberland*, which, as a casual appendix, has a "Vindication of the Philosophical and Theological Paraphrases of the Mosaick System of the Creation." Just before the end of the previous century he had published a shorter but even more ambitious book called *The Anatomy of the Earth*.[1] This is a curious but very entertaining pamphlet which combines the matter-of-fact style of late seventeenth century writing with the method of argument from analogy inherited from the Middle Ages. He compares the structure of the earth with that of an animal. The surface is the skin, which "became productive not only of Grass, Trees, and other Vegetables, as the skins of other Animals naturally grow hair; but, when it was in its full strength and vigour, it brought forth all kinds of Birds, Beasts and Serpents, as naturally as it now brings forth divers kinds of Insects, or, as the Skins of other Animals bring forth Lice." Likewise, the flesh is the subsoil; the bones are minerals; the bloodvessels are underground streams; the nerves and sinews are veins of metal; the belly is the centre of the earth. Indigestions and fevers in the body cause earthquakes and volcanoes; the circulation of the blood gives rise to springs and fountains. The Rector's observation is often keen and accurate, and is surpassed only by the ingenuity with which he uses it to support the wildest arguments. Thus, he pours great scorn on the suggestion that springs and fountains may be caused by rain and dews and "condensed air," for, he says, if this were true, they would dry up in summer and be more rapid in winter, which certainly is not the case. Surely nothing but the Cumberland weather could have produced that argument.

[1] Printed for J. Newton at the Three Pigeons in Fleet Street, 1694. It is reproduced in the *Transactions of the Cumberland and Westmorland Archæological Society*, New Series, vol. 5.

Words and Meaning

Any reader who wishes to get a detailed knowledge of the geology of the district will consult, of course, the authoritative books[1] on the subject. I wish to give here only a broad outline of the main features of the rock, and the way they affect the scenery and the life of the people.

The rocks of Cumberland and Westmorland, then, are of two sorts—sedimentary and igneous. If none of these rocks had been disturbed they would have rested one on the other like the layers of a huge liquorice all-sort with the oldest at the bottom and the newest at the top. This order has been broken up by cracks and bucklings in the rind of the earth, faults, and landslides and earthquakes, and also by the wearing away of the surface by rain and rivers and other erosive agents. But geologists are still able to get a very good idea of the order in which the rocks were laid down because of the fossils preserved in them. Enormous periods of time were needed for the deposition of each series of rocks, and during this time animal and vegetable life developed on the earth, and from their remains it is possible to estimate the period at which the rocks were found. Geologists have given names to these periods—they are not very pretty names, but they are useful, and I give below a table of the periods together with the chief deposits of each as they are found in our area.

Periods.	*Deposits.*
Post-Glacial	Sand-dunes, filling up of lakes, etc.
	Raised beaches.
Glacial	Boulders and boulder clay—modification of landscape by drift—scooping of valleys and lakes.
Jurassic	Lias—near Carlisle.
Triassic	Salt marls. Gypsum and sandstone —Walney Island.

[1] E.g., *The Geology of the Lake District*, by J. E. Marr; *British Regional Geology—Northern England*; and Professor Sedgwick's Letters printed in Wordsworth's *Guide to the Lakes*.

Periods.	Deposits.
PERMIAN	St. Bees and Penrith sandstones.
CARBONIFEROUS	Upper Carboniferous. Coal measures.
	Lower Carboniferous. Mountain limestone.
OLD RED SANDSTONE	Conglomerates.
SILURIAN	Silurian slates and grits of Westmorland and North Lonsdale.
ORDOVICIAN	Coniston Limestone series.
	Borrowdale Volcanic series.
	Skiddaw slates.

In Cumberland and Westmorland the older rocks are in the centre, with the newer rocks around them, rather like the rings of a tree. Thus we get a knot of Skiddaw slate, Borrowdale Volcanic Rocks and Silurian rocks, and round them a ring of limestone and an outer ring of sandstone, with a few patches of still younger rocks at the edge. But, of course, the rocks were not laid down in rings like that. It is rather that they were laid in layers, one above the other, and buckled into a huge dome. Then the rain got to work and peeled off the outer layers like slicing off the top of the onion, till in the middle the lower layers were exposed, and in the outer rings the upper layers. It was not quite so simple, because the laying-down and peeling-off process took place more than once, in many ups and downs, but the general effect is more or less the same.

The Old Rocks: Skiddaw Slate

The old rocks—and they are among the oldest in the world—are harder and tougher than the newer rocks, and they form the great central hump of the Lake District, with its spokes of fells and dales.

The oldest of the lot is the Skiddaw Slate. This is a mud-rock, laid down as the delta of a great river on the shores of a shallow sea. In comparison with the Borrowdale rocks it is softer, and though it is called a slate, it is not very slaty—that is, it does not easily split into thin slivers like roofing

14

slate. Here and there it does break up into small fragments, and makes screes, scabby and small and not nearly so impressive as those of Wastwater, but on the whole the surface disintegrates easily into soil so that grass can grow on it and heather. It wears smoothly, too, giving rounded outlines, with evenly falling slopes. These rocks occupy most of the north of the Lake District. Bassenthwaite, Crummock, Loweswater lie entirely in Skiddaw Slate; Derwentwater and Buttermere almost so; and Ennerdale Water and Ullswater have their lower reaches among it—though the Ullswater patch is separate from the main block. This main block has for its mountains Skiddaw itself, Saddleback,[1] all the fells around the Newlands valley, Grasmoor, Grizedale Pike and the fells around Whinlatter Pass, and westwards to the edge of the iron ore district. There are also a few outlying patches —that mentioned, around Ullswater, one near Shap, one across the Eden valley on Crossfell, and two in the southwest.

Skiddaw and Saddleback are the two most magnificent fells of this rock. They have long green slopes, more mathematical and ordered than the fells of the upper dales, yet sometimes with unexpected variations, like that surprising combe in the south side of Saddleback which gives it its name. They do not often break into crag, and for this reason do not look quite as high as they really are. Where the ice has sliced off their flanks, they can be abrupt and spectacular, diving down into the valleys with the running muscles of a sea-animal, but they can also be tamed, and, as landscape, dull (no part of Cumberland is dull in detail), as in the country north of Skiddaw. Yet tamed or fierce they are always animal and alive. The volcanic rocks are contorted and fantastic, like creatures of folk-lore, but the Skiddaw fells are like prehistoric monsters, still sleeping through the millennia of the rock, and sometimes not seeming to sleep.

---

[1] Saddleback is also known as Blencathra, but I find in practice that Cumberland people tend to use the older name for the village and the new one for the mountain. Moreover, Blencathra is associated in the minds of most inhabitants of Cumberland mining towns with the County Sanatorium for tuberculosis which is situated there overlooking the Keswick-Penrith railway.

The smoothness of the rock gives also an evenness of colour, different from the patch and jig-saw effects of the craggier districts, and this makes the fells look still more like animals, for grass or bracken or heather give a hide which bulges round the haunches and shoulders. Saddleback does not suggest any animal shape, yet it is always quietly watchful. Skiddaw is more of a pyramid, but an animal pyramid too, as if the pyramid could turn sphinx. But Black Combe (which is the largest outcrop of this slate in the south of the county) is the sphinx itself. Look at it from Silecroft shore, or Layriggs—the head has gone, certainly, but the chest muscles are there, and the paws with a huge gulley between them, slanting to Whicham, and the back stretching along White Combe, and the loins and ribs swelling above the valley. Even the last western outcrop of this slate, at Dent, near Cleator Moor, is also animal—a little pup monster, a Disney character, chubbily cheerful above the towns of the limestone district, the miner's pet, and a rare place for losing a reputation.

Each of the Skiddaw fells has its own individuality, yet they are all of the same family. They are epic or just narrative verse rather than the dramatic poetry of the volcanic rock. They are rhetorical rather than symbolic. Perhaps their finest and boldest effect is their size and solidity, the effect of sheer cubic content. Hollow out Saddleback and you have a dish-cover which would fit over London. All the people alive on the earth could easily be heaped inside the smallest of them. Moreover, many of them are rather isolated and you can see them complete and separate: Grizedale Pike seen across the lower hills on the western side of Derwentwater; or Skiddaw, seen from about the same place, slanting sheer from its top to Bassenthwaite. Most isolated of all is Black Combe, in the south-west, with only a low ripple of country to join it to the Eskdale fells ten miles away or more. Black Combe, indeed, is a familiar fell even to those who never visit the Lake District, for it dominates the coast from Scotland to central Lancashire, and can be seen from Liverpool and the Wirral. How many girls have walked on to the North Pier at Blackpool on a summer evening, and seen a round gumboil of a mountain heaving up into the sunset and dropping, apparently, straight into the sea? That is Black Combe, and that is Skiddaw Slate.

These Skiddaw rocks are of a dark heavy grey, sometimes with a blue-black tinge. In the deep ghylls which are often found around their spurs, the rock looks black at a distance. It is of no use for roofing slate, yet all round the lower slopes you will find small quarries where stones have been blasted for walls and building purposes. Walls and barns and the poorer cottages are built throughout the Lake District of the easiest material that comes to hand. Quite frequently blocks of slate and sandstone and even cobbles from the shore are all piled together where they are equally handy. And even in the district of the Skiddaw Slates the handiest stone is often volcanic rock from boulders which have been left there by the ice.

The Skiddaw Slate, however much it may be despised by builders and contractors, nevertheless paid its share to this rough stone-walling. The walls and the barns do not seem works of artificers—they seem to have grown like trees, for they are of the very stuff of the rock on which they stand. The stones of the walls are held together only by gravity, each stone fitted carefully against the others—there is no mortar, no soil. Yet they stand, and they keep their footing and balance on the steepest slopes, climbing high over crags even when there is quite an easy way round. On Saddleback the walls lie as if once they had covered the fell in a chain net, until it arched its back, and broke through at the top and left the tatters of the chain hanging about its flanks.

The quarries which provide the stone are no ill feature of the landscape. From a distance they may look like scars, but only the pock-marks on an old man's face, giving character to it. Individually, however, they are of great charm. I am thinking now not of the large commercial quarries such as you find among the other slates, but of small fellside pits, each to give a farmer stone to build a byre or make a road. There are scores of them all over the district, mostly abandoned, half-full of water. They are often on a steep slope so that one side of the quarry is level with the ground and the other high above you, the walls sloping up and round to it like a shovel that a grocer uses for weighing sugar. The rock is dark, and thorn trees bend over it, making it darker still. There are no ferns on the rock, but lichens and hairy bitter-cress which will grow anywhere. If the quarry is wide enough for soil to blow in there will be brambles on the ledges, hanging black-green and red throughout the winter. In winter, too, there is ice—not level, but knobbly stuff which breaks into brown chunks that can be rolled down the hillside to splinter as they bounce against stones. How often as a lad I longed for a house with a quarry in the back garden. One such house I know—the quarry is in the Coniston Flags, and two hard tennis courts have been made in the floor of it. In these quarries, too, you can see the variations and gradations in the colour and texture of the rock. Sometimes it is just dull grey, sometimes purple, sometimes green; and often you will see a band of quite a different colour running all round the quarry along the dip of the strata. That, surely, is a real rock-garden.

The Borrowdale Volcanic Series

After the Skiddaw Slates had been deposited, a number of volcanoes burst out in the district, perhaps still under the sea, and the land was heaped high with lava, breccias, ashes and volcanic dust. None of the volcanoes remain, of course, though it is thought that the main crater may have been near where Bassenthwaite is today, but the material which they ejected made the rocks which are now known as the Borrowdale Volcanic Series. These rocks form the central dome of the Lake District, and nearly all the dales lie among them. They run side by side with the Skiddaw Slates along the bottom of Saddleback; then skirt Derwentwater; across Honister, missing Buttermere and Crummock and leaving Ennerdale to the granophyre; down to Wasdale; then along the edge of the Eskdale Granite and the Black Combe Slate to the Duddon estuary. Their south-east boundary runs in a broadly curving line from Broughton-in-Furness, through Coniston, Ambleside, the Shap fells to the Eden valley. This includes nearly all the fells of the centre—the Scafell group, the Coniston-Wetherlam group, the Langdales, the Helvellyn range and the High Street range. Of the dales it includes Borrowdale, Wasdale, upper Eskdale, Dunnerdale,

18

Mardale and upper Patterdale. Of the larger lakes only Thirlmere and Haweswater lie entirely in volcanic rock, though Wastwater nearly does. These rocks were called by Professor Sedgwick "green slates and porphyries." Later geologists have divided them into groups, and I quote them, not because I pretend to be able to distinguish them, but because I like the sound of the names: Shap Rhyolite, Shap Andresite, Scafell Ashes and Breccias, Ullswater and Eycott Group, and Falcon Crag Group. They vary greatly in hardness. It is easy to see why, for the lavas, ashes and breccias[1] of which they were formed were of varying degrees of durability. This has had immense influence on the scenery. Lava being hard and the ash usually softer, we often get a terraced effect, steep lava cliffs and gentler ash slopes. But where the volcanic ash has been subjected to pressure and squeezed in at the sides, it turns to slate and then sometimes may be as hard as iron, and at others it weathers and rots along the lines of cleavage and breaks away in lumps or dribbles off as small stones. Look at the side of Scafell that drops down to Wasdale. Here is volcanic rock at its hardest, a sheer wall of rock which could take bombing and blasting and dynamiting as if they were flea-bites. The ice and the weather have made their marks, it is true, and there are long vertical grooves as if the rock had been combed with an iron comb. In the ghylls, too, there are trickles and slidings of scree, but still the rock is harder and more lasting than history. Where cleavage is greater, however, we find larger screes or a wreckage of broken-off boulders. The rain dribbles into wrinkles of the rock and there freezes, and, as it freezes, swells. This is a sort of geological rheumatism. The needles of ice swell in the joints of the rock, and split it, till deep cracks are formed, and the surface chips and flakes away. The screes which result are very characteristic of the dale scenery. A scree, academically, is a slope of loose stones in a state of unstable equilibrium—in other words, if you step on one it slides. Sometimes the stones are quite large, sometimes, if they are left undisturbed, soil accumulates and grass grows over them. Sometimes torrents form

---

[1] A breccia is a sort of conglomerate of bits and pieces of rock, some tiny, some of considerable size, all cemented together.

among them in times of heavy rain, and wash them into lakes or rivers, making little stony deltas.

The screes which the climber recognises, however, are the long cindery slopes of small stones which slither under the feet. The most magnificent examples in the district are those of Wasdale. Here, at the lower end of the lake, there is a huge curtain of scree, falling stones held in suspension, dropping 1,500 feet into the water. The screes, as they slide, grow and gather like streams, widening and curving, till at the foot they fan out into a series of scallops on the shore of the lake. The whole slope stands in fluted tapering columns, shaped very much like the fan-vaulting of a cathedral turned upside down.

To run down screes is one of the delights of the climber, when he knows how to do it—not, probably, the Wasdale screes, for there you are likely to end up in the lake, and it's not shallow. They are not as steep as they look, of course. If they were, the stones would fall. Wasdale Screes, seen from across the lake, look almost perpendicular, but the angle of the slope is really less than 45—they fall 1,500 feet in about three furlongs. Nevertheless, when going over the top of a scree for the first time, it looks steep enough. The secret of confidence is simple—when in danger, when giddy, when losing your balance, just sit down. The scree will not be far behind the part of you that sits. Scree running is really a series of strides with each stride carrying you many feet, according to the flexibility of the scree. You need good boots, or your ankles will be skinned. You need good socks, too, for I have found that after running down a scree holes appear, not at the ankles, but underneath the heels and the backs of the toes. Sometimes you may want to cross a patch of scree horizontally. This is difficult, as if you slide you have to climb the height you have lost. The method is to stand perfectly upright. If you lean in towards the scree your feet will push the stones in the direction in which they want to slide; if you stand upright the pressure of your feet helps to hold the stones steady.

Volcanic rock shows its character no less noticeably when it has a covering of soil. It is rarely an even covering, for crags and patches of scree break through in many places, but there is thin soil on the slopes, and more on the ledges and in the combes. The covering varies as much as the rock does. Here there is grass, here bracken, here (though less of it) heather. Up the ghylls gorse creeps, and, quite surprisingly high, rowans and thorns, often growing in the little bumps and saucers at the foot of scratchings of scree. Higher up, above the level of the trees, the vegetation is still variegated, spotted and striped, as if not even the grass could grow smoothly there. The colour, too, is variegated—brown and yellow and red among the greens and blues—and everywhere the rock is poking its fingers out, or crooking a neck round to have a look at itself. On Harter Fell, for instance, a hill in Dunnerdale which is not often climbed, the texture of the rock seems alive, as if the fell were continually scratching off the scabs of grass and herbs which try to cover it. Standing at the bottom you can scarcely see a path up to the summit, which does not dodge round outcrops of rock and scree. Yet Harter Fell is a comparatively tamed and docile mountain.

It is this texture which gives to the dales their unity— there is no clear division between dale and fell. Stubborn little fields of roots hang high among the crags, and rocks break out even in riverside meadows. The Skiddaw fells stand rather aloof above the lowlands: Skiddaw himself seems scarcely to have noticed Bassenthwaite Lake. But the fells of the dales are one with the becks and the ghylls. In the slate country, the normal level is that of the lowlands, and the mountains lift themselves above it. In the dales the sky line is the normal, and the valleys are carved below it.

The walker who goes to the dales goes for more than scenery. The landscape is magnificent when he can get high enough to see it, but it is not the landscape with which he is really concerned. It is rather the feel and the smell of the place, the living company of the dales: the little crags jutting up like gateposts, the linnets in the bracken, the Herdwicks rubbing themselves against the slates of a barn, the children throwing stones at an old bucket in the beck.

Yet, if you want views, the volcanic rock can give them right enough. Think of the most famous of them: Wasdale, looking up from the bottom end of the lake, or from where a shelter has been made by building two walls in a cross; Yewbarrow, on the left; Kirk Fell, half-hidden; Great Gable, plumb in the middle; then the lower Lingmell as a sort of foothill to Scafell and the Pikes; and the screes running along the edge of the lake. This is the most symmetrical, classical view in Cumberland. Gable, at the centre, is a pyramid, of whose depth and thickness you are aware immediately. It has a solidity like that of the Skiddaw fells, but it is hard and bony, the rock always ready to show its teeth, with wrinkles of screes which look sandy at a distance. On a clear day the mountains of Wasdale look as if they were expecting to be photographed, with a great double W of reflections upside down in the water. But it is rather a pity to see Wasdale in fine weather. To see it in its natural element you need a storm blowing up from Gosforth, clouds stuck against the peaks like cotton-wool, slanting graph-lines of rain, and the lake black as tar. Luckily, you are very likely to see Wasdale at its best if you go there in summer. And there are the Langdale Pikes, imposing whether you see them from the valley below, or looking level at them from any of the hills around. And Bowfell, the most graceful of all the peaks, slender, conical, concave, yet with a bite to it as if it were gimletting the sky. Bowfell, too, is probably the most visible of all the central peaks at a distance. Several valleys open up to it, and you can see it from the coast looking up most of the south-western dales, and from all the low hills round Windermere, and, of course, from the Scafell group. Walking in a mining town by the sea you turn a corner, and there at the end of a street, between the gasworks and the Roman Catholic chapel, miles away across the marshes, is Bowfell. There is magnetic rock on Bowfell which makes compasses go wrong. It certainly draws eyes to it.

Perhaps most famous of all is the view up Derwentwater, the trippers' view, but beautiful all the same. Go to the most obvious place, Friar's Crag or the woods beside it. Choose, if you can, a winter's day, with snow on the fells, and hoarfrost lying on the dead bracken till the woods seem to be ferny with ostrich feathers. There will be a thin cellophane of ice around the shores, but the centre of the lake is open,

Whicham Valley with Black Combe
Langdale Pikes

and the eye skids across it to the long view up the cleft of Borrowdale. One crag opens out behind the other, unfurling, like a metal rose, all the crags and peaks of Borrowdale, and, beyond, Great End and the Scafell Range against the sky. If the sun is out it will glint pink and gold on the snow and the shadows will be blue. It is not so solemn, nor so sculptured as the Wasdale view, but it is richer, more intricate, leading the eye outwards and ravelling it in a monkey-puzzle of fells—it would be pedantic to give them names. Now swing round on your heels and there is Skiddaw and all the fells of Newlands, Grasmoor and Grizedale, the rounded, sulky fells of the older slate. This is perhaps the most dramatic contrast between the Skiddaw slate and the volcanic rock.

The volcanic rock provides some of the finest roofing slates. The Borrowdale-Buttermere group of quarries produce slates of a beautiful bright green, which will shine like a spring larch among the chimneys, especially if the colour is emphasised by green paint on spouts and windows. Lucky is the townsman who sleeps with a bit of Honister Pass over his head. The Westmorland and Furness group of quarries include Loughrigg, Elterwater, Tilberthwaite and Saddlestone—the latter three-quarters of the way up Coniston Old Man. In some places the colouring matter is absent, and the slate is grey or drab. Where the quarries are high up on the mountain side the slates used to be brought down in wooden sledges. Now there are mostly rough roads up which a lorry can climb in low gear.

The rocks have many minerals, of which I shall write when I deal with industry.

The Silurian Rocks

The third of the great masses of the older rocks of the Lake District is that of the Silurian Rocks which form the southern slopes of the central dome. These are found almost entirely in North Lonsdale and Westmorland, touching Cumberland only in the extreme south. They lie below the curve which is the boundary of the volcanic rocks—Broughton-Coniston-Ambleside-Shap—and are bounded on the south by the limestone around Morecambe Bay, and on

Upland pasture, with distant view of
Coniston Old Man and Westmorland Fells
Little Langdale

the east by the Pennines. Ulverston, Kendal and Kirkby Lonsdale roughly mark the shape of the southern edge. The area includes Coniston Water, Esthwaite Lake, the vanished lakes of Kentmore and all but the northern tip of Windermere. These rocks were formed like the Skiddaw slates in a delta below the sea. The geologists have given them such names as Coniston Flag, Coniston Grit, Bannisdale Slates and Kirkby Moor Flags. Mostly they are grey rocks, weathering to green or purple, but duller, less sparkling than the volcanic rock. The Coniston Grit, at the Foxfield end, is a crumbling rock, easily broken into jagged ends like fractured bone, and with a distinct reddish tinge, rather strange among the usual greens and blues.

The Silurian rocks as a whole are not very assertive. They form, in the main, the easy-going country south of Coniston, near Hawkshead, on the Westmorland side of Windermere, and around Kirkby Lonsdale. The hills here are never very high. They are long, flat and smooth, with broad valleys dinted into them. This is not picture-postcard country. The hills shape themselves into languid-looking humps, often of rather desolate moorland. The lakes, too, are almost suburban. Coniston admittedly has the volcanic range of Dow Crags, Old Man and Wetherlam on one side of it, but the shores of Windermere are pretty and harmless. To sail up the lake on a steamer is like going out on a child's paddleboat on an ornamental water of a municipal park. It is ironic that, as Windermere is the most accessible of the lakes to Lancashire, it remains the typical example to thousands of day trippers. Already, at Bowness, they have set up their little promenade around the bay, with motor launches and putting greens and miniature Blackpool illuminations in the autumn.

Yet all this is foolish criticism, the result of staring too long at the bare bones of the central fells. For the Silurian country is good country to live in. It contains lots of homely valleys, cosy, bread-and-butter landscape: the Woodland Valley, the Rusland Valley with its damson trees, and all the little valleys which run down to the Kent.

You can see the contrast between the volcanic rock and the Silurian most impressively from the Coniston railway station. As you get out of the train, you find yourself on a vaulted platform, with a large round arch at the terminus end. Through the arch, looking so near that you feel you must be staring through binoculars, are the Yewdale Crags, along the flanks of Wetherlam. They are vicious crags, not very high, but fanged like a tiger, with slaverings of scree and bright green whiskers of larch and rowan. You walk forward and the arch widens and you see farther up Yewdale, with Raven Crag at its throat, and the road winding beneath Tom Heights on the way to Ambleside. All this is volcanic. Then you step through the arch, and Coniston village is below you, a row of villas and a neat wire fence leading to the lake. And, beyond the lake, the wavy, unemphatic moors of Silurian rock behind Brantwood. The lake itself is of a dull, drab green, like the paint on the railings of Sunday-schools, and it looks uncomfortably *damp*—the lakes of the Silurian country always look damp. Down the lake you see a quiet pastoral country, greener and more hospitable than the Brantwood fells, full of dimples and hollows, and little misty trees and farms. Wooden railings step out into the water like children hand-in-hand, paddling. Nevertheless, the Brantwood shore, which looks so dull from this side of the lake, is full of woods and ferns and birds and little sykes with golden saxifrage among the stones. You must learn to use the magnifying glass as well as the telescope when you look at the Lake District. And here, by the way, except for the distant hills of the Helvellyn Range, the landscape is all Lancashire.

Quarries

The largest slate quarries in the district, indeed in the North of England, are in the Silurian rocks at Kirkby-in-Furness. The rock is very strong and durable, known to architects as "Westmorland Blue Slate"—though it comes, now, from Lancashire. Locally it is known as "Kirkby Roundheads," which is the name inevitably given to all local cricket and football teams and the like. It is dark bluish-grey, rather a dull colour, and not, as you would think, a very exciting covering for houses. It makes you think of grimy, long streets in industrial towns. But when you have seen these slates, seasoned and purpled by age, dripping with rain, or steaming and faintly lilac under the winter sun, you will agree that they are not without beauty.

As building material none of the Lake District slates can compare with sandstone or limestone for variety. Nevertheless they are more colourful than is often thought. When the slate has weathered it often shows veins and crusts of mineral, green or brown or red, so that a street of houses, generally thought of as dark blue or grey, is seen, when the stone is dry and the sun clear but not too strong, to be dusted over with reddish-gold like a tiny fungus, or like pollen on willow catkins. Unfortunately the dry-stone walls, though they will stand up to wind and weather, are not impervious to the effect of heavy traffic, and houses near main roads often bulge out slowly and gently, bending the freestone window-sills till they crack and the wall has to be rebuilt.

One of the best ways to see the colour and texture in the slate is to walk down a back street in one of the mining towns on the coast. The front streets are often roughcast, or faced with prepared stone, but in the back streets the slate is left rough and jagged. In those streets built bit by bit—backyard beside warehouse beside chapel wall—the variety of the stone is obvious and interesting.

The Burlington Quarries at Kirkby have been worked for about two hundred years. The village, scattered into three or four hamlets, is on the lower slopes of the fells and on the marshes looking out to the Duddon Estuary. A terrace of brick villas, unfaithful to the slate, displays itself like a row of comfortable ladies in red crinolines. I would cheerfully put dynamite under most brick buildings in a slate country, but this brick puts a glow of warmth into the cold-looking Gawthwaite Fells. The church hides itself behind a bump in the wooded ghyll which runs up the fellside, and a narrow-gauge railway slants from the quarries to the railway station.

The quarries themselves are enormous cliffs, but beside them are terraces and platforms built out of slates, where once there were sidings, perhaps, or storage yards. Now they are grown over, and unless you kick at the soil under your feet you may not realise that you are not standing on solid earth. From here, as from almost any point around the Duddon Estuary, you can see the three main divisions of Lake District rock side by side. Across the estuary is Black Combe, of Skiddaw Slate—the deep combe which gives it its name is seen from here as a slice cut from a cake. Farther north you see the volcanic rock in the fells along Dunnerdale—a series of sharp hills, folding one over the other, Pen, Harter Fell, Stickle Pike, Caw, Dow Crag, and the Old Man—showing its hobnails on this side, very different from the view of him from Coniston; and on the skyline, the Scafell Range. Finally, look at your feet and all round you along the Ireleth, Kirkby, Gawthwaite moors, and across to the Woodland hills between Broughton and Coniston, and there you see the Silurian rock, modest, restrained, but hard as iron all the same.

Large quarries like those at Kirkby and Honister and those in the Coniston-Tilberthwaite-Langdale fells sign themselves boldly across the landscape. Many people think they harm it and have protested. It is true that they sometimes add a certain harshness to the scene, breaking up the tones of grass and bracken and heather, but I cannot feel that this is greatly to be deplored. For the quarries are true to the very nature of the rock. They introduce nothing alien; they have not got the stamp of some particular period or fashion, but are as timeless as the stone walls which they help to make. The buildings around them are usually of the good stuff of the rock, and the dumps of slate and rubble are so like screes that I can't for the life of me see how you can praise the beauty of the one and despise the other. And the rawness of the newly exposed rock is soon mossed over by the seasons. Even the most wilful exploitations of man are hidden by the silt of a few centuries—for instance, the bottom of Wastwater was once a slag-heap. The fells reclaim their own no less inevitably than the sea.

Coniston Limestone

A geologist, looking at that view from Coniston railway station, would have been aware of another rock, the Coniston Limestone, lying between the volcanic and the Silurian rocks. It lies between them both in space and time, having been laid down after the volcanic and before the Silurian rocks. It appears first at Beck Farm, near Millom, and then runs as a narrow strip along the division between the two slate rocks from the Duddon Estuary to Shap. In the north it changes from limestone to what is known as the Stockdale Shales. The limestone is hard and bluish, and where it crops up through the surface we get a little island of blue-white rock. A patch of it can be seen in Church Beck, where it flows through Coniston village. As this rock makes little difference to the scenery I will not say much about it, but to the geologist it is exciting because it is full of fossils— indeed it is one of the most fossiliferous of the older rocks of the world. Old John Bolton can write about it like this: "Probably smitten with the geological malady, your mind will be so much absorbed with the contemplation of the wonderful organisms by which you are surrounded, that, judging by ourselves, it will act upon you with a sort of mesmĕric influence, and you will ponder and dream over these strange but highly organised forms until you forget (for a while) everything else in the world."[1]

Igneous Intrusions in the Older Rocks

Long after the central rocks were formed certain igneous rocks were thrust up among them—probably in the period known as the Old Red Sandstone Period. The main masses are the granite of Shap, Skiddaw and Eskdale, the granophyre of Ennerdale, the micro-granite of Threlkeld, and the general mix-up of rocks on Carrock Fell, with another outside the lake area on Crossfell. There are also many dykes and minor intrusions, and a tiny patch of a rare and beautiful rock, Minette, on Sale Fell above Bassenthwaite.

The best known of the granites is probably that of Shap Fell, a pink rock which takes a high polish, when it looks like potted meat. It is widely used as an ornamental stone and seems to be particularly popular with post offices. Most of the granites are used for kerbs and setts and road material. If you look on the pavement in many a northern town you will find that you are stepping on slabs marked with Threlkeld Granite Company or some similar words.

[1] *Geological Fragments.*

The Eskdale granite is the largest patch of igneous rock and is easily inspected by the visitor because the Eskdale Miniature Railway runs through it. It varies in colour, sometimes being a dark rich red from hæmatite ore. Stone of this sort has been used for the older buildings of most of the railway stations on the line between Millom and White-haven. St. Bees station is naturally faithful to the sandstone which is named after it, and Sellafield blacklegs into a horrid unripe-tomato brick; but the rest are mostly granite. It is so dark a red that it looks almost like red sandstone, and, as the lintels and kerbs and many of the boundary walls and newer buildings are of this stone, it is easy to confuse the two. You can distinguish them, however, even from a pass-ing train by the way the stones are laid: the freestone is laid horizontally, like bricks; the granite is patchworked together in pieces of uneven size and shape, with the pattern of the interstices marked by mortar. Boulders of this granite have been carried southwards by the ice, and it forms much of the shingle between Walney Island and Ravenglass, giving the beach the lilac tinge of a sea anemone.

From the quarries at Broad Oak, near Waberthwaite, there is an overhead railway, with buckets that sail across the marshes of the lower Esk to Eskmeals, and add—to my mind—another attraction to the view. These aerial railways, and other elemental industrial structures like pitheaps, girders and pylons, seem to fit quite happily into the fells. Perhaps it is because against a landscape that is older than history the minor impertinences of man are trivial and temporal, whereas in an urban landscape, man-made and proportioned to man, they would be hideous and unman-nerly. Certainly I should be more perturbed to hear of a factory in Durham or Salisbury than on Corney Fell.

The little railway, however, runs in the next valley. It has a gauge of 15 inches, and was laid down in the 1870's to carry iron ore from the mines at Boot. After the mines were closed it continued, partly to carry granite, and partly to provide transport for the people of Eskdale and Irton. Then it was developed as an attraction for visitors, and though it lies a long way from any thickly populated area, it still . carries full loads of passengers in the summer. The L.M.S.

Railway Company has arranged excursions for as far away, I think, as Liverpool and Glasgow, which end with a ride up the "Ratty" and an hour or two at Dalegarth.

The railway is a joy to all children and everyone else, and the railway company has joined fully in the fun. The engines, for instance, are scale-models of those which cross the Rockies—not toys, by any means, but powerful Shetland ponies of machinery, which can face the steepish climb up the dale. The carriages are wooden and open like cattle-trucks, and you sit two by two, facing each other, and knocking your knees together when the train bounces downward on the return journey. At one time I think there were first-class carriages—incredible little coffins with lids on— but now it is a one-class train. The railway has its own signals and level-crossings, its own turn-table and sheds— indeed, everything is miniature except the fare.

The line runs from Ravenglass, not up Eskdale at first, but up Miterdale, the small valley which lies between Esk-dale and Wasdale. The sea at this point makes a three-pronged flank attack into the fells, and nowhere on the Cumberland coast does it skirmish so far forward. On this central prong you will see maritime scurvy grass growing beside the heather, and the fishing-boats are drawn up on the sand as if the hills were docks. The railway runs beside this estuary and climbs the slopes of Muncaster Fell. Here is the real granite country. It is on a small scale like the railway—no great crags or cliffs—but everywhere there are chippings and crusts of rock which sparkle like water in the turf. It is a jolly kindergarten country, which won't be acknowledged as Scafell's neighbour until it grows up. The children cheer as the train runs under bridges and across becks. They lean out of the trucks till you feel sure they will fall out. They snatch at heather and ferns and the white, frilly flowers of chervil, and if they are unwise enough to snatch at the bracken they are likely to get their hands cut by the sharp stalks. The train slows down in places, chugging up the hills, and the rowans bend over it, almost knocking the chimney off the engine. There are old thorn trees, too, and wild roses and golden-rod among the fern, so that if you are adventurous you can jump out and grab a handful and run back into the train again. At one place the line passes near the quarries and you can see screes of the pink rock, and whitish-pink dust from the crushing machine. At Eskdale Green it finds a dip in the hill and enters Eskdale close to the route of the Roman road from Ravenglass to Ambleside—which until then had kept to the south-eastern side of Muncaster Fell. It arrives by the tradesmen's entrance, wriggling round the walls and hedges of back gardens as if it were the Fylde tramway, running between Cleveleys and Fleetwood, and not in the wildest of all the dales. But it hustles to its terminus, with the sidings and the long restaurant building. The children get out. The rubble-tips of the mines which made the railway are near them; the marsh marigolds are growing in the sump by the station, and an ice-cream tricycle is waiting at the gate. There is Stanley Ghyll for the tourists, the Woolpack for the walkers, and all the rhetoric of Upper Eskdale for anyone who wants it.

The Newer Rocks: Mountain Limestone

After this great mass of the older rock of the Lake District had been laid down and humped into a dome the becks and rivers began to carve out the valleys. Then the land sank, there was a semi-tropical climate, and the carboniferous rocks were laid down. Up came the land again, and the new stone was shaved off till the old rock was exposed once more. Then another sinking and the Permian rocks were laid down at a time when desert conditions stretched to the Urals in Russia. Another elevation and these rocks were stripped away. Altogether it has been guessed that 30,000 feet of rock were removed in this way. But round the dome of the Lake District the newer rocks remain like the rings round Saturn. The oldest of these and that which forms the innermost ring is the Carboniferous or Mountain Limestone, which also forms the wall which runs vertically through the centre of northern England, the Pennine Chain. This has been called the backbone of England, and very rightly so, for it is really bone, the bone or the skeletal remains of millions of sea-creatures. The Pennines make the eastern boundary of the two counties and at places bulge farther west, especially in North Cumberland. The Bewcastle Fells, for instance, in the Border country, and the Alston Fells, are of limestone, but farther south, in the Ingleborough district, the chain swings into Yorkshire. In the Pennines the limestone is capped in places by millstone grit.

The limestone ring around the Lake District is broken and irregular, but only along the Cumberland coast is it completely missing. Let us start at its north-western tip and follow it clockwise. It appears near Egremont, and thence along the line of the mining towns of Cleator Moor, Frizington to Cockermouth. This is only a thin strip, but it is of great importance because here the stone contains hæmatite ore. Beyond Cockermouth it broadens and curves to the right, through Caldbeck to Penrith. Penrith lies at the jointure between the limestone and the sandstone of the Eden Valley, but the country between there and Ullswater is limestone. It continues thence roughly south-west, keeping to the edge of the Eden Valley, till it reaches the Yorkshire border, and here the Pennines themselves are part of the ring, to which otherwise they stand as a tangent to a circle. The southern segment is rather disjointed. There is a large patch around Milnthorpe and Arnside which pushes to Carnforth and up the lower Kent as far as Kendal. There are a few smaller patches round Grange and Cark-in-Cartmell and Low Furness; from Ulverston on Morecambe Bay to Askam on the Duddon is limestone, except around Barrow. Across the Duddon it appears again near Millom and Kirksanton. The Furness and South Cumberland deposits are small; but, like those of Egremont district, they are rich in iron ore.

The mountain limestone is one of the loveliest rocks to be found in the whole district, and forms a soft white ruff round the head of the older rocks. Not that it is always soft and winsome. It can be severe too. The Pennines are not winsome, especially on the Cumberland and Westmorland side, for while they slope fairly sedately into Northumberland and Durham, they descend on the west in steep escarpments along the line of the Pennine Fault. Particularly magnificent are the huge walls of white rock above the Eden Valley.

The colours of the limestone country are predominantly

white and green as against the grey, blue and purple of the older rocks. (In the hæmatite district there is red to add to the palette, but I will deal with this in the section on industrial Cumberland.)

The best-known part of the limestone country is that on the shores of Morecambe Bay. Probably the majority of people who come to the Lake District approach through this limestone area, passing through Carnforth, and then either to Kendal, or round the Bay to Ulverston on the west coast. As soon as you reach Carnforth you notice a difference in the very *feel* of the land. It is still an ordinary type of landscape, quiet, grassy and green, but you are aware how clean and washed it is after the griminess of central Lancashire. First you think it is just because you have got away from the smuts. But soon you realise that it is a *positive* cleanness, not just negative, not just the absence of dirt, but a real cleanness which shines out of the very rock. The little chips that break up through the soil here and there are as white as daisies. The stone walls, the cottages, the farms, even the station buildings round Carnforth look as if they have been scrubbed. Then as you move out of the town, by train or by road, you see low hills with shelves of white rock arranged one above the other. They look like rows of ivory-backed books standing on green baize. Even the roads have the same clean look about them, and the shining tarmac, with wide green verges and limestone walls, fits happily into the landscape.

Between Carnforth and Kendal the countryside is colder and bonier. The hills around Hutton Roof and north of Lupton are not bushy and billowy like Arnside Knott, but are almost bare, and seem at a distance to have been dusted over with lime or chalk. When you get close you find that the surface is covered with crusts and cobbles of rock, rough like slag. The beck bottoms are choked with accidental gargoyles of limestone. The villagers of lower Kendal collect the stones to make borders to garden paths, or even porches to front doors. I have seen monoliths and hog-backs of limestone, six feet high and more, propped against the walls in Burton and Holme. Many tons, also, have been sent to Blackpool and elsewhere for rockeries.

Farleton Fell and Hutton Roof Crag, between the Lancaster-Kendal canal and Lonsdale, and all the little hills around the River Bela, have their own acres of wilderness quite unlike anything else in the district. Here the rock is on the surface and the water has moulded it and carved it till it looks like cooled larva. There are waves and crests of rock, edges like pie-crusts, crevasses more than leg-deep, cracks and splittings, and tiny white patches of scree. Above Beetham are the Fairy Steps, where my grandmother was born. She was a stern old lady with a crutch and tight white hair, and when she told me years ago that she used to watch the fairies running up and down the steps it did not occur to me to doubt her. I don't think I doubt her now.

These upland commons are thatched with hazel and thorns and have clearings and clefts and glades among them where there is not even a dusting of soil on the stone. You can lose yourself easily in ten minutes, and be just as remote from the world and from men as if you were on Bowfell. Here grow the limestone flowers: lily-of-the-valley in late spring, and in summer, gentians, thyme, rock-roses, a sampler of tight-stitched colour, with here and there the tall yellow turrets of golden-rod or ploughman's spikenard.

Travelling north in the train[1] from Carnforth you come to the coast at Arnside, and at once you see the limestone at its most attractive. Arnside is at the mouth of the Kent, and can claim to be the port of Westmorland, though before the estuary was silted up small ships could sail farther up the river. It is a small, deliberate-looking village, running

---

[1] The train journey by the coast from Carnforth to Carlisle gives an excellent shop-window view of the geological formations of Cumberland and Westmorland. First you have the limestone of North Lonsdale, ore-bearing around Dalton, with occasional patches of Permian rock. Then on the Kirkby-Furness side of the Duddon you pass through Silurian rock and touch the volcanic at Duddon Bridge. Around Black Combe you are looking at Skiddaw Slate, and from thence to St. Bees, though the line is laid on Permian rock, you have magnificent views of the volcanic series up Eskdale and Wasdale, of the granite of Muncaster Fell at Ravenglass, and of the granophyre of the Ennerdale Fells between Seascale and Nethertown. At St. Bees there are fine sandstone cliffs, and between Whitehaven and Maryport the line runs through the Cumberland coalfield. From Maryport to Carlisle, though there is not much rock to be seen, the country is of sandstone again.

along the foot of a steep scarp. At high tide you can walk on the main road and spit into the sea; at low tide you are stranded at the edge of the Morecambe Bay sand. Acres of it stretch out, almost bridging the Fylde to Walney Island, an uncolonised county of sand, with its own relief and topography, its channels, islands, ridges and plains. In the evening, light runs like burning oil along the surface of the water in the channels, and the humps of the sand are slimy with the syrup of the sunset. Then the ripples which are almost imperceptible by day are ostentatious with their bars of red shine and shadow.

From Arnside to Kent's Bank the railway runs along the coast. Landward, there are fine limestone cliffs dropping sheer into—not the sea, but orderly marshes, for the sands have been ditched and drained here, and flat fields lie below the cliffs, with straight hedges along them and little canals. Once no doubt the cliffs dropped into the sea as they do at Humphrey Head, almost the extreme southerly point of Cartmel. The stone gets its claws into the water in the south of Cumberland, too, at Hodbarrow Point.

All along the shore by Grange-over-Sands the rock comes down to the sea not in cliffs but in a gentle, shelving shore. Here the water has lapped at the stone like a cat licking butter, and smoothed and rounded it till it has surprising shapes of the organic world—the shapes of beech boughs, and fungi, rhubarb leaves and roots and tubers. Here the water has left its billows and ripples on the rock, with some waves raised above the others and curled and crested as if they were about to break. And here pebbles have been trapped in hollows, and have scoured out pot-holes. And here little becks flowing from the hills have seeped deeply into the rock till it overhangs them like a balcony. At some places the shore seems crowded with bathers, all carved from the stone by Henry Moore. And in the sockets and navels of the rock the soil blows, and thrift grows, pink and papery, and in places the trees walk down to the water and bend over it as if they were washing their hair.

When you pass farther north into Furness there is not so much rock on the surface, but you are never unaware that you are in limestone country because of the glowing whiteness of the buildings. All of them, whether of rough or hewn stone, have a stubborn whiteness, even the ruins, and there are many of them, especially in the mining districts. Most of the ruins of Cumberland and Westmorland are of melancholy sandstone, or of slate which in collapse looks more like a rubble heap than a building; but these limestone ruins still seem sprightly and youthful. The farms on the fellside shine out as if they had been whitewashed, and the neighbourly rows of cottages which are common in Cartmel and Furness. The limestone villages, too, are attractive, and the market towns, Cockermouth and Ulverston, each with its eighteenth-century calmness. Ulverston, indeed, is situated at the junction of the limestone with the Silurian slates, so that the buildings are partly of the one and partly of the other. Those of hewn and shaped limestone have a characteristic smoothness, almost like that of pottery—Holy Trinity Church, Ulverston, is a good example. This stone can make even ordinary buildings look pleasant, and the rural schools of Furness are, from the outside, quite ingratiating with their white walls and red lintels—this is partly in contrast to the schools of the slate country, grey, dark, and Gothic, like monasteries turned desperate in decay.

The limestone goes on the razzle at Grange. Usually the promenade-balmoral style is depressing and vulgar, but the castellations and turrets, the bay-windows and porches, look playful and pretty in limestone, with trees about and the sea not far away. It is all a fancy-dress show, done in the best materials and with good drawing-room taste. The stone could not have chosen a better place for its frolic.

Limestone is quarried for many purposes, and in the industrial area it is used to smelt the iron-ore which it contains. The handiness of the limestone, and, in the Whitehaven district, the coal, has led to the development of the iron and steel industries close to the mines, and so once again the rock has directed the way of life of the people who live on it.

Coal

The upper rocks of the carboniferous series are the coal measures. We cannot claim that they form a ring round the district, for only about a quarter of the circle is found, just

outside the strip of limestone which runs from Egrement to
a little east of Caldbeck. The coal area is rather wide from
Whitehaven along the coast to Maryport, and thence curves
in a thin rim through the mining villages of Dearham and
Aspatria and peters out before it reaches the Eden Valley,
though there are beds of coal in the Ingleborough and
Hawes districts. The mid-Lancashire coalfield may be considered perhaps to be part of the southern edge of the ring,
and even—though this is stretching it too far!—the Durham
and North Yorkshire coalfields part of the eastern edge. As
the surface stone on the coal area is mostly a dirty-looking
sandstone, the traveller tends to connect it with the scenery
of the Permian rocks rather than that of the limestone. It is
a dark, dusty, blackberry-and-apple landscape, the features
of which I will discuss later.

The New Red Sandstone

The last main group is that of the Permian rocks, St.
Bees and Penrith Sandstone, and a few patches of magnesium limestone. This forms a horseshoe, hanging upside-
down so that the luck falls out. The left leg ends in the tip
of Furness, around Barrow, with a few isolated patches on
the shores of Morecambe Bay. It runs up the Cumberland
coast to Whitehaven, and from thence to Maryport it is
broken by the coal measures. Then it covers the mid-
Cumberland plain (though between Carlisle and the sea
there are newer rocks, Stanwix Shales and Lias). The
right leg is thrust down the Eden Valley, past Penrith and
Appleby to the Yorkshire border.

Sandstone is the least assertive of the rocks of the two
counties. In a few places it makes you notice it—in the
coastal cliffs, in the gulleys and river-beds of the Eden and
its tributaries, and in ravines like that of the Vale of the
Deadly Nightshade at Furness Abbey. In such places, the
rock pushes among the green, rather sombre and sullen.
In woods where it has flaked off into terraces, it stands out
among the trees, and the dead leaves pile upon it, brown and
muddy. Green and red are the colours, but not the green and
red of holly and berry, but a dark green and a dark brownish-
red which easily merge one into the other.

Often, however, you are scarcely aware of the rock. In the coastal strip between Millom and St. Bees you can travel for miles in the train without suspecting that you are on sandstone if you haven't seen a geological map. Here you are staring all the time at the hills of Skiddaw slate or granite or volcanic rock. Even the farms and villages and walls are of slate or granite, for it has been easier to quarry these in the low hills nearby than to dig deeper for the sandstone. Quite often barns and outhouses are built from cobble-ducks from the shore, so that they look like a bank of large shingle tipped on end. Sometimes the cobbles are laid in rows like cannon-balls, with a band of roofing slates, laid flat, between them. In the hedges, rows of cobbles and layers of sods are used in much the same way. When the sand blows against them, they are taken into the dune landscape as long banks of gorse, threaded here and there by barbed wire.

But nowhere among all this is there a sign of the sandstone, except in churches, where often the material has been brought from a distance. The sandstone first begins to show on the shore. The shingle in the southern part of the county has been mauve or pale lilac, from granite and slate and some limestone; now it grows pinker. If you pick it up you find many pebbles of red sandstone, rather like ginger-bread balls. They have been broken off the St. Bees cliffs and smoothed and carried down by the sea. At Seascale, when the tide is out, there are a few low, dark rocks, disguised with seaweed. Farther north at Sellafield there are blocks of a khaki sandstone piled along the banks of the Ehen to keep the flood waters in place. Here the river shies when it reaches the sea and wheels and flows parallel to the coast for a while, with only a bank of sand and shingle dividing it from the tide. From the train the sea looks higher than the river, and the sandbank is strewn with old tree-trunks, twisted and peeled of bark, like tree-creatures painted by Graham Sutherland. For miles yet there is just dune and glacial drift, and then suddenly the rock bites through at Nethertown. Here there is a superb red beach, slabs of stone, broken and flaked like ruined steps going down to the sea. It is a deep blood-red stone with the ripples of the prehistoric seas still

38

Coniston Water, from the North River Esk

lying on it, and huge fragments brought down by more recent tides, some of them smooth as chocolate. Now the St. Bees cliffs are already in sight, and the shore becomes redder, clotted thickly with seaweed, dark as blood in late evening. And at St. Bees there is a small, graceful curve of shingle, and then the south headland of Tomlin, a stubborn hull of rock, not jagged like the slates or modelled like the limestone, but shoving slabs and plates of rock into the sea like a battleship. The cliffs thrust out another headland and then curve in to the harbour of Whitehaven, where the coal suddenly comes up from underground and even the sea changes colour.

Going north the traveller meets the sandstone again at Maryport and thence across the Cumberland plain. This is much more typical of the sandstone country. The rock does not push its head up, but everywhere there are farms and barns and walls and villages of warm red stone. The rivers, often black from the little collieries hidden away in the woods, flow under sandstone bridges. The stone varies in colour, but is mostly dark red, and where barns and cottages have been whitewashed, the red soon shows through the white as I have seen iron ore showing through wood taken from the mines and whitewashed for sight-boards in cricket fields.

Sandstone disintegrates easily, so that the surface breaks into soil, and gives rise to the cosy, well-fleshed countryside of the Carlisle plain and the Eden Valley. Much of the former was covered with the old Inglewood Forest, and it is still better wooded than the rest of the country.

The crumbling of the stone has its effects on buildings, too, especially barns and old walls which are left uncared for. The stone rots into soil in crevices and crannies, and ivy-leaved toadflax roots there, mouse-ear hawkweed and the cresses. The buildings are integrated with the landscape. Even the squat, grim streets of miners' cottages at St. Bees and the villages nearby have a sombre glow of their own. The rooms are small, but the walls are thick and will not easily fall down. The old mill, near Wigton Station, is as mildewed as a bowler hat which has been kept twenty years in a damp cupboard. Wigton is built almost entirely of sand-

Clints, near Cockermouth
St. Bees Head and Fleswick Beach
from Tomlin

stone, and so is the fine market town of Penrith, and most of the older part of Carlisle.

The soft nature of the sandstone, however, has one great defect. Because of its workability, and because, perhaps, it has a warm, religious look, it has become the main stone for ecclesiastical building. Carlisle Cathedral, the abbeys of Calder and Furness, and nearly all the churches, old and recent, are built of sandstone. And the stone has crumbled sadly. In particular the ornamentation has been damaged. On the east end of Carlisle Cathedral the stone has worn and then flaked off, so that the figures have lost their faces, and sometimes the front of their bodies, as if they had been hacked off with an axe. Decorations of lesser relief—like the carvings round the door of the northern front of St. Bees Priory—have been mumbled and half-smudged away. In the same way, the many Norse and Anglican crosses up and down the two counties have suffered badly. Perhaps it is just as well that Long Meg is a toothless old hag or she might have been ground down to the gums by now.

These, then, are the main rocks of the Lake District, but while the rocks give the character of the land, they do not of themselves give it its personality. For this it needed a shaping influence, like a person needs to rub up against other people. We will consider what this shaping influence was.

NOTE

The following amusing account of the laying down of the rocks is taken from *Frae Pit and Farm*, a verse play in dialect by Alderman Charles Edmunds, at present (1949) chairman of the County Education Committee. It is reproduced here by kind permission of the author.

> Theer, whoar thoo's seaffly standan' noo,
> T'oald sea a dozen times bin throo'.
> Herdus, an' t'narrer hills on t'reet,
> Tho' standan' up et sec a heeght,
> Yance at girt watter boddam's stood;
> What's noo grey steann aw green-grey mud,
> Squeez't into steann, split inta pleatts,
> We ken them noo as Skidda Sleatts.

Than burnan' moontans mair ner yan
Spew't ashes, steam an' melted steann,
An' built up t'Rocks o' Borrowdell
For faddams mair than Ah cud tell.
Than cuh a warm an quiet time,
Wid tropic seas, chok full o' lime.
What yance war corals, shells, an' beanns,
Noo up as solid limesteann stan's.
Than aw gat land, wid swampy whols,
Whoar grew aw t'plants, et noo ur cwoals.
Noo up, noo doon alternately,
Noo whiles aw land, noo whiles aw sea,
Still wearan' off when up abeunn,
Still buildan' up when deepest doon,
Cuz Whitten sandstone efter t'cwols.
Than t'Permian breccia than in whols
In t'Trias marls, sea reed an' seappy,
Lig salt an' gypsum in hidlins happy.
Than cuh a time of arid sands,
Et t'sea laid doon in sandsten bands,
An t'St. Bees Sandsten' noo we meet,
Built up abuenn two thoosand feet.
Et udder rocks hev bin laid doon,
Thoo cud bet mair, than hoaf-a-croon,
Aw owre what is t'coonty noo.
For, nar tull Carrel City, thoo
Mit finnd some Lias rock,
Aw et is left o' t' newest stock.
Than t'Coonty gat a mighty bump,
An' was raised up intul a hump.
Aw t'newer rocks war worn away,
An' t' oldest browt tull t'leet o' day.
An' this explains a yah time riddle,
Hoo t'elder rocks ur aw in t'middle,
An' t' newer rocks aw lapt roon'd t'edges,
As roon'd a pond growe seaves an' sedges.

Chapter III

THE SHAPING OF THE ROCK

The Coming of the Ice

It has been said that when God made England His finger touched but did not press. This certainly is not true of Cumberland and Westmorland. He pressed there all right. What is more, He used His nails. And the nails were ice.

If the ice had not come the general shape of the country might be much as it is now, but its features would have been very different. There would have been few cliffs and crags; no waterfalls, no ghylls, and perhaps no lakes. There were two main invasions of ice to Northern England. From Scandinavia the ice sheet came to the north coast, but little of it crossed the Pennines. The Scottish ice came down the west coast, covering the Carlisle plain and the sea between there and the Isle of Man. It cut off spurs of the fells which formerly sloped gently to the coast, and pushed arms up the estuaries. It broke huge chunks off the Eskdale granite and left them on the shore of Walney Island and elsewhere to the south. It blocked up the mouths of some of the western valleys so that lakes were formed, as the "Whicham Lake" below Black Combe, which must have been rather like what Bassenthwaite is now. But, on the whole, the fells manufactured their own ice. I find it fascinating to imagine how this may have happened. Moreover, conditions might not have to change as greatly as we think for it to happen again. How often has a climber on Scafell or Helvellyn found snow in a gulley away from the sun as late as Whitsuntide or even midsummer! Imagine, then, that there was a small average fall in temperature throughout the year. Then we might expect that there would be a greater fall of snow, that the snow would melt more slowly, and that winter would come before all the snow had gone. If the fall in temperature were greater, there would be drifts of snow in the dales which the summer could not quite get rid of. And so each year the snow would accumulate and gradually glaciers would be formed.

That is what I think must have happened in the Ice Age.

Each dale had its own glacier which swelled till it overflowed the flanks of the dale and the whole of the lower hills were flooded with it. Eventually only the highest central peaks stood like an archipelago above the slow tides of the ice, and perhaps even these went under in the end. The reverse must have been the case when the ice retreated. First it descended the slopes of the fells, then it left bare the ridges between the dales, and finally the glaciers dwindled. This coming and going of the ice may have happened several times, with periods of comparatively temperate climate in between, but when, at last, the ice had gone it left a changed country.

What the Ice Left

The "deposits" are perhaps the least interesting of the glacial effects. There are huge daubs of boulder-clay all over the coastal lands, and dull, humpy moraines, where nothing will grow but sedges and sour grass. Frequently, among the fells, the glacial drift dammed up small valleys or combes and formed tarns, many of which, no doubt, have since drained away.

More amusing are the perched boulders, of which the Bowder Stone near Keswick is the most famous example. There are many of them to be seen, especially in the lower hills surrounding the central district. They look cheerfully ridiculous in their situations, like Humpty Dumpty, and there are often local legends to explain why they are there—legends usually connected with the Devil.[1] Often, of course, the boulders were left high up on the fell slopes, so that eventually they rolled down to the bottom of the valley. This is one of the reasons why such rivers as Derwent are chockful of huge stones in parts of their course.

Much more exciting than the deposits is the erosion of the ice.

Valleys

Let us look first at its effects on the shape of a valley. A cross-section of a "normal" valley is V-shaped, the sides

[1] The Devil plays quite an important part in Cumberland topography. On old maps there is even a village called Devil's Arse-hole. Laws of libel being what they are I shall not say where it was.

sloping evenly to the bottom. But when the ice got to work it planed the sides almost perpendicular and broadened the bottom till the valley became U-shaped. Hence in the Lake District we have dales with steep, bare sides, often cliffs or screes, at the bottom of which is a flat strip of fertile land running right up to the hub of the ridges. This is particularly noticeable from above, where the green ribbons of the dales can be seen below the brown, grey, blue and purple of the fellsides.

When the ice slices off the sides of the valleys it leaves the little tributary valleys hanging high and dry. Or rather, high and not dry, for the beck now drops steeply into the valley-bed. If the rock of the new cliff is hard, or if the rock on to which the water falls is softer, then there is formed one of the typical Lake District waterfalls[1]—usually a thin stream of water dropping from a considerable height. Dungeon Ghyll, Dalegarth Force, Scale Force, are falls of this kind, but each has its own character, and none conforms to a pattern.

Ghylls

More often, however, the beck from the hanging valley cuts out a ghyll, and descends not in one leap but in a jiggling chain of hops and hoops. Perhaps the best known of such ghylls is that of Tilberthwaite, where you can scramble for half a mile or more up a scaffolding of rickety bridges, many of which are no more than a plank thrown from one side of the chasm to the other. There are fine examples of such ghylls to be seen from the train as it rounds the spurs of Black Combe. Here little streams you can stride across have cut a gorge thirty feet deep or more, and when they are frozen in winter they hang down the black sides of the rock like rags of lace. When you think how short a time the weather has had in which to work on the rock (I have seen estimates of from twelve thousand to sixty thousand years as the time which has elapsed since the ice retreated—in any case, it is only a short time, geologically), you realise the great erosive power of even small streams.

[1] These are also caused, sometimes, by the deflection of a stream from its original course, and many coincide with faults.

The particular charm of these ghylls is often to be found where they are least spectacular, indeed, where they are not really ghylls at all, but merely gulleys carved out by a beck or a syke.[1]

Everyone who knows the district will have his own favourite beck, perhaps one which creates a little landscape of cliff and chasm for twenty or thirty feet. I remember with affection a certain beck above Coniston Water. It was September, and the scrubby wood was full of blackberries and browning fern. I had a farm dog with me, a young cur bitch which was afraid of water—rather oddly so, since all the rest of the farm dogs enjoyed swimming in the lake. The dog went ahead and out of sight, and eventually I found that it had turned into a little cleft and had run round the edge of the rock basin and could not find its way back. After spending ten minutes trying to show it where to go or trying to persuade it to venture into the water, I gave up and left. Ten seconds later the dog rejoined me, having solved its own puzzle in a dash of despair.

The cavern or grotto was formed by a quite small beck falling over a cliff about twelve feet high. The sides sloped very steeply, of smooth Silurian slate, and in the bottom was a pool, green and still as such pools are. Its sides went down in the same steep slope till they met at a sharp angle deep below the surface of the water. Directly opposite the waterfall the cliffs dropped to a sort of conduit where I came in and the water ran out. A few feet farther on it was again an ordinary little stream, bubbling and wriggling over the stones and the mossy roots of hazels.

Dunnerdale

There is no better example of a lakeless dale than Dunnerdale—at least, none I know better. It is narrow, compact, self-contained, and it does not dwindle away at its foot like Langdale or even Eskdale, nor splay out like the lake valleys of Wasdale and Borrowdale. Wordsworth, in his sonnets, follows it from its source to the sea, but it is better to track it backward. At Duddon Bridge you have the salt marshes

[1] A small stream, especially one which dries up in the summer.

on one side, and on the other the "jaws" of the dale—High Duddon on the Cumberland side and Bank End on the Lancashire side. The main road goes steeply up Bank End, so that at the very beginning you are able to look at the green water meadows beside Duddon Hall. The flow here is *andante cantabile* below steep woods. By the time the road descends to the river again you are more than half-way to Ulpha. Already the river is wilder, and has tossed the trees away from it. The road, too, has got rid of its walls, and the sides of the dale are steep and stubborn—not forbidding, or even imposing, but still a land of sheep and bracken and scree.

The river is confined for a moment between narrow rocks at Ulpha Bridge. It is very deep here, and green as bile. Below Ulpha Church it is wider—a gossipy Duddon—and someone has planted a row of conifers, well-spaced. At Ulpha Post Office you put your pennies through a slit in the counter like a collection box. Ulpha Church is on a little knoll. From here nearly to Seathwaite, the riverside is quiet farming country—a strip of Cheshire, a quarter of a mile wide, between the infertile flanks. Then the road leaves the river and wanders a little way to meet the biggish beck that bounces down from Seathwaite Tarn and its hanging valley. It is about here that there is a signpost pointing simply to

LANGDALE.

I hope they didn't take it down during the war, for it certainly would have puzzled any parachutist who tried to follow it.

The Duddon, here, is busy finding its way through the Duddon Gorge. It is not a gorge, really, but a cleft between two high crags, and the river batters through a barrier of rolled and tumbled boulders. Weasels run from side to side, jumping from boulder to boulder. Above this, the road joins the river again, and there is the lovely country of mid-Dunnerdale. It is wild and romantic, bright as a border ballad, red and green with rowan berries and birches. Yet it is intimate, too, keeping its pools and stepping-stones and bridges secret from all except those who search for them.

You can pass along the road at Birk's Bridge and never know of the leg-rock stalking about in its footbath.

Then the country changes. As you approach Cockley Beck you feel, as you do in nearly all the upper dales, that you are coming to the last edge of civilisation. Round the corner may be the tundra, or the snow-volcanoes of Iceland, or even—God knows—polar bears and trolls. The flanks slope up rather drearily, a sheep-bitten waste of brown and green. The mountains they lead up to—the Crinkles, Bow-fell, Grey Friar and Wetherlam—contain good country, but here they do not produce many views. Yet still there are those astonishing flat meadows, with cows beside the water and betony in the grass.

After Cockley Beck the dale is really ended, but the river swings to the right, up Wrynose Pass. The road follows it, in fact the road almost coincides with it, for it curves around its banks and continually crosses it in water-splashes. Here and over Hardknott the Romans marched, and here the army dispatch riders practised on their motor-cycles. There are rather sandy-looking banks overhanging the stream, and tussocks of coarse grass. Looking back, the head of the dale is shaped like the pit of a theatre. The Duddon now splits up into many tiny streams and the road goes over the pass by the Three Shires Stone and down into Little Langdale. The Stone, which marks more or less where Cumberland, Westmorland and Lancashire meet, is a sort of private fancy, of no antiquarian interest. But neither are we.

Lakes

The ice not only planed the sides of the dales, it wore away the bed too. In doing so it did not work evenly but in fits and starts, according to the varying hardness of the rock. Hence the incline from source to sea is no longer steady, but jerky. Very characteristic of the dales is a river which at times flows quietly through meadows and at times tumbles down a steep incline.

Frequently, too, the ice would gorge deep into the dale bottom and scoop back to the surface again. Then, of course, we get a lake forming, the height of its shore often increased by mounds of debris left by the glacier.

47

Many of the lakes have the character of wide, winding rivers: Ullswater never lets you see more than about a third of its length at a time. Ennerdale Water, too, though it widens like a club in its lower reaches, is narrow and river-like. Even Windermere, which does not really lie in a dale, has rather the nature of a placid European river, winding, narrowing and broadening.

Sometimes, because of the cleavage, the ice "plucks" at the rock so that the whole bed of the river falls perpendicularly for a short way, giving rise to the type of waterfall of which Skelwith Force is typical. Here the waters of the Brathay, which have been sliding along quite smoothly from Elterwater, suddenly drop twenty to thirty feet. Because of the weight of the water and because it drops, as it were, "solid," it is more impressive than falls which are higher. The water gains speed as it approaches the force, and then, because of the shape of the rocks, it twists in the air as it falls. The effect is not so much of movement as of continuity and even of rest within the turmoil. Though the individual drops which make up the fall are always passing and changing, yet the shape of the water remains constant, rigid as a girder, steady as the pikes which look down on it.

The Changing Landscape

Because of the immense ages of what we might call geological time we are inclined to think that the formulative forces belong to the past. But except for the ice they are still at work today—frost, sun, wind, rain, rivers. The landscape, in fact, is changing before our eyes and more rapidly, perhaps, than we think.

On the coast the estuaries are gradually being silted up. Ravenglass, which was a busy harbour in the time of the Romans, is now a village on an almost land-locked creek. Along the edges of most of the western estuaries, embankments and dykes have helped to drain some of the marshes and brought good fields to the farmer. Much more could be done, and perhaps the whole of some estuaries could be reclaimed. Plans have even been sketched out for a huge boom across Morecambe Bay which would create thousands of acres of new land.

Along the drier parts of the coast, also, changes are continually taking place. Dunes are blown into shape, are bound together by marram grass, and shift up and down on the flat coastal fields. Under the eye of the centuries they must seem to race about like huge brown waves. Nor does it need the centuries to make a change. I have seen a new dune landscape created in one night by a spring tide with a storm behind it. The dunes were sliced away as with a carving-knife along their seaward side, to make jagged cliffs of sand. Yet soon more sand drifted up, and a fresh map was laid out, of coves and combes, knolls and ridges, with the sea-holly and the restharrow growing as before.

The most interesting changes are taking place, however, in the lakes and tarns. All of the tarns are slowly filling up. Scores, perhaps hundreds, already have been filled and are now peat bogs on the fellsides. In some cases artificial drainage has accelerated the natural course of events, and in Kentmere whole lakes have disappeared. At the head of all the lakes there is a stretch of flat land which has been formed of the mud washed down by the main river of the dale. Ambleside and Coniston both show extensive marshy tracts of this kind. Sometimes, too, a large and powerful beck enters a lake half-way down its course. Then, if there are no strong currents, there is likely to be formed, stretching out into the water, a delta which will eventually cut the lake in two. This has already happened in the case of Buttermere and Crummock, and again in that of Derwentwater and Bassenthwaite Lake. The silting-up process has been particularly effective in the original Derwentwater-Bassenthwaite Lake, for there two considerable rivers were at work —the Greta and Newlands Beck. Both these pairs of lakes are apt to be reunited in times of floods. There are signs, too, that the same sort of thing was going to happen to Hawes Water if the Manchester Water Works had not taken it over.

Wind and Weather

Now the agent by which all these changes are brought about is the weather, and in particular the rain. And there is certainly a lot of it. Wordsworth admitted it 130 years ago:

"The country, indeed, is subject to much bad weather, and it has been ascertained that twice as much rain falls here as in many parts of the island."[1]

Seathwaite in Borrowdale is the wettest village in England, with 140 inches of rain a year. The Stye, above Borrowdale, has 165 inches. A mean average rainfall of 80 inches is common in the western dales, but when we get out into the central plain the rainfall is not much greater than that of the Midlands.

Moreover, as Wordsworth says: "The number of black drizzling days, that blot out the face of things, is by no means *proportionately* great."[2] When it rains, in fact, it rains "yal watter." No doubt the advertising committees of the holiday resorts in the Lake District will be able to prove that these towns enjoy more sunshine than most, but I remember many summers on the Cumberland coast when huge clouds rolled up from the Irish Sea, day after day, and hung about the tops of the fells. In the sultry days of July the matting of cloud hangs across the sky, not black or threatening, but never thin enough to let the sun through. The sea is grey, like lead; the smoke from the pit chimneys hangs in the air, spreading at last and mingling with the cloud; the dust settles on the bracken by the rubble-tips. Looking inland, the fells look flat and small, like a canvas backcloth.

Nevertheless, it is the climate which gives the Lake District much of its attraction. The aspect of the fells changes as quickly as the atmosphere, and the varying lights, the unexpected colours and the never-repeated shadows invent a new landscape every day. To quote Wordsworth again:

"Days of unsettled weather, with partial showers, are very frequent; but the showers, darkening, or brightening, as they fly from hill to hill, are not less grateful to the eye than finely interwoven passages of gay and sad music are touching to the ear. Vapours exhaling from the lakes and meadows after sunrise, in a hot season, or, in moist weather, brooding upon the heights, or descending towards the valleys with inaudible motion, give a visionary character to everything around them."[3]

[1] *Guide to the Lakes.*   [2] *Ibid.*   [3] *Ibid.*

So, early on an autumn morning, you will see a fellside above a lake draped in gauze like a ballet dancer. As the sun gets up the gauze rolls itself into coils, so that the flanks and the summit of the fell are bare, but bundles of mist still curl and twist in the combes and valleys. And earlier, before the sun rises, or rather when it comes to the edge of the horizon and the fellside is still in the slant of the shadow but the air and the trees are gleaming, then the light seems to trill like birdsong, and the air is unimaginably clear, and for hundreds of yards the gnats and midges become visible, little glints of light, rising and falling, with the swallows among them.

Snow

But if the summers are moist, the winters are mild. Average winter temperatures in the dales are about the same as those of London, and the latter has much greater extremes. Heavy snowstorms are not common in Cumberland. Only as we get nearer the Pennines, in the Crossfell, Shap and Sedburgh districts, do we often have heavy and prolonged snowfalls. The road over Shap is frequently blocked, and we hear of lorry-drivers stranded at remote farms, and of sheep being buried alive for days. But in the western fells the snow rarely lasts long—perhaps the salty air helps to melt it. In the first two winters of the war, however, there were snowfalls which isolated some of the coastal towns for nearly a week. Work was held up at a shell-filling factory for lack of material and the girls had a week's party on tinned food, sleeping in village houses and the canteen. Those who tried to walk home along the railway line arrived half dead, with stockings frozen to their legs. Yeast was dropped to some villages by parachute. These two winters made some of us hope (if "hope" is the right word) that we were going to have a cycle of hard winters, but more recent years have not borne this out.

When the landscape is covered with snow it takes on a new appearance. The change in colour is not hard to imagine. Upon the whiteness of the snow are cast deep blue shadows, and the sunrise is red and golden and green. But the fells seem to lose their perspective on a grey snowy day.

They look bigger, yet flat, too, and less solid. If there is no sun, the usual lines of the ranges are lost, and they become vague and strange. There is a khaki-coloured light which descends in the late afternoon and merges fell and sky together, and the sky seems heavier than the rock. When the sun comes out on the snow, and there is warmth in the air but no thaw on the ground, a mist forms, which clings so closely to the shape of the fells that they seem to have swollen during the night.

The tarns and reservoirs are usually frozen for part of the winter, and sometimes the larger lakes, but it is not often that these will bear from end to end. Probably the greatest frost within living memory was that of 1871-72, which lasted for sixteen weeks, when every stretch of water was frozen. More recently, in 1896-97, Windermere was covered with thick ice, and the railway company ran skaters' trips from London for 6s. return.

Local Storms

The Lake District has its own stubborn way of clinging to rain and storms while the rest of England is passing through a drought. Such was the case during the dry summers of 1943 and 1944. I think it was in 1943 that it rained on every single day of August. Often, too, in times of good weather, a sudden squall will arise over one or other of the lakes, making the shore trees creak and the water rock, and scaring the life out of holiday makers who have taken out a boat for some quiet fishing. Coniston and Ullswater are particularly notable for such storms.

A highly individual and famous example is that of the Helm Wind, which is experienced along the Eden Valley below Cross Fell. I have never seen a Helm, but it seems to be characterised by a heavy bank of cloud resting along the Cross Fell range, while three or four miles from the foot of the fell a long roll of cloud appears parallel with the Helm. This is the Helm Bar. Often the Bar is joined to the Helm at the ends, making an ellipse with clear sky in the middle. The wind rushes down the side of the fell till it reaches a point below the Bar, when it suddenly ceases. The wind is cold and violent, sometimes strong enough to uproot trees and overturn horses and carts, and makes a noise which has been compared to that of a railway train. Yet, however strong it may be, there is no wind at all beyond the Helm Bar, or sometimes a gentle breeze blowing *towards* it, as if to meet the Helm Wind.

The usual explanation is that a cold, wet wind blowing up the long peaty eastern slopes of the mountains suddenly meets the warmer western air on the crest of the ridge, and behaves rather like water falling over a weir. Perhaps similar conditions on a smaller scale are the cause of the sudden squalls on the lakes.

CHAPTER IV

GREEN THINGS ON THE EARTH

Trees

IT is quite unbotanical, but let us begin with the trees because they are the biggest and you notice them first.

When the ice retreated it was probably the sedges and mosses which colonised the land, then the alpine flowers, and then the trees. The first among the trees would be the birch, and it has remained the most characteristic of them all. In Iceland there are said to be forests of birches, perfect in proportion, but so small that as you walk among them they reach only to your shoulders. Perhaps such midget trees climbed up the dales and then, as the climate improved, developed into those we know today. For the birch is the loveliest of the trees of the dales. Borrowdale is famous for them, and Dunnerdale too, and it gives its name to such places as Birk's Bridge, Birker Moor, and Birthwaite (which is where Windermere Station is today). It is at its best beside a river—not the quiet sort of river that the willows and elders prefer, but a garrulous dale river. It climbs up and down the banks, and leans over the rocks and gets its food from between the boulders. It is not a tree which you notice at a distance; it never makes a show of itself; yet often when you come upon it suddenly, from below, the whole slants of the valley seem just a frame for the tree which riddles the sky in its leaves.

Its usual partner is the rowan, but the rowan on the whole prefers the smaller becks, where it is often the only tree. And though it lives in wild enough spots it is a meditative tree, not particularly graceful, and with rather drab leaves. It is only in early autumn, when the bunches of orange or red berries weigh down the branches, that it is as romantic as its name.

The rowan is also a tree of the fellsides, where only the juniper grows at a greater height. Round waterfalls it rises to 2,000 feet. Elder also climbs high alongside the becks, and hawthorn, each giving a crop of white blossom, the one

Bowder Stone, Upper Borrowdale
Goatswater and Dow Crag

in June, the other in May. The juniper may sometimes be seen in the lower dales as a tight dark flame of a tree, but more often it belongs to the desolate fellsides. Here it does not grow tree-like, but straggles as a thick bush, from a distance looking like gorse when kissing is out of season. It is then a shrub of the damp slopes, where the mist hangs in it, bunched over the branches like muslin over currant bushes. Then it seems a bitter, sullen green. Yet when you look closer, its leaves have an under sheen of blue, and the spider-webs are laid all over them, gleaming with the wet. You forget its shapelessness then, because of the patterns of spine and web and water.

The other typical fell tree is a foreigner—the larch. The larch has been severely criticised. Wordsworth spoke of its doing "great injury to the appearance of the country." Yet any tree which can make itself so well at home deserves, at least, "naturalisation." Throughout these pages there will be no attempt to discriminate between indigenous plants and those which have come to the district, perhaps in sacks or seedbags to begin with, and then settled down and lived like the natives.

The larch has certainly settled down, and there is not a lovelier green among the fells than the April green of the larch. It washes in a great gush up some of the ghylls, and well deserves to be defended by Faber, much less of a poet than Wordsworth, but, in this matter, surely clearer sighted.[1]

It is another stranger, the sycamore, which is often the only tree on the coastal flanks of the mountains. It grows in clumps around the farms, tall and lean, not spreading, but sometimes bent by the perpetual gales till its upper branches hang over the roofs.

In the lower dales there are alders, oaks, wych-elms, old thorns, and fine yews. In the Silurian country, between Coniston and Windermere, many trees have been planted— spruce, firs, cedars. Here also there are unexpected trees,

[1] "There is no other tree on earth but thou
Which brings the sky so near or makes it seem so blue."
(Rev. E. W. Faber, 1814-63, who lived many years
in the Lake District.)

E

Coniston Water (down lake)
Windermere, looking west

like the magnolia, which grows near Coniston Lake, and the almond around Keswick. Yews are particularly plentiful on the limestone: there is a wood of them near Beetham, dark and Gothic, like a crypt with red pillars and blue-green fan-vaulting.

Lake Woods

The dale country is not a country of forests, with green-sward and undergrowth and great trees. Its typical woods are more like spreading thickets, with some chestnut and oak, but more often slender-trunked trees. There, as by the streams, the birch grows, and the hazel, on steep slopes, with bramble, and tutsan tangling round the roots. There is not much soil, and the roots grip the stones, where the little becks scour them clear of moss. Here in early March there is a time when the hazel catkins are hanging and yellow, but still, not flicking their pollen about. The sky is often grey, and the grass still dark and the bracken brown, so that the catkins glow with a pale light of their own.

Later, when the catkins are dropping, it is the gean, the wild cherry, which is the most handsome tree of the dale woods, frequent but not clustered, blue-white, the colour of skimmed milk, above the still-brown bracken.

The woods are full of tits of all kinds, and the rocks are whiskered with fern. Sometimes they descend to lake-level, and even when they don't there may be a long line of trees along the lakeside. Coniston, Windermere, and particularly Ullswater in parts, are bordered by trees which curve over the edge, making a little tunnel along which you can walk on the rough slate beach. There scarcely seems to be any soil, and the slates squelch under your feet and the drift-wood branches crack, but still the trees can find something to feed on. Perhaps the dead rats and birds, and sometimes sheep which float to the shore, help to provide animal manure. This is the lakeside landscape of Beatrix Potter's *Squirrel Nutkin* and other stories. Tilberthwaite Farm, at the head of Coniston Lake, was owned by Miss Potter, who left it to the National Trust.

Ancient Forests

Cumberland once had three great forests, two in the north —Inglewood and Allerdale—and one on the mid-west— Copeland. The term "forest," of course, meant originally any land enclosed for the protection of game, but Inglewood at least was well wooded and famous for its timber. Inglewood occupied the valleys of the Caldew and the Petteril, and Allerdale was to the west of it, but as land outside this area was also afforested by Henry II, the Cumberland forest stretched from the sea to the east of the Eden Valley. North it went as far as Carlisle, and south to the route of the present Workington-Penrith railway. It must have been one of the largest forests in England.

Within this area the Crown had exclusive right to the red deer, the fallow deer, and the wild boar. Severe laws were passed to protect the game. No one was allowed to kill a deer, or even (in the time of Henry II) to walk the bounds of the forest with dogs or bow and arrows without a warrant. These laws caused considerable hardship to farmers, who were unable to prevent the deer straying out of the forest on to cultivated land. Hence it was not unusual for them to ask that a certain area should be disafforested so that they could take measures against the pests. There is a case on record in which the monks of Holme Cultram Abbey petitioned for the freeing of the island of Holme Cultram, which was two miles from the forest, but to which the deer used to stray and which was protected for that reason.

Inglewood not only had its game and its poachers, but also its outlaws, whose fame was scarcely less than that of Robin Hood of Sherwood:

> Mery it was in the grene foreste
>   Amonge the leves grene,
> Wheras men hunt east and west
>   Wyth bowes and arrowes kene;
>
> To raise the dere out of theyr denne;
>   Suche sightes hath ofte bene sene;
> As by thre yemen of the north countrey,
>   By them it is I meane.

57

The one of them hight Adam Bell,
The other Clym of the Clough,
The thyrd was Wyllyam of Cloudesley,
An archer good ynough.[1]

Modern Afforestation

These ancient forests have disappeared, yet there are still many plantations, especially in the lower reaches of the dales and along the west coast in the Gosforth and Muncaster districts. Recently, too, the Forestry Commission has bought estates for large-scale commercial afforestation. Since the proposal has met with much opposition it may be worth while to consider it in some detail.

First of all, the Commission has agreed not to buy any land in the centre of the district, thus leaving free the mountain block and the dales in which lie Derwentwater, Crummock and Buttermere, Ullswater, Grasmere and Rydal. Their chief present properties are in Ennerdale, around Whinlatter Pass, the spurs of Skiddaw above Bassenthwaite, and upper Eskdale around Hardknott Pass. In addition, if opportunity rises, the Commission proposes to buy estates in Miterdale, mid-Eskdale, Dunnerdale as far as Ulpha, all round Coniston Water, except for the head, and also between Esthwaite and upper Windermere. Many of these places are already planted or are being planted, and the controversy is concerned chiefly with the proposal to extend afforestation in mid-Eskdale and Dunnerdale.

The chief objection is that commercial planting damages the beauty and character of the district. It is the planting of conifers which is objected to, not that of hardwood or deciduous trees. Hardwood plantations are a delight in all the valleys where they appear. The Commission has agreed to plant hardwood wherever possible, but this, unfortunately, does not apply to much of the land it has bought. Moreover, on the wet fellsides, practically the only tree which will grow profitably is the Sitka Spruce, a tree of uniform shape and colour throughout the year.

To one who is used to the greys, purples, and soft greens

[1] *Adam Bell, Clym of the Clough and William of Cloudesley—Oxford Book of Ballads.*

of the rock and the turf, the colouring of the spruce is sombre and dull. Moreover, it is necessary that the trees should be planted regularly, in straight rows. In the early stages, when the trees are small, the effect is as if the fells had been combed.

To all of this objections have been made—yet I feel that the objections have been based on a wrong way of looking at the Lake District, or indeed at any part of the world. It is wrong, I think, to regard the District as an album of views, the sole purpose of which is to please the beholder. The District, indeed, is a living part of the countryside, having its own function in the life and economy of the nation. Its beauty is only a by-product. And in any case its beauty is not to be assessed only in terms of "views." Which is the more beautiful—a young spruce tree or Bowfell?

In any case, I do not think that conifer plantations invariably spoil the landscape. The dark colouring, the geometric lines and rectangles, give an oddness to the scene which I find not unpleasing. It is strange, it is sometimes harsh, but it is neither sentimental nor sham, and it is the sentimental and the sham which are the great dangers to the Lake District.

Mr. H. H. Symonds, who has written with great love and knowledge of the fells, is eloquent against the conifers.[1] "Bird life perishes," he says, "for there are no berried trees as plant life perishes; the barren undergrowth of a coniferous woodland is a pale, bloodless thing."

Now I have had much experience of conifer plantations in the New Forest, and I certainly would not call them "pale and bloodless." They are dark, certainly, but it is a thick, frightening darkness. These plantations are of Scots pines rather than of spruces, and though there are few flowers, they are not without life. Every now and then, in the half-dusk, you will hear the song of the robin, dripping like a trickle of liquid light, or the brighter trill of the wren. Thrushes, too, are not rare in the pine woods, especially at the edges, and you will see the jay flying low among the trunks. It is a tense, wary, surprising world.

This may seem a poor substitute for the wheatear and the

[1] See *Afforestation in the Lake District,* by H. H. Symonds. Dent.

ring-ouzel and the fellside orchis and saxifrages. So it is.
But remember the real function of the trees. Trees (in commercial plantations) are grown to be chopped down, and
when this is done it will be found that they have helped to
bind and conserve the fellside. The exposed slopes of Cumberland and Westmorland, especially those towards the sea,
are subject to great erosion. Unless they have trees to protect them they will soon be bare rock. The Manchester
Water engineers realised this, and planted trees around their
reservoir of Thirlmere, to prevent soil being washed into
the lake. I myself know a fellside where a wood was cut
down during the war years of 1914-18. At first it was
thickly covered with flowers; now it is bare as bone.

Even on a slope which is fairly bare to begin with, the
planting of trees helps to hold what soil there is and creates
more from leaf mould—this is particularly the case with
hardwood, of course. Then, when the trees are felled, you
will find within a spring or two a thick growth of brambles,
primroses, wood anemones, bluebells, foxgloves, and, nowadays, rose-bay willow-herb. The richness of an area of felled
woodland is of great contrast with the bareness of the surrounding land.

Some of the people who object to the planting of conifers
recoil also from the time when they will be felled. They are
pained by the thought of chopped trees, of the noise of the
lorries, and even of the ruts in the road. For such people I
feel that one of their main motives is a dislike of change.
Nostalgia is a powerful emotion. The fells make their first
appeal in childhood and adolescence, and the memory of
them becomes private and sacred. Then it seems sacrilege
to build a house, to change a stile into a gate, or to alter the
shape of a hedge. There is no harm in such nostalgia, but it
is as well to recognise it for what it is.

Another objection to afforestation is that it will injure the
Herdwick sheep farming. I am not competent to weigh the
economic advantages and disadvantages of sheep and trees.
While planting is going on a reasonable number of men will
be needed, but afterwards only very few—certainly not
enough to affect unemployment in the mining area of west
Cumberland, to relieve which is one of the aims of the

scheme. But, later, there will no doubt be sawmills and accompanying industries.

The Herdwick industry does seem likely to suffer, as several of the more important farms have been taken over, and these are very necessary for breeding a local type to which new blood cannot be introduced from outside the area. Also the afforestation of the lower slopes, leaving land above 1,200 or 1,500 feet for pasture, is going to deprive the sheep of their winter feed.

Nevertheless, while I have the greatest respect for many of those who have objected to afforestation, I feel that their attitude is based on the desire to *preserve* the Lake District. Now that seems to me deplorable. Lord preserve us from the preservers. I am hag-ridden with the prospect of the dales becoming a museum, a Piece of Old England, with the children standing at road ends to sell daffodils to motorists, and the older people allowing themselves to be photographed for a contribution to the "Missionary Box"—this has been known to happen in Hawkshead. And the only way to prevent this is for the dales to continue as a living, economic unit, in whatever way they can. The farmer, the shepherd, the miner, have a natural respect for the land. It is the holiday-maker, the grouse-shooter, the artist, however susceptible to beauty, who looks upon the district as a means of satisfying his own wishes. The farmer, the shepherd, the miner, go about their business and don't give a damn for beauty. Yet beauty is often a by-product of their work. The stone walls were not built for the sake of beauty; neither were the bridges, nor the farms, nor the warehouses of Ambleside and Hawkshead. Yet they are part of the charm of the countryside. If necessary, I would rather see the whole of the dales covered with mining shafts and chimneys than with select verandas for tourists and æsthetes. The colliery coast around Moresby gives a far nobler view than the promenade at Bowness-on-Windermere.[1]

[1] It may be added that much could be done to modify the geometric effect of the conifers by planting an irregular surround of native trees. If these included berry-bearing trees, like rowan and guelder rose, there would be no loss in bird-life.

Flowers

If you want to know what flowers grow in Cumberland and Westmorland you should consult the County Floras. Yet, to anyone but a botanist, the County Floras may be deceptive. To a botanist, a flower is of interest largely in proportion to its rarity. But it is not the rare flowers, on the whole, which make up the true botanical character of a county, it is rather the special balance of common and less common flowers. Thus it is exciting to know that Alpine Campion (*Lychnis alpina*) grows on Hobcarten Fell, but this adds only a tiny speck to the floral picture. On the other hand, you catch the true tang of Cumberland when you know that Alpine Campion's two common relations, Red and White Campion, are known as fadder-dees and mudder-dees, because if you pluck the red flowers your father will die, and the white flowers will likewise do for your mother.

I want, therefore, not to give a list of rare or even common flowers, but to try to say what flowers are typical of one or two types of country in the district.

Flowers of the Fells

As we climb the fells we recede, as it were, into the bare country of the tundra. The tops of the highest fells (over 2,700 feet) are classed in Watson's mid-arctic zone. These include the Scafell, Bowfell and Pillar groups, Skiddaw, Blencathra and Helvellyn. They are mostly bare rock with little vegetation of any sort, and the two characteristic plants are the dwarf willow (*Salix herbacea*) and *Carex rigida*.

From thence downward, to 1,800 feet, is Watson's infra-arctic zone, which again is mostly rocky fellside, but touches also one or two of the highest tarns, of which Sprinkling Tarn below Esk Hause is the most important. Here there are lots of alpine plants: the saxifrages—purple (*S. oppositifolia*), clustered alpine (*S. nivalis*)—together with less alpine species, no less lovely, like mossy saxifrage, and yellow mountain; rose-root (*Sedum rhodiola*); and moss campion (*Silene acaulis*). Here, too, we find alpine varieties of many familiar lowland flowers—of hawkweed, mouse-ear chickweed, lady's mantle, and even scurvy grass. Some quite ordinary meadow flowers manage to survive at 2,000 feet or a little lower, especially around becks and other moist places—yarrow, common tormentil, and several of the buttercups.

As we come lower down the slopes there are many stonecrops and saxifrages, and the foxglove, especially where timber has been felled—in the lower regions, rose-bay willow-herb is becoming equally common.

Round about 1,500 feet, or even as high as 1,800, the bracken appears. It is usually rather thin at the top, but on the lower slopes it makes a thick jungle, waist-high, or even shoulder-high. It is exhausting to force your way through it in mid-summer, when the flies buzz round your head and you cannot see where you are putting your feet. Then you realise the toughness of the stalks, and the sharpness of their edges if you happen to run your hand along one of them. But the bracken is surely one of the best of all mountain coverings. It does not go into dead black for half the year like heather. Only for one month at the height of the summer is it dull—before that it is the quick green of larch, and afterwards it mellows through yellows, browns, reds and purples, and even keeps on smouldering under the snow, so that the green of spring comes up among the brown of the previous year. In many of the fellside farms the bracken is cut for bedding, and as it lies to dry it flames almost as yellow as the gorse, and then, when it is carted away, it leaves a sober patch of stubbly turf, making the fellside piebald.

There are the heathers, too, at about this height, and spreading indeed from shore level to the tops of the fells. And there are the berried plants—bilberry, cowberry, bog whortleberry and, much lower down, cranberry. The stone bramble also grows among the hills. Of all these the bilberry (*Vaccinium myrtillus*) is by far the most common. It seems to choose not the steep slopes, but flat terraces and combes, and peat bogs, where, perhaps, old tarns once stood. There, in summer, it is a dark, rather bitter green, with the berries, like purple pearls, hidden till you move the leaves. But in a good season you can sit and fill your pocket with berries without moving from one place. The bilberry is one of the plants that town children know about, and each summer they go in crowds to the moors and gather berries. They gather cranberries, too, from the mosses beside the estuaries and sell them to the bakers, who make tarts out of them. The cranberry, after it has been cooked, is a ripe, juicy fruit, which you can burst with your tongue against your teeth.

By the becks, as you come down the fellsides, there is golden saxifrage, like greenish-yellow hair among the rocks. Lower down, where the becks are slower and there is more soil around them, you find water crowfoot and wood anemone, and great masses of ramsons, which look like Christmas-tree decorations and stink of garlic if you tread on them. Buckbean and grass of Parnassus are two of the loveliest of the flowers of the mountain mosses, and both grow also near the coast. I have found grass of Parnassus in the drain of a war-time aerodrome. To a casual glance it is not particularly impressive, rather like a bleached meadow buttercup. But when you look inside, its petals are streaked as with watermarks on writing paper. There are ten stamens, pure white: five of them are barren, shaped like Spanish combs and tipped with little yellow globes, and five are fertile, bearing anthers. The fertile stamens are bent over the centre of the flower when it opens, little fists clenched across the breast, but they straighten out one by one, making patterns of stretched and bent stamens which vary from flower to flower.

The mimulus, or the monkey-flower, is an American species which has settled in the becks, often quite swift ones, where it strains and tugs with the current, rocking its yellow trumpets, spotted with red. And another American flower is sandwort-like claytonia—not the common perfoliate claytonia of the south, but *Claytonia alsinoides*. It seems to have been introduced not so very long ago and is spreading rapidly, and is found not only in swamps and streams, but also on dry walls and as a garden weed. The Himalayan balsam, which is such a feature today of canals and drains in central Lancashire, is also beginning to appear in the district.

Mountain Pastures

Of all the Cumberland flowers those of the mountain pastures are to me the most exciting. It is hard to say how these differ from the flowers of the fells or of the lowlands, yet they do, and you cannot mistake the new character of the plants the moment you turn away from the lowlands or step down from the mountains. This character is the same wherever the mountain pastures are found—in the dales, in the lake country around Coniston and Windermere, and in the little Westmorland valleys around Kendal.

It shows itself even in the grass, which seems dark green, wide-bladed, cool and sappy, fed on the mists. And among it you find orchises of many kinds, and cow-wheat, betony, lousewort—all half-secret plants, of dark, brooding colours, rich orange or purple. Typical, too, are the marsh marigolds growing as common as buttercups in the damp fields. They are usually a mountain variety (*Caltha palustris*, var. *minor*), with flowers of a darker yellow growing close to the ground—there are acres of them beside Torver Station beneath the cliffs of Dow and Old Man. Another of the Ranunculus tribe common in the dales is the beautiful globe-flower (*Trollius europæus*), with huge yellow sepals enclosing the flower like the rind of an orange. Frequent also is lady's mantle, not very conspicuous, but making a flat green covering still darker than the grass.

Even the flowers which are also common in the lowlands —wood-sorrel, dog-violet, sweet violet, bluebell (which, as in Scotland, is usually called the wild hyacinth), moschatel, with dog's mercury, primrose, and enchanter's nightshade at the edge of woods—seen here have a darker, richer look. They all have that rather intense appearance of flowers which feed among thunderclouds, or of the orchises which look as if the grass were sweating blood. Bistort or snake-weed is also common, and is used in herb puddings. There are some nutritious-looking plants in the graveyard of St. George's, Millom, but no one seems to want them.[1] When the leaves grow in spring, they have the same dark colour as the mountain grass, and they seem to grow thickly in

---

[1] The rather uncommon winter heliotrope grows in the same churchyard.

isolated patches. But when the flowers are out, held on high stalks, like pink ears of wheat, they are paler and gayer than most of the mountain flowers. In Cumberland they are called Easter Magiants or Easterman Giants. The derivation may be from the French "mangeant," because it is used as a vegetable, but perhaps there is a reference to Magi, for the leaves, though not the flowers, help to announce Easter and spring. Still more delicate is the mountain pansy, usually called the yellow mountain pansy (*Viola lutea*), though the pure yellow forms are uncommon. They occur around Dockray in Matterdale, however, and higher up the same valley, around Dowthwaite Head, are thousands of the blue variety, taller than the dog-violet, and with their two upper petals elongated like rabbits' ears.

Of the more conspicuous flowers, the giant bellflower (*Campanula latifolia*) is one of the most attractive. It is very frequent in the dales, growing in the dirt at the roadsides, and it climbs quite high in places. Water ragwort also grows up to 1,500 feet along the streams, but the most noticeable of the Compositæ is golden-rod, which grows on the slate rocks, in fellside woods and along the lake shores. Water lobelia is there too.

Around the fellside farms are to be found many of the flowers which have escaped from the gardens and manage to fend for themselves. The yellow Welsh poppy is one of the commonest, and you will also find Solomon's seal, lungwort or Adam and Eve, snowdrops and daffodils. Perhaps the daffodils are really wild in parts. No doubt many of those which grow beside the rivers have spread from bulbs washed from cottage gardens, but in some places, as near Broughton Mills in the Lickle Valley, there are fields of them, growing as thick as corn—small, pale-flowered blooms on short stalks. For some reason the daffodil is one of the few flowers which the boy from the town is ready to pick. Buttercups, stitchwort, loosestrife—he would not be seen dead with any of these; but daffodils, primroses and bluebells are flowers which he can gather without being "sissy," and he does gather them in huge bunches, and brings them home tied on to sticks cut from the hedges. Single daffodils may also be worn in cloth caps or as a buttonhole with a blue serge suit.

Most people know Dorothy Wordsworth's description of the daffodils by Gowbarrow Park which inspired brother William's poem, but her journal is full of lesser-known passages about flowers. Always she sees things vividly and tenderly, and she transcribes something of the very dialect of the mountain pastures and the dale villages: "Wednesday, 12th May.—A sunshiny, but coldish morning. We walked into Easedale. . . . We brought home heckberry blossom, crab blossom, the *Anemone nemorosa*, marsh marigold, speedwell—that beautiful blue one, the colour of the bluestone or glass used in jewellery—with the beautiful pearl-like chives. Anemones are in abundance, and still the dear, dear primroses, violets in beds, pansies in abundance, and the little celandine. I pulled a bunch of the taller celandine."

Flowers of the Coast

After the fells the best places for flowers in Cumberland and North Lonsdale are along the coast. Here again there are a good many rare-ish flowers, but it is the more abundant which give character to the scene. The two lengths of rocky coast—limestone in North Lonsdale and sandstone in St. Bees—offer the rarer cresses, viper's bugloss, and such ferns as sea-spleenwort, but it is the dunes and marshes which are the most exciting places for the flower-seeker who is not primarily a botanist.

The dunes stretch from Walney Island to St. Bees Head, and from Maryport northward along the edge of the Solway. Here, tipped over the ground, are great splashes of colour in summer, the soft colours of women's dresses, pinks, mauves, pale yellows and orange. Lady's bedstraw is yellow and frilly, and never seems to get dirty. Yellow stonecrop is also pale, but a more acid colour, pressed closer to the dune. The Isle of Man cabbage, one of the rarer brassicas, grows here and there, lemon-coloured and rather tender-looking. You can slip out and gather it when the train stops at Seascale Station. Then there are fat dandelions when the sand has more soil in it, and hawkweeds by the million that I cannot recognise. On an afternoon of late summer when the wind blew from the dunes, sitting at a window in a street of a coastal town, I have seen a parachute flight of hawkweed and dandelion "clocks," thousand upon thousand, floating and skating across the roofs for hour after hour.

At Seascale the special decoration of the coast is the bloody crane's-bill. Its leaves cover the clayey dunes like green coco-nut matting, and the pink cups are so lovely that many visitors think the plant is a garden escape. It grows northward in the county but not southward (except for a patch on the extreme tip of Hodbarrow Point), and it spreads itself again on the shores of Walney. This long island, bent like the head of a harpoon round the peninsula, is now a suburb of Barrow-in-Furness. At Bigger Bank there used to be a putting green and ice-cream booths, but past the golf-course, towards North Scale, the coast becomes suddenly as wild as anything between Silecroft and Seascale. Because of some twist in the line of the dune, you do not see the Duddon Estuary, and the shore seems to go straight on to the foot of Black Combe, with the light-ship off Selker Rocks near Bootle. There is bright, granity shingle, and sea-birds and porpoises out to sea. Yet the shipyards are only a bus-ride away.

Here there is not only the bloody crane's-bill, but also a sub-species (*Geranium sanguineum lancastrienses*) native only on Walney Island. Its petals are streaked and paler than those of the normal form, as if they were shy about the swearing. Another crane's-bill very common on the dunes is herb Robert, while a very similar flower, hemlock stork's-bill, is more restricted to the coast. Restharrow crawls on the sand, throwing out its little pink sweet-peas, but it is a sticky plant and gets clart up with sand, so that there is no pleasure in gathering it. Sea bindweed crawls, too, but manages to keep itself clean. It has flowers about the size of those of lesser bindweed, but pinker. Devil's nightcap, the greater bindweed, sometimes grows, especially at Seascale, which is particularly rich in flowers. Here for a few hundred yards the coast suddenly becomes respectable, trying to look as if it were in Sussex. There are large boarding houses of purple brick on the low cliffs, a girls' school, a boys' pre-paratory school, and a swagger golf-course. It is not sur-prising that the visitors take the bloody crane's-bill for a garden escape. They probably think that the local council planted out all the burnet roses which grow there—the whitest and most genteel of all the wild roses.

On the whole, however, the white flowers of the coast are not very respectable in appearance. They are rather things like sea-kale and the marine variety of scentless mayweed. But in early spring the whitlow grass (*Draba verna*) grows all along the dunes, wagging its tiny white flowers rather gaily. Thalecress is also fond of the sand. It grows straight out of a little rosette of leaves laid on the ground and is more sedate than most of the cresses.

There are many more flowers of the dunes—harebell, heartsease, eyebright, the yellow-horned poppy—but perhaps you remember most vividly the sea-holly, beautiful at all times: in early summer, when the leaves are sprayed with silver-gilt, and in late summer when the shining blue flowers are fully out. If you bring it home it will last unchanged for months without water, unlike the sea-spurge, which often grows beside it, and which, when gathered, soon saps its life away into a nasty-smelling limpness.

The Coastal Marshes

As well as the dunes and the rocks there are the salt marshes at the mouth of several of the rivers, and especially along the Solway. These marshes have a strange attraction of their own, and even when, as at the mouth of the Duddon, and around Workington and Maryport, they are soiled and smeared by smoke and scum from the iron and steel works, they do not lose their character. They are neither land proper nor sea proper, and yet they are not a clean border-line like sand and shingle and dunes. At low tide they show acres and acres of grass. The tide rises and you do not see it because it is in the gulleys, and then in a short while the marshes seem to become lakes or fiords or even, if it is stormy, the open sea.

The turf of these marshes can be as soft as a mouse's hair. Sea-washed turf from Silloth and places round Morecambe Bay is famous for bowling greens. Because it takes its feed more from the sea than from the weather, this turf always has an underlying greenness, but after it has flowered, the seed pods throw a thin brown muslin across it so that it looks at the same time to be shooting and yet half-dead.

There are many small flowers of these marshes—sea-plantain, buck's-horn plantain, sea milkwort, saltwort, sea-lavender. Spring squill does not seem to grow at all in Cumberland, which peeves me greatly, for Bentham and Hooker describe it as common on "the western and northern coasts of Great Britain." Yellow flag, the wild iris, grows often at the point where the salt marsh joins the river bed at the foot of the dale.

But there are three flowers which are specially character-istic of the marshes, each at a different time of the year. First there is the scurvy-grass, which comes into flower in April in the mud at the side of the gullies, and looks like the white rock of cottage gardens. Many people despise this plant, perhaps because it often grows near the mouths of sewers, or gets clogged with coal-dust, as in Workington Harbour, or with red ore-dust in the iron country. Individually, it is one of the more untidy and less attractive cresses, but in bulk it shows a welcome mass of white when the rest of the marshes are still the purply green of winter. Its leaves, too, before the dirt gets on them, are a bright and shiny green. This plant is found in abundance on the shores of the arctic seas, and the Elizabethan sailors used to eat it as a cure for scurvy in the days before lemons and bottled vitamins. It must have been nearly as unappetising as boiled cabbage.

After the scurvy-grass has dropped its petals and pro-duced globular pods, the thrift comes, the flower of the threepenny-bit. It grows on the drier parts, those which are covered only by the spring tides, and it is often so thick and close that the mud-flats look pink. When it fades it remains there, stiff and brittle, the colour of faintly charred paper, hissing quietly in the wind.

Lastly, in the autumn, much less in numbers but indi-vidual and charming, comes the sea-aster, which looks like single mauve flowers of Michaelmas daisies, sometimes very short, sometimes a foot or two in height.

The salt marsh pushes its fingers surprisingly high into the fells. In Dunnerdale you come down the daffodil woods below Stickle Pike, and then at Duddon Bridge, with the

Grasmere, early morning
Grasmere, north end

river among the boulders, and hazels, cherry and spindle-wood all round you, you notice the salt only a few yards away. Below Muncaster, the marsh is wedged up among the granite hills of lower Eskdale. Moreover, before the land had settled to its present level, the tides were twenty-five feet higher, which must have made the sea stretch well into Westmorland along the Kent, and as far as Woodland up the Duddon Estuary.

The Solway

But the greatest of all these marshes are those which border the Solway. The Solway is a county of its own. No one who has not lived beside it (and I have not) can see it except as a stranger. Yet even a stranger cannot deny its personality. As soon as you round the northern point of St. Bees Head there is a new vista. You see the sea sweeping inwards almost to Carlisle, and, beyond, the hills of Kirkcud-brightshire and Annan, with Criffel dominating them as Black Combe dominates the South Cumberland coast. This is the land of enormous mudflats and sands; of the tide which comes in like a galloping horse (as Scott describes it in *Redgauntlet*); of moss-troopers and smugglers. Here are the little ports—Allonby, Silloth, Bowness and Port Carlisle; here are the war-time aerodromes; here is the now disused viaduct from Bowness to Annan which was planned to make a new north-west route to Scotland. Not far from Maryport (the name is modern) Mary, Queen of Scots, landed after her flight from Scotland; at Burgh-by-Sands Edward I prepared to subdue the Scots and died there before he started.

Flowers of the Lowlands

The fells and the coasts have each their own special flora, but the lowlands, the everyday working part of the country, have only the general sort of flowers which they share with the rest of England. There are plenty of rare ones, of course, but it is not the rare ones I remember.

I remember instead: cornfields, bright in spring with the chalky yellow of charlock, which disappears as the corn over-tops it, so that first it is yellow, then yellow shot with green,

F

Ullswater, stormy day—looking up lake
Buttermere, down lake

then green shot with yellow, then just green. The blue corn-flower is almost unknown, but the corn-cockle has been appearing more often lately, perhaps because war-time seed was less carefully sorted. Chicory also gets sown with the corn, and produces its flat flowers, pinned against the stalk like blue catherine wheels.

I remember fields in autumn, the smell of mangolds in the mist, and the roots bulging almost out of the soil, with the tops gnawed off where sheep have broken in. There, in the soil, is a tangle of weeds going to seed—chickweed, knotgrass, common persicaria, black bindweed, and the ragged and spiky hemp-nettle. Corn-marigolds flower right on to December, shining out through the damp air, brighter even than the dead bracken and the oak leaves. Ragwort also persists, its slow smoulder going out clinker by clinker as each separate flower-head turns to seed or blackens unfer-tilised. And in the hedges, red campion, dove's-foot crane's-bill and hawkweeds cling on grimly.

I remember the half-tame flowers around old cottages which have crumbled and fallen: these are the once wild flowers, grown and tended in gardens, which now manage to struggle on by themselves, long after the garden has become field or verge to a lane. Such are comfrey, feverfew, soapwort, lesser periwinkle, green alkanet, large red dead-nettle with its spotted leaves. And on the walls of more imposing ruins, the castles and abbeys, there are mouse-ear hawkweed, rue-leaved saxifrage and the wallflower.

And I remember with special joy the flowers of railway sidings and cuttings: colt's-foot along the banks in March and primroses in April. Between Dalton and Carnforth there are many patches of cowslips, which grow profusely in the limestone country, and also push into the slate along the Kendal-Windermere line. Soon after the primroses comes a time of sudden and transient whiteness along the railway banks, when the despised ribwort plantain hangs rings of white anthers around its dark-brown knob. If the stalks are twisted round the heads in a loop and tugged sharply, the heads will fly off as from a catapult. Then in summer there are tall, handsome flowers like the dog-daisy and yellow toadflax, and in the goods-yards, among the buffers and sleepers, tangles of wild carrot, crepises, cinquefoil, ivy-leaved toadflax on the walls, hogweed and many kinds of vetch. The greater bindweed climbs up stalks of sorrel like a spiral staircase, and curls around blocks of wood or pieces of iron left lying about, lolling its white bells on the rust. In the cinders of the track the least toadflax grows all along the West Cumberland coast. Perhaps the seeds are wafted by the draught from passing trains.

Flowers of the Mines

Finally, there are the mines. The collieries are not well off in flowers, and in any case coal dust and the coal slime quickly rub the freshness off a bloom, though along the coast from Whitehaven to Harrington there are patches of yellow bird's-foot trefoil in the black soil. The iron-ore mines, however, are rich in flowers. The heaps of rubble which lie about are evidently good soil for plants, for they are soon grown over till they look not like scars, but like rich red ploughland going back into fallow. There is always much waste land among the mines—land which has subsided, or has been dug up a bit, and has huts scattered about on it, and sleepers, old pylons, bits of machinery lying around everywhere. Among the old railway tracks and the cinder paths grow all the small, tight flowers of thin soil—strawberry, yellow stonecrop, blue bugle, crosswort, hedge bedstraw, silverweed, lots of crane's-bills, with the potato flowers of bittersweet twisting among them all. Willows grow in abundance, and brambles, with great fat berries which perhaps take their colour and tang from the iron they feed on. During the war one mine—technically a prohibited area—issued permits at a shilling a time to gather blackberries, the money going to the Red Cross. Where there are old hedges they are usually neglected, and the thorns have grown into trees, tall and bent above the mound of sods, each incredibly senile like characters in a Yeats play. In the shadow of the hedge grows the moschatel, small and unnoticed, yet perhaps the commonest of all spring flowers in West Cumberland.

There are bigger and handsomer flowers too—perforated St. John's wort, foxglove, rose-bay willow-herb, codlins-

73

and-cream, and greater mullein. The mullein would be one of the most striking of our wild flowers if all its flower heads came out together. Instead they come out first at the bottom, as if a lamplighter were climbing its fat stalk, and as each flower head lights up, the one below goes out.

And where there is water there are forget-me-nots; the brooklime, the bluest of the speedwells; figwort, smelling like rotten meat; marsh cinquefoil, the colour of chocolate; twayblade and prettier orchises. In some places there are more exciting things, especially around Workington, where, in the marsh wastes behind the harbour, rare and even foreign flowers spring up from time to time, the seeds having come there among the ships' cargoes.

I have heard it said that the mining district of Cumberland is a land which has been exploited by man and then abandoned. It has certainly not been abandoned by nature. Some of the pits are caving in, the water is breaking through the dykes, the old buildings and pithead gear are falling, but the cresses and the buttercups reclaim the soil. Man struck the rock and the rock gushed blood, but the bloody crane's-bill grows on the red scabs of rubble.

Ferns

Of mosses, lichens, horsetails, grasses and fungi I won't try to speak, but the mountains of Cumberland and Westmorland are, of course, a fine place for ferns. Many of the rarer species grow there—Tunbridge filmy fern, Wilson's filmy fern, oblong Woodsia (*Woodsia ilvensis*), holly fern, oak fern, green spleenwort (*Asplenium viride*). The bracken I have already spoken of, and parsley fern is also very common, but is much more confined to the rocks and hills. It is a lovely little fern, with its barren fronds very like the parsley leaves that it is named after, and its fruiting fronds quite distinct, with narrowed segments, standing more upright. When the latter are covered with spores, they are a rich chocolate brown, beside the barren fronds, which remain a light green throughout the summer. It is fond of old walls and rocky slopes where water slithers down.

The walls of the farms are usually half-covered with the common maidenhair spleenwort and wall-rue, and often there is also hart's-tongue and scaly spleenwort or "rusty backs," which looks like a hart's-tongue with hair behind the ears. In the fellside woods the hard fern (*Blechnum spicant*) is abundant, its thick bush of barren fronds growing in damp places, with the fruiting fronds straight up the middle, like long combs with half the teeth knocked out. The lady fern is at her loveliest in these woods, great fountains of soft green fronds, with the male fern ("meckans"), in lots of its slight variations, to keep her company, and many of the complicated species of shield and buckler ferns. In the lower woods the royal fern still survives, though it is constantly dug up for gardens and backyards. It is called "bog onion" for some strange reason, and grows most regally in the peat bogs just above high tide level on the western estuaries.

Adder's tongue and moonwort belong more to the lower meadows. Adder's tongue, for instance, appeared very plentifully in the park and children's pleasure ground of a small mining town during the early summer of the war. Thousands of people walked over the spot every week, children rolled on the grass, and girls and young men strolled there, but the fern is small, rather like a dock-leaf, and few noticed it. After two or three years it dwindled and disappeared, as inexplicably as it came.

Gardens

Gardens are partly the work of God who makes the country and partly of man who makes the town. But in Cumberland and Westmorland God does more than His fair share. I am thinking not of the gardens of the great houses of the lowlands, Lowther Castle, Rose Castle, Sizergh Castle and the rest, with their lawns, rose beds, and topiary art, but of rough-and-tumble, half-wild gardens of the lower fells and the dales.

First there are the farms, small, square and perhaps whitewashed, with half an acre or so of fellside walled off from the rabbits. Often the ground is steep and rocky, with only a few apple trees planted there. The blossom on the apples tosses in the wind like foam and the trunks creak in stockings of whitewash. Perhaps there are damsons, too, as in the Rusland Valley, where thousands of trees flower every spring. White is the colour of the fellside farms, bright white in spring against the grey and green; white of white-wash, and of blossom and of washing too, tugging and twirling on the clothes-line stretched from tree to tree. And earlier there is the white of snowdrops. Then the daffodils: not white, of course, but having something of the same Easter cleanness and freshness. It is in these orchards, not in fields or by the riverside, that the daffodils look their best, when they strain and rebound in the winds.

Lower in the dales, and around the shoulders of the mountains, and especially in all the low hills around Coniston and Windermere, there are larger gardens, but still shaggy and half-wild. Here are the small manors, often fortified at one time against Scottish raiders, and the country houses built in the nineteenth century for settlers among the lakes. They are mostly dark, these gardens, with firs and monkey-puzzles throwing shadows over the roofs, and the crags in a great wall above them. There are hollies, too, grown into trees, and yews and other dark-leaved trees and shrubs, and the pale Solomon's seal, hanging its white chessmen under the leaves.

But the dominant plant is the rhododendron. Many people do not like rhododendrons. They belong to the Asiatic mountains, but if they are at home anywhere in England it is surely here. They grow into huge bulks, scarcely shaped like trees, but solid as rocks. They bulge around the houses in waves, sometimes overtopping the chimneys, so that the roofs look half-submerged like the farms of a drowned valley. The steep gables and dormers of dark green slate jut out among the darker green leaves. In spring the bushes flower, and the most common of all the colours is a dark, stained-glass red, glowing intensely among the almost black leaves. The blackbird nests there, and the mountain thrushes and all birds whose songs flash and flicker in the evening dusk.

Chapter V

CREATURES GREAT AND SMALL

1. *Mammals*

THE Lake District would seem to be a splendid place to find those rarer and fiercer animals which have been hunted out of the rest of England. A few centuries ago you might have met the wolf, brown bear, wild boar, wild ox, badger, red deer and fallow deer. Even a few generations ago there were the wildcat, the polecat and the pine-marten. The red deer still exists, like the fallow deer, in parks; the badger seems to have become extinct about the end of the eighteenth century, though it has repatriated itself recently; the pine marten lingers on. The rest are only a memory.

But what a memory! Think of packs of wolves on Skiddaw or the Ullswater fells falling on the flocks of the Wigton plain and the Eden Valley. Early man no doubt had often to protect his sheep from wolves, and wolf hunts must have been common even in Saxon times. The Reverend H. A. Macpherson[1] says that he cannot find evidence that the wolf still existed in the Lake District much later than the end of the thirteenth century. Tradition, however, believes that it persisted a great deal longer. In Furness it is thought that the last wolf was killed on Humphrey Head in the fifteenth century. Certainly packs of wolf-hounds were kept at some of the castles and manors as late as the reign of Charles II, but the mouse-trap is no proof of the mouse.

The brown bear was not so common, but its remains have been found in a cave on Arnside Knott. It is not impossible that specimens may have been shipped from Ravenglass to the Roman arenas. Badgers, too, were often captured alive so that they might be baited by dogs. Throughout the seventeenth and eighteenth centuries the dalesmen seem to have been set on exterminating any vermin which they thought might harm their sheep or fowls, and they were encouraged in this by the churchwardens, who paid rewards varying from sixpence to five shillings for the heads of

[1] See Macpherson's *Fauna of Lakeland*.

badgers, foxes, polecats, ravens and the like. The skins of many of the animals brought good prices at Kendal and Ulverston.

The pine-marten began to get scarce in the second half of the last century, but it was still fairly common among the highest fells of Eskdale, Wasdale, and the Coniston district. It was called the sweet-mart to distinguish it from the pole-cat or foumart (foul mart), and both were often hunted with packs of dogs. Neither of the animals had much chance on level ground, but in their own country they gave rise to exciting chases among the crags and screes. The foumart, however, was commoner along the peat bogs and rough mosses around the Solway and Morecambe Bay. The pine marten still exists in some of its haunts, but the polecat seems to have disappeared, though several polecat ferrets have escaped during recent years and set up for them-selves in the fields.

Two other members of the same tribe are still common throughout the district—the weasel and the stoat. Neither is very popular, though both probably do more good by killing rats than they do harm, but they are both beautiful little animals. In particular I enjoy the sight of the weasel running along the boulders at the side of rivers, like an enormous and agile caterpillar. Its lishness and its apparent freedom from the usual restrictions of legs and joints make it look less like an animal than like an animate line running about in one of Walt Disney's abstract cartoons. The stoat does not change colour in winter here as often as it does in Scotland, but I have seen a pure ermine at a beckside only a few yards from the warehouses and hen-huts of a mining town. The otter, the water-weasel, is common too, and there are many meetings of otter-hounds, especially on the two rivers, the Eden and the Lune.

As for the fox, it is probably more at home in the Lakes than in any other part of England. Mass gas attacks would no doubt exterminate it, but, barring those, it holds its own without any need of preservation. Fox-hunting is no gentle-manly pastime here, but a practical, organised system for destroying foxes. Upland farmers lose too many hens and geese, and even lambs, to have chivalrous or sentimental feelings towards the fox, and are not unready to use gun and trap. Even gun and trap will not root a fox out of his earth among the rocks, so that the hunt is necessary to farming economy. This was recognised during the war, when the huntsmen of the Eskdale and Ennerdale pack were released from war service as a result of a farmers' petition.

Deer

The fox, the stoat, the weasel are able to look after themselves. This is hardly the case with the deer, which were once the wild aristocracy of the Lakes. The native deer is the red deer, which roamed the mountains and dales at the time of the Romans, giving not only their flesh for food but their horns for rough drinking cups and the like. Fine herds of red deer lived in Ennerdale, Wasdale and Eskdale as late as the seventeenth century, and their antlers are continually being found in the sands of the estuaries. Direct descendants of these herds still live in a wild state at Martindale, beside Ullswater, and wander over Helvellyn and also in many parts of Westmorland and High Furness.

The Romans may have introduced the fallow deer to the Lakes, or perhaps it did not arrive until later. It was once very common, especially in south Cumberland and around the lower reaches of the Leven and the Kent, where, as in other parts of the country, it is still preserved in parks. Near Millom Castle there are several fields called Sewel, which were evidently on the borders of the deer park, since "sewell" means a line of feathers fastened to string to keep deer from straying. The roe deer is confined now to the Border country above Carlisle.

Herdwicks

The deer have charm and an honourable history, but they can no longer claim the freedom of the fells. They are rather pensioners, permitted to live on as part of the decoration of the landscape. Their ancient inheritance has passed away from them, and if any animal can claim it surely the herdwicks can. These sheep are not wild, nor are they able to get on without the aid of men, but they have adapted themselves completely to their habitat, and they play an essential part in the life of the dales. They owe their existence not to sentiment but to practical value.

No animals look so much at home on the fells as do the herdwicks. They are small black-faced sheep, lithe and vigorous, able to climb like goats and to leap over any but the highest wall. They are lean about the legs and the flanks, though the wool which covers them like upholstery often hides this. It is only when they are allowed to laze about and batten in the riverside meadows that they put on flesh and give the sweet mutton they are famous for. When they have been clipped in summer they look quite naked and white as they climb among the rocks, or perhaps yellow if they have been dipped too. But when their wool is long it is usually grey, with bits of dead bracken and bramble and dung stuck to it. Sometimes you will see a sheep dragging by its wool a branch of thorn six feet long or more.

There is a legend that the herdwicks first came ashore from a wrecked ship of the Armada. That they came by sea is very likely, for it seems almost certain that they were brought to the district by the Vikings from Iceland or Norway. If that is true they belong to the same stock as the shepherds, and they have much the same individualistic habits. Each sheep belongs to its own flock and each flock to its own farm. The flocks are not collected and owned separately but are usually rented with the farm. When the tenant leaves he makes up for any deficiency in the flock or takes the benefit of any increase.

Each flock, too, has its "heaf" or pasture on the fells where it spends the summer and autumn. The sheep often know their own heaf so well that they will return to it from a long distance. Their memory is remarkable and rather fantastic. Canon Rawnsley tells of a flock which, having got used to leaping over a hurdle at a certain place in a lane, continued to leap whenever they passed there long after the hurdle had been taken away.[1]

Because the sheep wander freely on the fells, it is inevitable that some of them stray from their own heaf. The farmers, therefore, meet twice a year at a few traditional places, and there exchange and restore any sheep which may

[1] H. D. Rawnsley: *By Fell and Dale.*

have been lost. The identification of the sheep is easy to the shepherd because of a careful and elaborate system of markings. The sheep are smitten on the body with red ruddle or tar, or sometimes even with blue or green. The marks are usually stripes, pops (*i.e.*, round blobs), or initials, and are placed on different parts of the body. In addition the ears are cut in some distinctive way, or the horns are burned. Each farm inherits its own lug-marks, and in some cases this may go back to a long history. Certainly the habit has descended from the Vikings, to whom "lug-marks" were "law-marks." The ears may be cropped (*i.e.*, the end of the ear is chopped clean off) or forked or ritted (slit). They may be fork-bitted (*i.e.*, a V-shaped notch is cut out of the side of the ear), or key-bitted (a square notch). And as there is a top side and a bottom side to every ear, and two ears to every sheep, the number of permutations and combinations of the marks is very great.

In 1817 J. Walker of Martindale compiled *The Shepherd's Book*, which catalogued the lug-marks and smits belonging to each farm in the fells west of the Eden Valley. Several revisions were made and books were brought out for other parts of the district. I have beside me one of the latest and most comprehensive of these volumes, Gates's *New Shepherd's Guide*, published by the *West Cumberland Times* in 1879. This has nearly 500 pages, with an engraving of the same two prize sheep repeated three times a page with a romantic background of tree, lake and sky. On each engraving the smits are stamped in black and red and the lug-marks are indicated diagrammatically. Under each engraving is a technical description of the marks and the name of the farm and farmer to whom they belong. They are arranged roughly in townships and cover all the central fell and dale area. I open at the parish of Whitbeck:

John Grice, Far End;
cropped near, upper halved far, stroke down near lisk, pop on tailhead.

William Thompson, Barfield;
cropped and ritted near, stroke from shoulder blade on near side over back, and to lisk on far side.

James Robinson, Hall Foss;
cropped near, ritted far, three red strokes
down far shoulder in the form of a crow's
foot, J.R. on near side.

 George Kirkby, Beckside;
cropped and under key-bitted near, under
halfed far, three short strokes over back.

The shepherd used to count his sheep by a set of Celtic
numerals which came down from the early British tribes
who lived in Cumbria before the Saxons and the Northmen
came. The numerals are in groups of twenty. When a
shepherd had counted to twenty, he put up a finger and
started again. When all five fingers were up he had reached
the hundred, and he put a pebble in his pocket or a mark on
a wall. Here is one version:[1]

> Yan, taen, tether, mether, pimp;
> Teezar, leezar, catterah, horna, dick;
> Yan-dick, tan-dick, tether-dick, mether-dick, bumpit;
> Yan-a-bumpit, tan-a-bumpit, tedera-bumpit, medera-
>   bumpit, gigot.

Sheep-dogs

It is impossible to think of the herdwicks without thinking of the dogs which herd them. The fell sheep-dog is not
at all like the collie which wins prizes at shows. The value
of a sheep-dog depends on its ability, not its looks. The
dogs, indeed, are rarely pure in breed, and it is not unusual
for them to have quite a strong mixture of foxhound. If the
dog lives at a remote farm, it is often suspicious of strangers,
regarding the whole fellside as his own backyard. If, however, it lives at a farm by the roadside, where it is used to
passers-by, it is more likely to be very friendly, so friendly
that it may seem to be fawning, especially if it has been
taught to creep.

The sheep-dog is indispensable to the shepherd. The skill
of the dogs is known to everyone, and is demonstrated at

---

[1] Quoted from *Millom People and Places*, by Frank Warriner.

its highest in the sheep-dog trials held at Eskdale and else-where. Something of this skill was shown to the rest of England in the film *Owd Bob*, where the shepherd was played for some odd reason by Will Fyfe—a man with an accent as urban as that of the Cockney or the Lancashire mill-hand. The ordinary shepherd does not ask his dog to do elaborate tricks, however—he asks only that it shall manage the sheep quietly and intelligently, working over rough country and long distances. He will stand on a rock and with whistle, shout and wave of the arm will direct the dog over operations which may cover a good many acres. I have known a farmer send a dog on an errand which in-volved its being completely out of sight behind a bump in the ground. He could tell by the movement of the sheep whether the dog was working as hard as it ought to, and when it began to slacken off he would blow on his whistle to encourage it.

There are many stories of the wisdom of sheep-dogs. One —and I am assured of its truth—pleases me greatly. A farmer from Ulverston[1] sold some sheep to a farmer from Kirkby Lonsdale. The buyer, noticing that the Ulverston man had a very good dog, asked for the loan of it to help get the sheep home, and promised to send it back by pas-senger train. When he got to Kirkby-Lonsdale, however, he shut up the dog, hoping that it would eventually settle down in its new home. To inquiries from the owner he said that the dog must have gone astray on the railway journey. One day the dog broke out, had a look round the farm, picked out the sheep which had belonged to his real master, separated them from the rest of the flock and drove them back along the roads to Ulverston. And the Kirkby farmer could say nothing about it, as he should not have detained the dog!

2. *Birds*

In some ways the north-western corner of England is not very rich in wild birds. There is little of the fat farm land, with orchards, copses and hedges, which make the south of

[1] I have deliberately altered the place-names.

England such good country for the birds. Moreover, the district lies too far north for the full tide of summer migrants to break on it. The warblers, for instance, begin to get thinned out in numbers by the time they reach the Lakes— only the willow-warbler and the whitethroat are really common everywhere. The nightingale does not come at all, at any rate as a nesting bird. There are persistent rumours nearly every summer of nightingales reaching the south of the district. I have known charabanc trips run for people to listen to the song. No doubt any bird which sings at night is likely to be mistaken for a nightingale, but these may have been stray cock birds from Cheshire or the Midlands which had failed to find a mate. Hoopoes, bee-eaters and other exciting continental species which are always turning up in the southern counties are met with only as very rare passage migrants in the Lakes.[1] In the same way, the district is too far west for the main stream of the winter migrants which arrive from Scandinavia and the Arctic. They are often seen, especially on the slopes of the Pennines or the western marshes, but rarely in such numbers as appear on the Northumbrian coast and in East Anglia.

Still, within a small area the district offers a great variety of country, including two types which have a specialised bird life—the mountains and the coast.

Birds of the Fells

The highest fells have little to offer to the birds, and those we see there are usually high fliers rather than high nesters. Nevertheless, the wheatear nests nearly up to 3,000 feet, and a bird like the black grouse has been found nesting at 2,200 feet.[2]

The characteristic birds of the upper fells, however, are the birds of prey. And of these the raven is the patriarch. Ravens must have been common once, as you can tell from the many crags and hills named after them. There are not so many of them now, but they are holding their own on

[1] For an authoritative account see *The Birds of Lakeland*, edited by Ernest Blezard. Carlisle Natural History Society (1943). This book makes no mention of the nightingale.

[2] *The Birds of Lakeland*.

most of the central falls. I have watched one soaring (appropriately) over Raven Crag in Yewdale, high above the dale, circling lackadaisically, not seeming to be searching for anything, but merely taking a stroll through the air.

The golden eagle and the sea-eagle have both nested in Lakeland in the past, but of present residents the two most notable hawks are the peregrine falcon and the common buzzard. The buzzard belongs entirely to the fells, but the peregrine nests also at St. Bees Head. I confess that these and other birds of prey are only names to me, for I can't for the life of me tell them apart, probably because I have never learned to use binoculars effectively.

The smaller birds I know better. Chief among them is the wheatear, which flicks ahead of you as you walk, always keeping an eye on you but never flying too far off. It makes its call, clacking little stones together, and bobs its white rump, and though it lives quite high up on the fells it is also common along the dunes on the coast. Two other birds which range from coastal level to the tops of the fells are the skylark and the meadow pipit, both of which tend to leave the highest reaches during the winter. The skylark is practically the only song-bird to be heard on the tops, and sometimes you have the unusual experience of seeing and hearing it flying *below* you in the air. As you get a little lower down the fellsides, where gorse appears and small thorn trees and rowans, there are more birds. The stonechat, so familiar in similar localities in the south downs, is not common, though you'll find it often enough among the gorse of the dunes. It adjusts itself very quickly to the industrial landscape, and you will hear it clicking in scrubby whinbushes along the railway lines, or sticking out its red chest among the iron-ore waggons and broken bits of machinery. In the hills this bird is replaced by the whinchat, a quieter, less dapper bird, which watches you with a supercilious, white eyebrow.

There was a time when another chat, the redstart, was regarded as the typical bird of the dale villages and farms. Now it is much less common, certainly in the western districts, and it is the pied flycatcher which takes your notice. It is enchanting, partly because it is so unself-conscious. It sits on the telephone wires or on the tiles beside an old mill

or a pub, always busy, but always unharassed. It is like a
very effective shopper who stands still when nothing is
doing, but snatches as soon as there is a bargain. And then,
when the prize is safely in the basket, it returns quite unper-
turbed to the same place in the queue. Then there is the
ring-ouzel, the blackbird with a white collar; and the blackbird, too, nests as high as there are sparse fields and hedges
to give it cover. Odd blackbirds are sometimes seen at surprising heights. Of the other thrushes, the missel-thrush is
commoner in the fells than the throstle, and its burr-r-r-ing
call—like the sound of a motor-cycle exhaust at a great distance—is typical of fellside gardens. The winter-visiting
thrushes, fieldfare and redwing, are both common, the fieldfare on the higher land. By the becks there are the wagtails,
pied, grey, and (less often) yellow. Pied wagtails are common
round all the dale farms, and nest as high as 2,000 feet. They
are one of the few birds which can adapt themselves to life
both on the fell-tops and in the towns, for they are great
haunters of bowling greens and cricket pitches. I have seen
them running about bowling greens when the game has been
in progress, looking rather like little black-and-white jacks,
taking no notice of the players, and merely side-stepping
when the woods come along. Large numbers roost in the
winter on the glass roof of Carlisle railway station.[1] To
people used only to the pied wagtail the first glimpse of a
grey wagtail, with its yellow belly and markings, is always
a surprise. This, too, occasionally visits the bowling greens
when it is migrating, but it belongs more to the becks. My
happiest memory of this bird is of a pair I saw at Burneside
on the Kent. The river makes an S-curve among the
meadows and boulders and carves deeply into the slope
below the Vicarage garden. The flow is not very great, as
part of the water has been tapped off a little bit higher up.
Among the roots of the trees are claytonia and moschatel.
The cows come down to the water from the children's
playing field. Beyond, low hills border the valley towards
Staveley. Then suddenly there is the paper-mill, a large
barren-looking building, mostly of slate, with a row of pink
rhododendrons beside the rubbish-heaps. The water which

[1] *The Birds of Lakeland.*

Ennerdale, foot of the lake

has been drawn off is now returned to the Kent, vomiting from pipes, and goes rocking through the village, black as Spanish water. And here the grey wagtails were—skittering from stone to stone in the river, rocking above the grey water, bright as whin flowers in a slate quarry.

The dipper belongs to about the same sites as the grey wagtail. Its most characteristic appearance is on a stone or shingle in a quick-flowing beck, when it puts down its shoulders and butts into the water like a Rugby player going into a scrimmage. It is also seen very often flying across lakes and tarns only a few inches above the surface.

There are also the game birds, blackcock and red grouse, with the partridge common enough, but restricted to cultivated land; and the plovers, the lapwing and the beautiful golden plover, especially on the limestone. All these belong more to the lower moors than to the fells. So too does the curlew. Its long note, like water gurgling from the mouth of a medicine bottle, is one of the loveliest of all sounds on the black moors above the coast. It is a sound that touches all senses—ear, eye, nose and skin—one with clouds and mists and the smell of young bracken. Curlews and lapwings are two of the birds which share winter and summer residence between the coast and the fells. In spring and summer there is nothing more characteristic of the moors and the scraggy fields below them than the creaking of the lapwing and its contortions in the sky. As you walk along the turf one pair after another begins to fratch and feint as you enter the nesting territory. But in winter the lapwing loses its love of solitude, and congregates in large numbers on the salt flats of the estuaries and in the marshy fields around the mining towns. Great flocks are blown across the roofs and chimneys, flapping above the pit-smoke. Their white flanks shine as the wings go up; then down come the wings and the birds are green again, winking like eyes in the sky. This double life, between coast and fell, is fairly common with Cumberland birds. Even such a typical coast bird as the shelduck breeds often in the lower western hills. From thence it flies to the estuaries for food, and when the young are fledged, it marshals them in a little battalion down by lane and beck to the shore. Many of the sea-

Wastwater (Great Gable centre)

birds, particularly waders and divers, take up stations on the lakes.

Birds of the Dales

As you get nearer to cultivation the ordinary birds of arable land begin to appear. Yet somehow they are always more exciting seen, say, on a thorn bush, or in a cottage garden, against the slope of a bare fellside. For even the broadest and most luxuriant of the dales seems always a desperate outpost on the edge of the wastes, and the most civilised of rivers is likely to bare its teeth if it has a sudden rocky step to manage. So that the suburban birds are adventurers here. The bullfinch, for instance, is much at home in many a southern orchard, but I remember one I saw at Kirkby Lonsdale. It was at that famous and rhetorical view from the churchyard, the view that Turner painted—the summer-house he used was burnt down recently, and a family of dogs cremated in it. There the Lune comes down with the sweep of an old master. Beyond, to the right, are the hills of the Yorkshire Border: Middleton Fell, Foul Moss, Casterton Fell. There is a broad valley, flat alluvial fields below the steep hills, with farmhouses standing about like feudal halls. The river flows along towards Devil's Bridge, the shingle shining white in the sun, and the cherry trees in April are like beds of shingle in the woods. The bracken is still brown, and the hard woods unleaved, and the firs dark. It seems a perfect site for a monastery—the curve of the river, the rich fields, the bridge, the highroad, the sheltering cliff of the town, the medieval glitter on the young leaves. Here great trees stand right up from the riverside to the cliffs above, and suddenly among the branches a cock bullfinch flew, rising vertically as if it were jerked on a string. It perched for a second, red, lavender and black, the colours deep and intense, like a broken bit of stained glass tossed into the air.

So it is with the other birds of the dales. Listen to a wren singing among the rhododendrons in early morning, with the dew on the spider-webs, and the sun rising through the mist. It is a more intense, more vibrant song than you hear in the Home County avenues.

The wren's song always attracts me most when it is among
dark trees in a wood. Then it has a vivid aural brightness.
So, too, has the clatter of a jay, which is a most common bird
of the dale woods. You see it flying in curves and zigzags,
at undergrowth height, missing the tree trunks without
seeming to see them. Jays have a habit of clinging to their
own patch of wood whatever may go on outside, like rabbits
hiding in the last swathes of grass while the mower circles
round them. I have seen a patch of wood in Sheffield, looped
with roads and houses, where seven jays flew within sound
of the buses. The woodpeckers are all present in the dale
woods, but are not common. Hawfinches are on the increase, especially near Coniston. Siskins occur, and wax-
wings come on occasional visitations. In the second and
third year of the war, when there was an invasion of wax-
wings to the north of England, one of them lived for several
days among the allotments of a mining town in South
Cumberland. The tiny goldcrest and the tree-creeper are
common, especially in coniferous woods, and both of them
may be expected to take advantage of the new afforestation.[1]

The birds which are most at home in the woods, however,
are the tits, all of them—great-, blue-, cole-, marsh-, willow-,
and long-tailed tit. My eyes cannot distinguish between the
marsh-tit and the willow-tit, but ornithologists say that the
latter is the commoner bird. Blue-tits seem to grow on
birches—the trees are not complete without these little
yellow and blue fruit to make the end twigs hang down. The
long-tails, too, jerk about between the trees, or run among
the wickerwork of the branches, signalling with their tails
like a boy-scout with flags.

[1] In view of the argument which has been put forward that afforestation
will be harmful to bird life, the following paragraph may be quoted from *The
Birds of Lakeland*: "In recent years much replanting has taken place, almost
entirely conifers, and what influence this will have remains to be seen. A
good deal of this has been and is being carried out on the bare sides of the
Lake mountains, and on the uplands adjoining the Scottish borders, ground
formerly treeless, and this may in time attract species to which a bare hillside
offered little in the way of food and shelter."

Birds of the Coast

The coast from Carlisle to Carnforth offers several kinds of country. There are the salt marshes of the Solway and Morecambe Bay, with sand and mud flats especially around the latter; there are the sandstone cliffs of St. Bees Head, and the limestone rocks of Humphrey Head; there is much dune land between Maryport and the Solway, and along southern Cumberland and Furness. And there are stretches between St. Bees and Silecroft, where the fells come against the sea without any preparation. It is as if a designer had sliced the landscape with a knife, thrown one half away, laid a band of sand and shingle against it and called it the shore. Practically all of these areas can be surveyed from the coastal railway journey, and, curiously enough, a train gives quite satisfactory glimpses of wild birds. It is noticeable that while most birds are worried at the approach of man, they do not mind being near sheep or cows or horses. Perhaps it is just because man moves jerkily, and goes balanced on his hind legs in an odd manner, and is noisier than most animals. Perhaps it is because clothes do not merge in with the landscape like wool and hide. But perhaps the birds realise that there is something alien and artificial about man, that he is not one with the natural order, that he does not *belong*. Anyway, most birds which nest in solitary places are perturbed at the presence of man. They seem to worry much less about trains and cars, evidently accepting them as strange but harmless animals. Herons jut up their heads like periscopes and go flapping through the air if a man comes near, but they will watch passing trains without any alarm. In the Morecambe Bay stretch between Carnforth and Ulverston, the railway line several times runs out far into the sand and crosses the river mouths by viaducts. Here you can see the waders, redshank, greenshank, snipe, and the gulls floating about in the pools, rocking like moored boats. The two pied birds of the sea (black and white at a quick glance, tortoiseshell and white when you look closer), shelduck and oyster-catcher, are very common about here. The woodwind call of the oyster-catcher, rising in pitch and quickening in rhythm as it gets excited, is very typical of the wet sands, and is heard at night flying over the coastal towns as it feeds with the tide, day and night. You will also see the comorant, the vulture of the estuaries. In winter it congregates like the devils in *Paradise Lost* along the channels of the rivers, far out in the sand. It seems to suit this limbo between land and sea and heaven and hell, when the mists smudge the view of the shore, and the winter sky is as brown as the sand and the sand as wet as the clouds.

From Seascale to St. Bees and again north of Workington, the line runs beside a shingle beach. Here another little pied bird catches the eye, the ring-plover. When it runs among the pebbles you can hardly tell it is a bird—it is more as if the pebbles themselves were wriggling; and when it stands still, unless you have spotted it carefully, it disappears altogether.

The Solway is a great haunt for the wild fowl, and so, too, is Morecambe Bay. Here you find enormous numbers of geese on the salt marshes—the pink-feet commonest in the north and the grey lag in the south. But there are other species: barnacle-goose, bean-goose, brent-goose, and rarer visitors. It is astonishing how a bird so large and distinctively shaped as a goose can camouflage itself on a marsh where there is no cover. A gaggle of grey lag have been pointed out to me and I have had to stare for half a minute before spotting them. Even then they looked more like a flock of sheep, having the dirty-wool colour of sheep in the winter light, when marsh, mud and sand, sky and the distant hills are all grey or grey-brown. Swans also come to the estuaries and many kinds of duck. Birds of the open sea occasionally visit or are blown in by storms, petrels and skuas, and the less common gulls and terns. In 1943 there was brought to me a little auk which had had its brains dashed out against a telegraph pole near Bootle. It was strange to hold this bird, which I had only seen because it had been caught by gales from the Hebrides or even the Arctic, and yet to remember that it was one of the most abundant birds on earth.[1]

St. Bees Head is the most popular spot on the coast for the true sea-birds. Here there is a double headland, built of sandstone, in great slabs and buttresses which provide pro-

[1] See James Fisher: *Bird Watching* (Pelican Books).

tection for the birds and many ledges and shelves for them to nest on. Anyone who tries to climb the cliffs from the shore is likely to be cut off by the tide; anyone who tries to reach the nests from above is likely to have dislodged fragments of rock dropping about his shoulders. There are razor-bills here, and guillemots, herring-gulls and kittiwakes. Cormorants roost, but have not yet been proved to nest. Fulmar petrels hang around in the breeding time and look as if they will soon settle down. There are stockdoves, too, and puffins. Here, until the middle of the last century, lived the Cornish chough, that red-legged crow, which clung on like the memory of the Celtic tradition long after the Saxons and the Normans had driven away the language.

Except for a few bird-watchers and egg-collectors, the cliffs belong entirely to the birds. There is no road to them, and no railway running along their base. They jut out into the sea in a blunt promontory, with coal and iron ore mines ringing them in on the landward side. The tourists and the coastal traffic do not pass near them. When the tide goes out there is only the vicious slabbed shore, blood-black with seaweed. There, throughout the summer, the white birds squat on the red rock, or circle screeching over the sea and return to their perch. The droppings whiten the stone.

The Gulleries

The most spectacular breeding places along the coast are the gulleries on the dunes, of which the best known are at Ravenglass and Walney Island, where black-headed gulls nest in large numbers, together with other gulls and terns. That at Walney Island is perhaps a little more favoured by the rarer species, but the Ravenglass gullery is by far the bigger. Indeed, two-thirds of the black-headed gull population of England and Wales (100,000 birds out of 150,000) nest there. There, too, or at Walney or both, you will find the common gull, herring-gull, lesser black-headed gull, Sandwich tern, roseate tern, arctic tern, common and little terns. To spot these in flight or find their nests you need the help of an ornithologist, though it is easy enough to pick out the terns from the gulls.

92

The three rivers, Irt, Mite and Esk, flow more or less parallel till they reach the lower ground by the coast; then the Irt turns south and the Esk turns north and both meet the Mite at Ravenglass, where there is an opening to the sea. Between the south-flowing Irt and the sea a long spit of dune land pushes downwards from Drigg to the mouth of the Mite, and in the same way a spit pushes up from Eskmeals. The Eskmeals dunes are used as a gun-range by Messrs. Vickers-Armstrong—whether or not the atmosphere is healthy to birds it certainly doesn't attract man, though I have heard of an Eskdale archæologist searching for prehistoric arrows while naval guns were being tested above her head. But the opposite dunes are given over to the birds and can be approached by walking along the loose sand from Drigg or by taking a boat from Ravenglass. The amphibious operation is much to be preferred. You are advised, also, to go at high tide, when you get a longer sail and avoid having to walk across a hundred yards or so of sea mud like black semolina pudding.

Ravenglass is probably the most attractive village on the whole of the Cumberland coast, yet somehow it seems to have escaped the tourists. Perhaps that is why it is still attractive. It was once a port of some importance, and has that rather ghostly, nostalgic look that all decayed ports have. But there is nothing "quaint" or self-conscious about it. It is still a practical sort of place for people to live in— houses of slate, or sometimes of granite from the Eskdale quarries, or even of cobbles from the shore. It accepts the sea as part of its environment, and the main street marches straight down to the shore as if no one would think of going anywhere else.

A man in a rowing-boat takes you across the three-prong estuary to the gulleries. You do not come across the gulls at first—there are only large dunes, some of them bare of even bent-grass, great waves and hills of sand. Looking back there is a strip of sea, and the village low on the shore, and then the roof-line of the Wasdale fells—Gable, Scafell, the Screes. You stare from the sand to the rock. The water seems more alive than either. You are at a last outpost of land, on the fringe of civilisation, as far removed as if you were in the Hebrides or the western isles of Ireland.

Then you find the gulls; or they find you first. They do not leave the nest readily—not till you are near them—but as you reach the suburbs of the colony one or two outlying pairs take to the wing, and then as you go forward the rest get up and soon there are thousands of gulls flying over your head. The air is like a blizzard. The birds swoop down to shoulder height, sometimes looking as if they were going to dive-bomb you, sometimes actually striking with the wing. They dive and sweep and loop and curl, thousands and thousands of them, squawking and screeching, but they never seem to collide. After the first angry flight those birds settle whose nests are not too near you, or stand on the sand, screeching, with wings half-stretched. But round about you the dipping and diving still goes on. You need an old mackintosh and a cap, for there are droppings everywhere, and a stench comes from the ground. The nests are so close in places that you can hardly turn round without stepping on one. They lie under tufts of grass, on little terraces of dunes, and on the bare sand. There are thousands of greenish-brown eggs and broken eggshells, and young birds in all stages of development. The fledgelings look like tiny ducklings, and will let you pick them up without showing any signs of nervousness, except, perhaps, to wet your hand.

If the keeper is with you, he will be able to distinguish the screeching of the rarer birds from that of the gulls, and he will show you their nests, and, if any eggs have been laid since last he was there, he will scribble over them with an indelible pencil to make them worthless for collectors.

In ordinary times the eggs of the black-headed gull are protected, but during the war large numbers were gathered and sold. A certain area of the dune is covered every day, so that it can be certain that the eggs are fresh. Then, after some time of this, the birds are allowed to lay in peace. To plain sandwich cakes the eggs give a slightly fishy taste, but this can easily be overcome by adding a strong flavouring like chocolate. Even in normal times many are stolen and find their way to market, especially from the smaller inland mosses which are easier to reach than Ravenglass. In the course of transport they usually change into plovers' eggs and so fetch a better price, but there is no need to pretend they are plovers' eggs in order to enjoy them. Boil lightly, or bake slowly till they form into a jelly inside the shell, and serve cold with salad.

PART II

CHAPTER VI

THE COMING OF MAN

THERE are many other creatures in Cumberland and Westmorland beside the mammals and the birds. There are insects, creatures that creep or crawl, or fly or sting. The *Victoria County History* lists 226 species of spiders or spider-like creatures in Cumberland alone. Then there are the fishes—plaice, dab and flounder[1]—along the coast, and the many other sea fishes which occasionally visit the Cumberland and Lancashire waters; the fish of the lakes—pike and char; and the salmon[2] and trout of the Eden and other streams. Of these and many more I will not speak, but of the mammal who came last, or almost last, there is much to be said, for Man has helped to change the land and develop its character.

In sketching the history of the district I will be much less concerned with politics and affairs of State than with the way in which various races, tribes and groups came and settled on the land, and helped to breed its people and to give them their traditions. Some of these settlers have left monuments on the surface of the land—barrows or burial mounds, monoliths, crosses, churches; others have left few visible signs, but remain still in the very speech and way of life of their descendants; others are remembered only on a page of a history book or in a romantic tale. But all of them have helped to define the meaning of Cumberland, Westmorland and North Lonsdale, and all at some point have touched the life both of the Mardale shepherd and the Workington miner. The levelling tidal wave of modern civilisation is sweeping over the Lakes as over the rest of the world, washing away landmarks and leaving behind foreign wreckage, but as yet the shape still stands, the marks are not obliterated, the accent is still to be heard.

[1] Called "flooks" locally.
[2] Salmon fishing is one of our oldest industries.

Early Man

During the early Stone Age, when primitive man was living in the south of England, the north was covered with ice. It was not until the ice began to retreat in the New Stone Age that man appeared there. First he made summer settlements on the coast of Northumberland and Durham, living a sort of Eskimo life, mostly on fish.

These people were long-headed, and buried their dead in long barrows. They were followed by the round-headed folk. Neither of these races was very numerous, nor can have had much influence on the physical type which was eventually to inhabit Britain.

The Early Britons

After the round-headed folk came the races who were to provide the first real stock for Cumberland and Westmorland. They were Celtic, the Goidels, and the Brythons. The Goidels are represented today in the Gaels of Ireland, the Hebrides and the Isle of Man; the Brythons in the Welsh, the Cornish and the people of Brittany. Cumberland became, as its name implies, Welsh. Its language was Welsh when the Romans came and remained so long after they had gone. In view of this it is remarkable that few Celtic names remain in the Lakeland landscape: a few important towns like Carlisle and Penrith, one or two mountains; but in the villages, the nooks and crannies, the homes and the dialect, only a few traces.

The tribe which occupied Cumberland and Westmorland was the Brigantes, a war-like people who continued to live in Bronze Age conditions long after Iron Age culture had been introduced in the rest of England and the Romans had conquered the country. Furness seems to have been comparatively populous in the Bronze Age, and the inhabitants of Urswick must often have looked from the fells to the Roman galleys sailing past Walney Island[1] to Ravenglass. There was a pre-Celtic village not so far away around Devoke Water, on the northern slopes of Black Combe,

[1] If the level of the land has been raised since Roman times it is possible that Walney Island was then several islands.

with hundreds of burial cairns scattered round it. Others are found at various places in the district, and also fortified positions on higher ground intended as a refuge during raids.

They chose, on the whole, bleak and wild places, like the fells above the upper valley of the Calder, in what is now called Copeland Forest. No doubt it was more of a forest in those days, and the tribes could get some shelter among the trees, and so also could the game and the birds. But still the camps must have been high and cold, with mists from the sea rolling up the western dales, and the cloud-rack often hanging over the fells like a thatched roof for days on end, so that they would have to climb down to see daylight. Devoke Water lies black and dead-looking, with scarcely a reed to smudge the line of its shaly shores.[1]

These Celtic tribes were very poor. Comparatively few ornaments and implements have been found belonging to them. Copper was available, and the amount of tin required to make bronze could easily have been imported, so that the slowness with which they adopted the Bronze Age culture is probably due to their poverty. The country in which they lived gave little chance for any form of livelihood but that of hunting. The valleys and even the moorlands were covered with thick scrub of thorn, hazel, birch, wherever they were not just swamps. Only the fells were really bare of wood. And where there was a chance on the lower fell-sides to clear the ground of stones and till it with spade and hoe the soil was poor, the mists hung about it, and the winds blew through the meagre summer. Many skeletons of the Early Bronze Age show signs of extensive arthritis. Crops were poor and ripened late. If the weather broke in August, the becks were choked and the fields became bogs. Then there were no crops at all. There is no hectic summer in these uplands as there is in the Arctic tundra, giving quick growth for a week or two. There are only the months of longer days when the farmer waits for the sun, and the bracken mellows in September, and the weeds are tangled and heavy with seed, and the corn blackens before it ripens.

It was a hard life, often a long and disappointing life, but

[1] Nevertheless, it is quite famous for its trout.

the Celtic tribes did not give in. They stuck to Cumberland. Beside the Derwent and the Ehen and the Duddon they stayed, even as the miners stayed there in the hard, long years of the industrial slump.

The Megalith Builders

About this time, or later, in the Bronze Age proper, there came a race which has left very remarkable memorials of itself. These people came from the coasts of France and Spain, and wherever they settled they built stone circles or erected single monoliths. *9/0/9*

In the north-west there are none of the more magnificent megalithic remains like those at Stonehenge or Avebury, but there are many smaller examples, and nowhere are they so strange and compelling as on the moors or on the bare Cumberland coast. It is as if the rock has become articulate. The three largest are those at Little Salkeld (Long Meg and her Daughters), at Castlerigg near Keswick, and at Swinside near Broughton-in-Furness. There are circles in various states of preservation at Burnmoor near Wastwater, at Elva Plain near Bassenthwaite, at Gunnerkeld, Gamelands and other places near Shap, and elsewhere, as well as fragments of circles, single monoliths and cairns. Not all these were built by the same people, and some may have been used by successive races down to the Celts and even perhaps the Norsemen.

No one can be sure of their purpose. Many of the smaller ones, certainly, were burial grounds, but the popular belief that they were temples or gathering places is probably true of at least some. The fact that many are situated beside a good well or spring seems to suggest that there was a settlement near them. Moreover, such settlements would tend to be on higher ground because of the forests and swamps which covered the dales and the lowlands at that time.

Of the circles which remain more or less intact, some of the bigger stones have toppled over and some have been removed by farmers, but the rest must look much the same as they did to the people who put them in place. The surroundings, too, especially of those among the higher and wilder fells, can have changed little in two or three thousand years. If we cannot understand the purpose of the circles surely we can feel their meaning in our bones. There is an ache of worship in the stones, more primitive, but no less apparent than in a Gothic cathedral. For my part I find these structures more moving than many elaborate works— the simple geometry of circle and vertical, the bare sexual symbols, male and female, the functionalism of the design and its fidelity to the material. No architect has ever worked in greater harmony with the landscape than these ancient people who made the rock grow fingers, using the materials which were handiest. The greater circles are built of fragments of volcanic rock such as were left about the fellsides by the glaciers. Long Meg[1] is of sandstone, but this is an exception.

The circles differ a good deal in detail. That at Gunnerkeld, near Shap, is of the rare type which consists of two concentric circles. One on Knipe Scar, also in the Shap district, is not built of large stones, but "is a space of rocky ground from which the stones have been cleared in a circle, and the pieces used to fill the vacancies between the 'clints' left standing and the spaces where none previously existed."[2] Long Meg and her Daughters is a fine example of a large circle with a gateway and an external menhir—Long Meg herself. Keswick Circle is similar in construction, though not so large and without the menhir. It has also a sort of internal chamber, which may have been a burial place or perhaps holy of holies. Swinside Circle is smaller, but has a gateway like the others. The stones when they were set up must have been so close that they touched one another and made a perfect stone fence.

Of the three larger circles that at Keswick has the most magnificent site. It stands on a little rise, an outcrop of Castlerigg Fell, as on the middle hump of a saucer, with the dip of valleys round it on nearly every side and beyond them a circular rim of mountains. Standing at the gateway and looking across the circle, you see the shallow valley of

---

[1] Her daughters, however—*i.e.*, the stones of the circle itself—are of volcanic rock.

[2] *Transactions of the Cumberland and Westmorland Antiquarian and Archæological Society.* Volume VII. New series.

Naddle Beck, very green among the rougher fell. Parallel is the larger St. John's in the Vale, seen through a gap in the low Naddle Fell, and beyond it the Helvellyn range. To your right, across the valley where Derwentwater lies (unseen from here), is a long folded horizon of Derwent Fells, Buttermere Fells, Grasmoor, Grizedale Pike, and the Lorton Fells. Behind, nearer and more solid, Skiddaw and Saddleback. Its more immediate surroundings are much tamer—two metalled roads along the side of the field, a couple of stiles and a notice:

Visitors
Are Requested
Not to Write
On The Stones.

It's a good job that was not there in Keats's time.[1] The distinguished poet with whom I visited the circle promised, however, that she would not break the command. Nor will I.

I pass on therefore to Swinside, which has its place in my memories of adolescence. There is an age about fourteen or fifteen when a restlessness comes over a boy, and his bones seem to be trembling inside him. This restlessness may break out in many ways—in games, in religion, in gangs, in girls. In a few unhappy cases it does not break out at all. But for some boys there are times when it gives relief to be among romantic scenery, mountains and wild rocks, to be alone or with a friend of the same age, above all to walk or climb or cycle, to get on and out and away. I was such a boy. And there was one day—I must have been about fifteen—when the fit came on me in early afternoon in November or December. I set off from home about half-past one. I did not know then where it was going to lead me, or even that it was going to lead me anywhere, yet, for some

---

[1] Keats visited Castlerigg Circle and it is generally thought that this was the source of his simile about the gods in *Hyperion*:

"... like a dismal cirque
Of Druid stones, upon a forlorn moor,
When the chill rain begins at shut of eve,
In dull November, and their chancel vault,
The heaven itself, is blinded throughout night."

queer reason, even the beginnings of that afternoon are clear in my mind. I went along the road out of the town, past the football field, where a younger boy (he was to be killed in France) joined me, and walked about a mile along the road which led through the Green to Broughton-in-Furness. It had snowed during the week, and there were still whips and slashes of snow on the fields, and more on the slope of the lower hills. On the tops of the fells there would be thick snow, but the clouds were too low for me to see. By the time I got to Green I realised that I wanted to go to Swinside. I passed through the village, up the hill by Thwaites Church and on to Broadgate. It was now a race between me and the light, for already it began to get dark. I turned off the main road and along the track which led to the circle, and soon I was out on the open moor. There was snow everywhere, flat and desolate, with tussocks of grass pushing through like hairy warts. The clouds were not far above me, thick and yellow-brown, rubbing the tops of White Combe. The snow was yellow-brown, too, and you could not tell where snow ended and cloud began. The clouds lost their yellow and darkened to brown. There were shadowy mists, and the sort of silence which makes you feel that the air is a solid block and you are embalmed in it. I was thoroughly scared, but I determined to go on till I could see the stones. They stand on a sort of plateau or flat-bottomed combe, with the smooth fells of Black Combe range surrounding them on three sides like an ancient earthwork. On the fourth side the ground slopes steeply to the Duddon Estuary, but this is not visible from the circle. It is dreary, slovenly country, with not much rock showing, and the grass sour with bog. And there at last I saw the stones, huddled and hooded, black against the snow which was mounded against them on one side. There was no comfort about them; nothing human, nothing you could touch. They were as frightening as the moor; yet they were not just part of it. They were separate, persisting through the centuries in some dumb, motionless struggle. They were in opposition to the moor, struggling against it, just as I was—but they were not on my side. Their struggle would endure through God knows how many centuries more, but mine—well, I turned and

Long Meg and her Daughters,
Little Salkeld

went as fast as I could down the snowy track and the main road, and walked home while the farm windows were lit in the mist, till I found a friendly schoolmaster and his wife with whom to share the last couple of miles.

I have seen the Swinside stones many times in summer, and in spring when the circle is full of bluebells though there are none outside—but it is this winter view which I remember. Then more than ever they were as they have always been. Surely there are no monuments of the past in England so evocative as these circles and monoliths, for they have not changed, they have never become museum pieces, they go on existing in their old way.

Oddly enough, however, these Neolithic remains do not seem to touch the imagination of the local folk. In all the times I have visited the stones, not once have I seen anyone else there, and I know a man who passed that way on business once a fortnight for years and never climbed over the stile to look at them. The Swinside Circle is certainly harder to get to than Long Meg or the Keswick Circles, but there must be nearly 150,000 people living within twenty or thirty miles of it, and I doubt whether more than one in fifty has been to see it. Moreover, the destruction that has gone on among these monuments makes you gasp. In the Swinside district of South Cumberland there were once at least five other circles—at Annaside, Gutterby, Kirkstones (two) and Standing Stones, Kirksanton.[1] Scarcely anything remains of any of these, though two of the Kirksanton stones can be seen from the train just north of the village, standing like huge gate-posts. Other circles have been cleared away by the farmers, or the stones have been blasted for making walls and fences. Vanished circles have been recorded near Dalston, Lamplugh, Motherby, Ullock, and one or two near Keswick, as well as that at Castlerigg. That called the Grey Yards on King Harry Fell, not far from Carlisle, must have been next to the largest in the county. These and others all seem to have been destroyed in the last two centuries. There must be many more of which we have no record. This is one of the most thoughtless, unnecessary and unreasonable acts of destruction in our history.

[1] Standing Stones is a burial place.

Hardknott Pass

The Romans

The great colonising power of the Roman Empire made its mark upon Cumberland and Westmorland, but its lasting influence was not great. The other races who lived among the fells, the Stone Age men, the Celts, Angles and Norsemen, were all assimilated into the common stock, however little trace of them may remain. The Romans were never assimilated—they were always foreigners.

The term race can hardly be given to them, for the Roman army of occupation was drawn from the wilder provinces of the Empire—from the farther parts of Spain and France. Often the soldiers were not Roman even in the sense in which St. Paul claimed to be so, though at the end of twenty-five years' service they could acquire Roman citizenship. Nevertheless, the domination of Rome was very great for some centuries, and the stamp of it still stands on moor and valleys.

For the first twenty years or so of the occupation of Britain the Romans did not try to subdue the north. Instead they had an alliance with the Brigantes which enabled them to avoid the difficult work of conquest in hill country. The Brigantes themselves broke the alliance, and the Romans began to impose their order on the tribes between the Mersey and the Clyde on the west and the Humber and the Forth on the east.

Their method was to divide the land into districts for administration, and to build forts at road junctions and other suitable places. Each fort held a garrison of 500 or 800, and could call on the help of the legions if serious trouble broke out. The legions were quartered at Chester and at York, so that the working of the scheme depended on good communications north of these points on either side of the Pennines. The main north-western road ran from Ribchester through Overborough and Boroughbridge to Carlisle, with a parallel road through Lancaster and Kendal. From Carlisle there was a road to the Northumberland coast, and a communication with the line of forts along the southern shore of the Solway, at Maryport and elsewhere.

One of the most exciting of the roads branched off via Kendal and Ambleside to the coast. There was a direct route from Ambleside over High Street to Brougham. Between Ambleside and Ravenglass the road crossed by Wrynose and Hardknott to the fort above mid-Eskdale, and thence to Ravenglass. Here the Romans took advantage of the natural harbour to make a port which was probably intended as a base for the invasion of Ireland. The present track over Wrynose and Hardknott does not follow the exact route of the Romans, but otherwise the road across the passes must have changed little in the centuries. Certainly the surface has not improved much. The size of the area and the distances between the forts made military occupation difficult, especially in the Scottish districts, until the Emperor Hadrian decided to shorten his lines and to establish the frontier at the Solway-Tyne gap. Thus was built Hadrian's Wall, the most imposing of the Empire's defences both then and now. It was a fine structure partly of stone, partly of turf, to begin with, and later all of stone. There were guard-forts with sally-gates every mile, and look-out turrets in between. Later a line of large forts was added about seven miles apart. The forts along the coast from Bowness to Maryport and Moresby acted as a sort of continuation of the wall-defences against raiders who might come across the Solway by the sands or by water.

The Wall, as it remains, appeals to the sense of history rather than to the imagination. It looks rather futile as it runs across the bare North Cumberland and Northumberland moors, curving up and over the bumps like a huge weasel. Moreover, when it was decided to subdue Scotland proper, the Wall did not provide a really good base. It was too defensive, too static. A supply base was organised, therefore, behind the Wall, and from thence the invasion of southern Scotland was carried out. The Lowlands were occupied and a temporary frontier made at the Clyde-Forth gap, where a turf wall was built. North of that there were outposts controlling the routes into the Highlands. The district between the two walls now acted as the foothills of a defensive zone, where delaying actions could be fought before the forces retired behind the main Wall—it is the Siegfried Line tactics.

The Caledonian tribes did break through several times.

however, and eventually the Lowlands were evacuated, and a series of strongly fortified positions were built north of the Wall, from which it was possible to patrol the neutral districts. But when the Empire caved in at the centre, the peripheries had to crack, and the north was flooded with centuries of almost unrecorded history.

Before the Romans left, the Brigantes had achieved a level of civilisation quite unknown to them before they became part of the Empire. Native troops were trained as legionaries, and agriculture had improved immensely to provide the vast amount of grain and fodder needed by the garrisons on the Wall. The hillfolk probably remained suspicious and unfriendly, but large trading towns developed at places like Carlisle. Around most of the larger forts, too, there grew up British villages of shopkeepers, traders and camp-followers. The Roman soldiers frequently married British girls, and these, though they were not allowed to live inside the forts, adopted more or less the Roman way of life. Thus we had small centres of civilisation, not only along the main roads, but also at the outposts.

Such an outpost must have been Ravenglass, the port on the west. Travel inland was by the land route to Ambleside and Lancaster, but the chief communication with the Empire was by the galleys which came into the Irish Sea. To the south, the hulk of Black Combe blocked off all sight of colonial power, and inland there were the thick forests of the lower hills, and the long winding march over the passes, where the inhabitants lived a wretched life in mud hovels or crude stone huts. The soldiers tried to get what home comforts they could, and built a bath-house[1] on the bleak coast. It stands today; indeed, its walls are among the highest above ground of any Roman building in Britain. Oddly enough it does not look very old. It has rather the appearance of a ruined barn, made of rough stones and cobbles with some cement. No doubt it was patched up by later peoples and converted into a dwelling-house or perhaps into byres. At any rate, there it is in a sparse plantation by the shore, the niches in the walls, the lintels still intact. I have known a more decrepit-looking structure hold up plans for widen-

[1] Walls Castle.

ing a road until the owner could be traced and the property bought by the County Council.[1]

After the Romans left their way of life survived for a long time in these settlements. Probably the Britons moved from the "native suburbs" into the fort itself, or they would make use of it in the times of the Scottish raids. But gradually barbarism grew over it like forest over a ruined town and the Empire was forgotten.

The English

In the centuries which followed the departure of the Romans the tribes between the Clyde and the Mersey were gathered into the kingdom of Strathclyde. Of this kingdom we know very little, but by the seventh century it had already begun to disintegrate. Before that two small English kingdoms were established on the north-east coast: Deira round about the Yorkshire Wolds, and Bernicia from the Tyne to the Forth. Gradually these were unified into the great kingdom of Northumbria, which extended its influence to the western coast and governed the Celtic tribes of what are now Cumberland and Westmorland.

The main area of English colonisation was on the north-east coast, however. The people of the hills on the north-west remained predominantly British and kept their own language for a long time, though there were English settlements on the lowlands and at places on the coast.[2] The domination of Northumbria was very strong for a time, but later it began to decline, and it is possible that the territory between the Solway and the Duddon regained its independence and formed a kingdom in alliance with the British tribes of the Scottish Lowlands. If this is so it was only a temporary come-back of an ageing fighter. Eventually, as

---

[1] Miss M. C. Fair tells me that recent research has revealed a much fuller system of coastal roads than was first thought to exist. Maryport and Ravenglass each had four or five roads linking at the harbours with sea-borne traffic from Chester or Lancaster. The whole of the Cumberland coast was carefully patrolled so that the Wall could not be turned from the sea.

[2] There is a group of typical Anglican place-names in the West Cumberland industrial area: Workington, Harrington, Frizington, Hensingham, etc.; and another in Furness: Aldingham, Pennington.

elsewhere, the English influence was to flood over the land —the language became English, the country became part of England.

But just because the English influence is the most widespread it is the least interesting. It gives the people of Cumberland and Westmorland only what they have in common with the people of the rest of England. Their peculiarities, those traits and traditions which give character and personality, come from the Norse ancestry or, less markedly, from the British.

The English, however, were responsible for the first development of a type of monument which is rather characteristic of the lowlands of the dale countries, though it is not confined to them. This is the sculptured stone, usually a cross, which was set up at market-places or in churchyards or beside graves. There are some fragments of Celtic carvings which may be pre-Saxon, but the finest work came with the English, and is seen especially in the great Bewcastle Cross.[1] This has lost its cross-head but still stands over fourteen feet above its pedestal—a massive piece of sandstone, about twenty-one inches thick at the base. The west face bears three panels with sculptured figures, one of John the Baptist, one of Christ, and the third of an unknown person—evidently a contemporary. At Irton, in the valley of the Mite, is a smaller cross, carved with scrolls of fruit, leaves and flowers, and panels of geometrical pattern. It still has its cross-head, with the arms "free" (*i.e.*, without a wheel round them), and the "armpits" are cut in a curve which gives grace and movement—steady but turning on four separate axes, all bearing relation to the centre of rest at the mid-point of the cross-head.

There are several of these Anglican crosses, and more made by the Cumbrians themselves under Anglican instruction. These are clumsier, less sophisticated, more rustic, the most characteristic ornament being spirals of plait-work. These crosses are scattered round the county— at Beckermet, St. Bees, Dearham, Aspatria and elsewhere. And there are fragments in other places—broken bits of

---

[1] For those who find Bewcastle rather out of the way, there is a fine cast of the cross in Tullie House Museum, Carlisle.

shafts built into church walls, fragments of different styles
and periods heaped together, wheel-heads set beside shafts
to which they do not belong. In places where there is not
even a cobble left there is a tradition of a cross now disappeared. For the country people seem to have treated these
crosses as they treated the megaliths—not even the Christian symbol could save them. One cross, and that a fine one,
the Giant's Thumb of Penrith, was once used as a pillory.
Others have been broken up and built into walls or used as
shafts or bases for sundials or fonts, even as rubbing-stones
for cattle.

The Norse Crosses

The Cumbrian cross began gradually to give way to that
which is characteristic of the next race to come to the dales
—the Norsemen. There are a good many crosses which
show Norse, or Celtic-Norse influence, including the well-
known Giant's Grave at Penrith, which has two hog-backs
(curved grave-slabs lying not flat but on their sides) and
two pillars. But by far the finest of all the Norse sculptures
is the group at Gosforth.

The Gosforth group consists of the remains of two hog-
backs and three crosses, all of about the same period and
possibly by the same hand. The standing cross is a particularly exciting work. It is placed in the churchyard, a little
way from the main road, in a village which is cosier, more
Tudor-looking than most Cumberland villages. Your first
impression is that it is so slender, so *thin* indeed, that it
might easily snap. It looks thin because of the shaft which
is round like the trunk of a tree and plain, and then, about
four feet up, breaks into pattern, narrows and is cut into
four faces. Above, it tapers to the smallish wheel-head cross
at the top. It has not the serenity of the Irton cross, with that
look of a work of art conceived in a flash whole and complete, but its detailed carvings tell a more complicated story.
On the eastern side is a crucifixion—a rather stiff and
warrior-like Christ watched by a soldier and Mary Magda-
lene with long, spiral hair. Above the crucifixion is a fear-
ful dragon, its body knotted like a hank of knitting-wool
with a head at each end. And at the lower head is the figure

of a man wrenching open the dragon's jaws with his foot. This, we are told, illustrates the old Norse story of Vidar the Silent, who was to avenge the death of Odin by opening the jaws of the dragon wolf.

Here and elsewhere in this cross Christian and pagan symbols are linked together. The stag chased by dogs or wolves represents the Christian; but other figures seem to illustrate quite faithfully stories of the *Edda*.[1] This and other sculptures where there is similar blending of Christian and pagan symbols must have belonged to a time when the Norsemen had been converted to Christianity, but had not yet forgotten their old mythology and the stories told by the skalds. Indeed, it may be possible that they half-believed both Christian and pagan myths simultaneously. Certainly the Dragon, which is slain very convincingly by St. Michael on the Dragon Lintel at St. Bees, looks more as if he comes from the *Edda* than from the *Revelation of St. John*.

Crosses of this type have become popular in the district as war memorials or gravestones—usually with the wheelhead, and with Norse or Celtic carvings. The Ruskin memorial in Coniston churchyard is an example. Of red sandstone, greening with age, they are mostly inoffensive, and indeed seem to belong to the tradition of the district. I think it is a pity, however, that they have so often been designed by antiquarians. Had they been left to the local masons, there might have developed a small school of sculpture, crude no doubt and unscholarly, but really alive. As it is, we have only a number of period models in stone.

The Norsemen

The race which made these Norse crosses was the last to invade the dales in force, and it was in many ways the most important. It has left its names hacked in the rocks and scotched over the lowlands; it has left its language in the dialect; it has left its character in the life and outlook of the people. Yet curiously enough this invasion is unrecorded in our history. There are a few vague references to Cumberland and Wales in the works of early Scandinavian historians—that is all.

[1] See W. S. Calverley: *Early Sculptured Crosses of the Diocese of Carlisle.*

The evidence for this invasion rests largely on place-names, but it is none the less convincing. The whole of the north of England was subjected to Scandinavian raids during the ninth and tenth centuries, but the raiders were Danish rather than Norwegian. The Danes harried the north-east coast and settled in Lincolnshire and Yorkshire, where there are a great many place-names which are purely Danish. From these settlements they pressed north into Tyneside, and ranged across the country even to the British kingdom of Strathclyde, and they are reported to have sacked Carlisle. In Cumberland and Westmorland, however, the names are not Danish but Norwegian. There are many places in Norway today whose names are very similar to those of places in the Lake District,[1] and the resemblance is even stronger in the case of Iceland. This seems to be because in Iceland, as in Cumberland, the invading race tended to call its settlements after the name of the chief or warrior who took possession rather than after the nature of the land. An enormous number of place-names in the Lake District contain an Icelandic surname as part of their etymology. As we move out of the dales, south into Lancashire, east across the Pennines, or north into Scotland, we find that the number of Norwegian place-names diminishes and gives way to those which are Danish or Saxon. This surely shows that the Norse invasion of the dales did not come from any of these directions, and that, on the contrary, those Norwegian names which are found outside the Cumberland and Westmorland borders are due to infiltration from within them. We are left with only one way open—the west, the sea. From the sea, therefore, we feel sure that the Norsemen must have come, and though history does not confirm this, it gives so much contributory evidence that we can no longer doubt its truth.

By the ninth century the Norsemen had established in Iceland a civilisation which was really one of the wonders of the Middle Ages. A few bands of farmers and fishermen in that grey, stubborn land between the glaciers and the sea had found a way of life with a true heroic clang which still

---

[1] See *The Northmen in Cumberland and Westmorland*, by Robert Fergusson. Here are some of the examples he gives: Braithwaite—Braathveit; Seathwaite—Sjöthveit; Micklethwaite—Myklethvet; Rusland—Rüsland.

rings across the centuries. To the races who had learnt the arts of civilisation from the Romans and were now re-learning it from the monks, these Norsemen seemed only barbarians, raiding, plundering, destroying. Iceland was to them the island of robbers among the dark Arctic seas. But had there been no Greece and no Rome, no Empire and no Catholic Church, it is likely that a fierce civilisation would have spread down from the north, making a Europe the like of which we cannot imagine today.

Iceland still haunts the imagination—a grey island of ice mountains and hot springs. Yet the myth may be far from the truth. It is deceptive, for one thing, to speak of Iceland as the cradle of the pure Nordic race. For there the Norsemen came into contact with the Celt, and it may be the mixing of these two races and traditions which caused the peculiar ferment like a volcano among the snow. The Norseman was an individualist, a fighter, hard as nails; the Celt was more of a tribesman, a dreamer and an artist. The influence of Celtic verse-forms can be seen in the Sagas.

The Norsemen swept down, colonising the Faroes, the Shetlands, the Orkneys, and harrying the whole of the coasts of Scotland and northern Ireland and England. They took possession of most of the islands along the west coast of Scotland and Ireland, and made settlements on the mainland. Ireland they seem to have colonised on a larger scale, and they set up a kingdom on the Isle of Man. From thence they probably made excursions into Pembrokeshire, for there are a number of Scandinavian place-names around Milford Haven, but their main objective beyond Man was Cumberland.

Looking east from Snaefell, over the miles of the quiet Irish Sea, they would see the outline of a country not unlike their own—a line of peaks against the sunrise and the great hump of Black Combe. When they sailed across they would find a land of dales divided from each other by high ridges, a land well suited to the life of small individualistic communities such as they were used to. It would be a land on a smaller scale than Iceland, but less severe. In each of the tiny dales there was a small strip of really fertile land, which would be more productive than the barren acres of the subarctic. It was a cosier, more friendly country. They must have felt at home there almost at once.

Nor is it likely that they met with great opposition. The English were in the lowlands about the Solway Firth but not along the rocky coast. The British tribes which still remained in the hills had been dwindling in power and numbers for centuries. As late as the middle of the ninth century, however, they were still sufficiently powerful to be troublesome to the Saxon kings, and in 945 King Edmund, in league with (oddly enough) the King of Wales, organised a punitive expedition against them. A battle was fought against the Cumbrians under the command of King Dunmail. The king was defeated, and the Cumbrian kingdom came to an end for ever. Tradition points to Dunmail Raise, the pass between Keswick and Grasmere, as the site of the battle, and a rough heap of stones is looked on as the king's grave.[1]

We cannot be certain what happened to the Cumbrians after this. Perhaps they emigrated to Wales; perhaps the survivors were allowed to linger on among the mountains. Certainly they would be in no state to offer much resistance to the Norsemen. Edmund, indeed, handed over Cumberland to Malcolm, King of the Scots, but it is unlikely that the latter would be able to spare soldiers to protect that wild district so far from the centre of his kingdom.

At what part of the coast did they land? Here we can only guess. But the Solway as far down as Whitehaven was in the hands of the English, and the southern shores of Morecambe Bay would not greatly attract the Vikings. This points to the coast between St. Bees Head and Humphrey Head, which, indeed, is the most readily accessible from the Isle of Man. If the invaders came in any force, strategy would seem to suggest the Furness peninsula, where they could assemble and drive inland—the country to which it leads, Coniston and Kendal, is as Norse as any. But if, as I fancy, the Norsemen settled in small batches, then more probably they would choose the wildest part of the coast, between Seascale and Kirksanton, from any part of which they would be able to slip almost unnoticed into the fells,

[1] In fact, he died at Rome thirty years later.

and thence up Wasdale, Eskdale or Dunnerdale into the heart of the district.

When I think of this invasion, I like to picture Gutterby (with its Scandinavian name) as a place where landings were made. Ravenglass, a few miles north, offers a better harbour, but here the Britons may have persisted in some numbers, clustered round the old Roman fort. Gutterby, with a bare coast and the barren mountains above it, was likely to be less populous. It is certainly secluded; as late as the eighteenth century it is rumoured to have been used by smugglers— also from the Isle of Man. Even today it is scarcely known. The main road does not come near the coast, and there is only a rough cart-track from Whitbeck, which peters out when it reaches the fields above the shore. A path, which is partly a watercourse, gouges through the clay to the sea-level, making a dell rather like a Dorset chine. By the sea you find great banks of shingle, curving in a tiny cove, with red cliffs around it, the whole similar to the bays along the Yorkshire coast, but quite unlike what you usually find in Cumberland. Half-buried in the shingle is part of the hull of a twenty- or thirty-year-old wreck—I have sheltered behind it from the biting midsummer wind. Currents often throw up drowned bodies on this shore. It is famous, too, for crabs.

The Norse Heritage

Once the Vikings were settled among the dales neither Celt nor Scot nor Englishman could shift them. There they were and there they stayed. The nature of the land encouraged them to set up a system of land-owning very similar to that of Norway. In Iceland their society had been more aristocratic because it required capital to settle in such a barren country at so great a distance from the home base. But in Cumberland and Westmorland there developed a number of small, isolated communities, with families each owning its farm of two or three hundred acres or less. The feudal system modified this to some extent, particularly in the lowlands, but the independent farmer remained until quite recently as the "statesman" or "estatesman." The boundaries of their small fell farms are marked by the stone walls which can often be seen straddling little knots and climbing steep scars where there does not seem the slightest need for them.

The independent character of the dalesman, his hardiness, his suspicion of "foreigners," is undoubtedly due to his inherited way of life. What else in his nature belongs to his Norse ancestry it is difficult to say. Purely physical characteristics have scarcely survived the centuries. Perhaps the dalesmen do tend to be taller and fairer than the average Englishmen—perhaps not. It depends mostly on the way you look at them! The Herdwick sheep may have remained truer to breed. The love of country sports, and especially of wrestling, is certainly inherited from the Vikings, but so far as I know none of the tales of the skalds have come down to us in local folk-lore. Nevertheless, the *Edda* is illustrated on the Gosforth Cross, so the stories must have been familiar to the people at one time.

I like to fancy that I can see something of the gesture of the sagas in the tall stories which are popular among the Cumbrians. Exaggeration is a convention in northern conversation, and often bewilders southerners. Will Ritson, landlord of the Wasdale Head Inn in the last century, was famous for such stories. He told of a wounded eagle which was put in a chicken run and mated with a foxhound bitch to breed winged hounds that hunted along the screes. It is a long way from that story to the sagas, but the fantastic touch is there, and the homely touch too. The Sagas have a high swagger, but they are ready to get down to earth. The sun glints on the brass helmets and the ice, but the soil is not far beneath.

It is said of Will Ritson that he entered a competition at the dale sports for the man who could tell the biggest lie, but when it came to his turn he asked to withdraw.

"Why?" he was asked.

"Because I cannot tel' a lie."

He won. There, too, is the shrewdness that was also found in the Norse tales.

W. G. Collingwood thinks that the tradition of the skalds may have had a faint echo in the way in which some of the older dalesmen used to break into impromptu rhymes. He quotes John Audland of the early nineteenth century, who, having lost a law-suit at Ulverston, expressed himself extempore in verses of "very nearly the old *Edda* metre":

> God mead men,
>   And men mead money;
> God mead bees,
>   And bees mead honey;
> But t'Divil himself
>   Mead lawyers and 'tornies,
> And pleaced 'em i' U'ston
> And Dalton i' Forness.[1]

This rhyme, like the Sagas, had been passed on by word of mouth before being written down. But I cannot feel that Lakeland dialect verse as a whole has even the remotest ring of the Sagas, nor has that of the Cumberland laureate. It is notable, too, that Wordsworth made very little use of Norse vocabulary in his poetry, in spite of his theories about the use of common speech. Skelton, who was born at Armathwaite Castle in Cumberland, is much nearer the language of the people, but he derives more from Anglo-Saxon poetry than from Norse.

But these are all dim signs of the Norsemen, romantic images blurred by the mist. It is easy to delude yourself that you have found such signs when you are hoping to find them. "Bill Stubbs His Mark" has bamboozled more than Mr. Pickwick. And when you think you have found a typical Viking of the dales, he is likely to turn out to be a Cockney who has settled there because of his wife's health.

There are, however, other signs which are not so easily mistaken, nor easily forgotten, for they are engraved across the landscape like the names on a map. Fell, scar, scree, ghyll, dale, tarn—these Norse words at once name the landscape and evoke it. Their synonyms have nothing like the same rugged force. No one could confuse a fell with a hill, or a down, or a tor. They belong so particularly to the north

---

[1] Quoted from *The Life and Death of Cormac the Skald,* translated by W. G. Collingwood: Holmes, Ulverston. "Mead" and "pleaced" are practically bi-syllables.

that the southerner uses them almost self-consciously, while
they spring naturally to the tongue of a Cumberland or a
Westmorland man, whether he be a shepherd of Matterdale
or a miner of Wath Brow. There are others not quite so
familiar which have the same concise expressiveness—pike,
dodd (a small hill attached to a larger one), knot, nab (a
projection), haws (literally a neck—hence a pass—but the
name is often given to wide expanses of grassland, even on
the dunes), sike, force or spout (both waterfalls), mire.
Many, too, are known as common suffixes in place-names—
Thwaite: a clearing, the best known of all; there must be
more than a hundred places in the Lake District whose
names end with "thwaite"; and surnames, too—my own
middle name is Cornthwaite. Then there is biggen (a building), seat (a dwelling—usually on the side of a mountain),
keld (a spring), wick (a bay), and so on. There are scores of
examples, even among the most familiar names—Bassenthwaite, Newbiggin, Seathwaite (seat plus thwaite), Thelkeld, Keswick, Langdale, Scafell Pike, Esk Haws, Airey
Force, Gibson Spout, Nab Scar, Hardknott, Skiddaw Dodd
—every visitor to the district will remember at least one or
two of these. There are other endings, too, like -land, -side,
and -ness (a promontory), which may come either from Old
Norse or from Anglo-Saxon, but where the other part of the
name suggests a Norse derivation. Even such very English-
looking words as "mere" and "water" may in the dales be
just anglicised versions of the Norse, for they are often
found linked to Scandinavian surnames. Buttermere, Windermere, Grasmere, Ullswater, Elter Water and Thurston's
Water (the old name for Coniston Lake) are thought to
contain the Scandinavian names of Buthar, Windar, Gris
(this means swine), Ulf, Eldir, and Thurston (or Thorstein).

Sometimes the names have changed so much in the course
of time that it is hard to suspect that once they had a Scandinavian ring. Who would have thought that Dolly Waggon
Pike was not a pure English folk-tune sort of name? Moreover, as I write, I look out of the window to a small knot of
Silurian rock. It is built over now, being once the oldest part
of a market village, which, when industry came to the lowland fells, became the suburb of the new town. The slates

pile up each behind the other, in all the sharp angles of roof and dormer window and gable end. There are chimneys spiking up like fir trees on the fellside, and red sandstone lintels, and here and there a wall of red or yellow brick. From hidden plots of garden the tops of thorn and elder puff among the chimneys like green smoke, and at the top is a tiny non-conformist chapel of buff sandstone. The prosaic, nineteenth-century working- and middle-class houses are given a spur by the slope of the hill to make a mining-town St. Michael's Mount. Its name is Holborn Hill, but this is no nostalgic glimpse at the metropolis, but the memory of Hallbiörn, an old Viking.

Very rightly it is the fells themselves which preserve the Norse names. Some of the rivers go on whispering quietly in Celtic (the Derwent, for instance), but the fells carry the names of the men who claimed them as their natural home. But if the fells are the tombstones of the Vikings, the dialect is their living testimony. The dialect of the whole of the north of England and of Lowland Scotland shows strong Scandinavian influence, both in vocabulary and in pronunciation. It is not true to say that there is one dialect in the district—there are several. The speech of the coastal dales varies from that of the Yorkshire border, and Westmorland has a decided dialect of its own—softer and spoken more in the front of the mouth. Around Carlisle the speech merges into Lowland Scots. The colliery district of Whitehaven and Workington has a dialect quite of its own, which seems to have developed by crossing Tyneside and Cumberland; and Barrow-in-Furness speaks a language common to most of the towns of the north.[1]

The true dale dialects, however, are all full of Norse words, and have a peculiar clicking, cracking tune which sounds harsh at first, but which has a music of its own. In the broadest dialects the vowels are nearly all diphthongs or triphthongs; in fact, in three words out of four the dalesman seems to use a sound which perhaps can be suggested by ee-y-ah, though there are slight variations of colour within this pattern which differentiate the vowel. Thus a farmer speaking to me of a foxhunt on screes on a frosty morning

[1] There is, nevertheless, a distinctive Furness dialect.

118

*Penrith Castle, looking across town
to Beacon Hill
Carlisle Cathedral—nave*

said: "Nee-yah scee-y-ant at ee-y-al," and there was no doubt whatever that he meant: "No scent at all."

Later Immigrations

For a thousand years the land has remained predominantly Norse. The dialect is dying, the stock is breeding thin, but the place-names remain. No subsequent race has made anything like the same mark on the land. In the seventeenth century Dutch and German miners settled in Keswick and Coniston and were merged into the local life. Many Scottish farmers foraged across the Border and have settled there. But the most exciting of recent immigrations has been the return of the Celts. In the time of industrial development they came from Ireland, Cornwall and Wales, laying claim to their old valleys and marshland. In some of the mining towns around Whitehaven a large percentage of the population is Irish Roman Catholic, and in one place in the south of the district the Chairman of the Town Council spoke with a Cornish accent as late as 1946.

Carlisle Cathedral—choir
Doorway, St. Bees Priory Church

Chapter VII

RAIDERS AND MISSIONARIES

I HAVE dealt with some of the races which have come to Cumberland and Westmorland and settled in the dales. There are also two other groups of people who have influenced the two counties greatly from the outside, though they cannot be called "settlers" in the ordinary sense. These are the Scots and the Christian missionaries. Each, in a different way, has meant much to the life of the Cumbrians, and each has left signs in stone.

The Scots

In the Lake District proper it is possible today to forget that Cumberland is a Border county. The expresses that rattle past the little towns of Burton and Milnthorpe have "Edinborough" or "Glasgow" on the carriage windows, and the corridors are purring with Scots talk, but the country outside seems peaceful enough, and the country folk have a confident, self-contained way which does not suggest alarms and intrusions. When you begin to descend the northern slopes of Shap, however, you know you are heading for Scotland; and when, along the coast, you go beyond St. Bees Head, the sky begins to widen above the Solway, and you sniff at the wind from the Scottish Lowlands. And when you are in Carlisle, there is no longer any doubt. There are Scottish voices all around you, in streets, in cafés, in shops and markets. The station has an anxious bustle and jostle which you would not find at other junctions, however busy. As soon as you come out of it you see the two law-courts, plain and round like rooks in a chess-set, dour and grim and guarded. They were built in the nineteenth century, like much of the Gothic you'll find in the city, but the Border watchfulness hangs over them like a heritage or a curse.

The Frontier Wars

It is not part of the purpose of this book to try to tell the complex political history of the Border counties. Perhaps it will be enough to say that the Border Wars fell roughly into two periods: in the first the boundaries between England and Scotland were being determined; in the second these were really settled, but a series of raids and counter-raids continued.

As I have said before, soon after the Norman Conquest King Malcolm of Scotland seized the land north of the Duddon. William Rufus went north in 1092, captured Carlisle and built the castle. From then onwards the English kings regarded Cumberland as part of their dominion, though there was still a long period of doubt about administration. During the reign of Stephen the Scots overran both Cumberland and Westmorland, and King David of Scotland set up residence in Carlisle. Both Stephen and David died about the middle of the twelfth century, and Henry II was easily able to wrest the territory from the hands of Malcolm, the boy king.

For a long time the Scottish kings continued to lay claim to the northern district, but in the thirteenth century understanding between the two countries improved, helped by Pope Gregory, and when Edward I came to the throne there seemed good hopes of happier relations. Soon after his accession Edward stayed in Carlisle, visited Lanercost Priory, and hunted in Inglewood Forest. Everything in the greenwood seemed to be lovely.

These years of frontier wars were unsettled, and at times cruel and murderous, but compared to the years which followed they were fairly peaceful. The people on either side of the Border knew at least when there was a war on and when there wasn't. It was a time of watchfulness and alertness but not of continual fighting and destruction.

In all these years the king-pin of defence was Carlisle Castle. There were other castles, too, but Carlisle was the main defence. When the Normans began to set up their baronies in Cumberland they built fortresses of the motte and bailey type, but these, because they were of wood, were easily destroyed by the Scots. About the time that William Rufus fortified Carlisle, other castles were being built of stone, and these contributed to the defence of the Border. There was Liddel Strength, practically on the frontier, Brougham and Appleby, commanding the fords over the

Eamont and the Eden; and Brough, commanding the pass over Stainmore into Yorkshire. On the west, stone castles were built at Egremont and Cockermouth, and farther south, on a little hill commanding the shallow valleys which slope to Morecambe Bay, was Kendal Castle, where, centuries later was to be born the only one of Henry VIII's wives who was also his widow. The latter three, however, could not have played much part in the defence of the Border, though they testify to the general feeling of unrest.

Nearly all these castles are in ruins, unlike the pele towers which were to follow in the fourteenth century, most of which have become farmhouses. Cockermouth, at the junction of the limestone with the slate, is one of the loveliest in decay; Kendal splendid in its situation; Appleby grim and stubborn; Liddel swathed with ballad and tradition like ivy. But perhaps, by a freak, Egremont is now the most romantic of them all, for Egremont, like Cockermouth, is in the limestone country, and here the limestone yields iron ore. Egremont, therefore, rises above a town which has known the grimmest of the Border struggles of this century and the last—the struggle of man with the rock, and later with unemployment and poverty. The Castle grounds are now a public park. You can walk along paths and inspect the herring-bone masonry, and see yellow groundsel growing on the red stone. Inland are Pillar and the Ennerdale Fells, rounded and humped in shoulders and haunches; seaward, St. Bees, the coast, and the long sweep of the Solway up to Scotland. Great milky mists blow up from the sea, and the sun is bright on the roofs, but the stone of the Castle itself is dark and sullen. Much blood has soaked into it. Below, among the streets, are the mines, the shops, and the heaps of rubble, red as the Castle walls. The one-track railway runs down to Sellafield, and twists northwards among the mining towns of Moor Row, Cleator Moor, and, farther away, Frizington, Rowrah, Lamplugh. There is red rust on the lines and weeds between the sleepers; the signals are all down, for the line is rarely used now except for a Sunday-school trip to Seascale.[1] The Border warfare is not

---

[1] Recently a not very successful attempt was made to revive a passenger service on the Sellafield-Egremont-Whitehaven route.

over in these towns; hardship is not just a tradition, and the earth bears scars more recent than those the Scotsmen left.

Carlisle Castle

Carlisle Castle, however, was the centre of the defence. An invading army could by-pass it, but could not ignore it, and so long as it remained untaken no occupation of the Cumberland Plain could be secure. It stands to the north of the city, on a promontory between the Eden and the Caldew, with the Petteril not far away to give another water barrier. Square and solid, looking north-west to meet the challenge, it is a practical building which may, perhaps, have been of use in Border wars, but which is now more concerned with its present-day function of barracks to the Border Regiment. Nothing in Carlisle is preserved for tradition or sentiment; everything exists because it serves a thoroughly useful purpose. That is why the city has never become a museum, but is still alive and exciting. A thousand years easily pass away in Carlisle, not because the city is too dreamy to notice them, but because it is so busy that it has never really changed. Except for a few motor-cars, factories and cash chemists, Carlisle is essentially the same Border town that it has been for centuries.

The Scottish Wars of Independence

Towards the end of the thirteenth century the Scots found a new leader, William Wallace. In 1298 he ravaged the northern counties as far as Durham. Edward took a great army over the Border and annihilated the Scots at Falkirk. Wallace was betrayed and beheaded. But then Robert Bruce arose. Edward gathered another army, was carried in his litter to Carlisle to pray for the defeat of his enemies, but died at Burgh-by-Sands on the Solway, looking across at the country he had come to invade.

Edward II was no match for the Bruce and was defeated at Bannockburn, and from that time the northern counties lay open to the invaders. Carlisle Castle was besieged several times without success, but the castle was now of little importance, for the aim of the Scots was not to occupy the land, but to plunder and pillage.

This period was the most ferocious in the whole history of the Border. Farms and churches were burned, cattle driven off and slain, women raped, children impaled on spikes, abbeys plundered, monks killed, nuns stripped and violated. The northern abbeys naturally suffered most, Lanercost and Holme Cultram, while the monks at Calder were so dispirited by continual burning and pillage that they tried to go back to their mother-church, Furness Abbey, and when they were turned away, went over the Pennines and founded Bylands Abbey in Yorkshire. Soon, however, the foraging bands went farther afield. In 1316 they went down into Yorkshire and west as far as Furness. In 1319 the Bruce burnt the bishop's palace at Rose Castle, plundered Holme Cultram abbey, went south through Copeland Forest and across the Duddon to Furness (where the Abbot paid ransom), ravaged around Cartmel Priory, crossed Morecambe Sands and burnt Lancaster to the ground, and then returned to Scotland by Carlisle.

It soon became obvious that a new system of defence was needed. Cockermouth, Naworth, Millom, Penrith, Workington and other castles were fortified and in some cases given permanent garrisons. Castles like Penrith, however, were not intended to provide much active defence, but merely to act as a shelter for men and beasts while help could be brought from the garrison at Carlisle.

Gradually the barons and landowners began to take matters into their own hands. They realised that what they were up against was not large-scale, organised war, but a series of short, improvised raids. What they needed was a system of many small local defences, where each landowner and his tenants could hold out for a day or two, or even an hour or two—the raiders could not afford to waste time, and there was little likelihood of a long siege. Wooden buildings were useless—they went down before fire every time. So there began to be built those pele towers which are such a characteristic feature of the Border landscape.

They are oblong or occasionally square buildings, with walls five to ten feet thick. The general plan was that of a basement with two or three storeys above it, the upper floor divided by partitions into different apartments. The en-

trance was by a low doorway that led to the basement, giving
no chance for invaders to rush in. In case fire should be put
against the door, it was heavily barred and studded with
iron. And if by any chance the invaders did get through,
they had to fight their way up a narrow, twisting staircase
to the floors above.

These towers were given over almost entirely to defence
and not to comfort or elegance. The lower windows were
nothing but slits to let in a little air and light. Upstairs, in
the women's rooms, there might be small double windows
decorated with trefoils and the like, which became more
elaborate as the centuries passed on and peace was more
assured, but the general appearance is one of gaunt, massive
strength, stubborn, practical and dour. In the sandstone
country they were built of dressed stone, but in the lime-
country they were made of huge blocks of unhewn rubble
and stand as grey and bare as slag. Hazleslack comes into
mind, on the slope above the quiet Kent valley.

The building of towers and castles and the fortifying of
manors was so widespread in the fourteenth century that I
am tempted to quote a list of some of the names, not for
instruction, but merely to show how they sprang up in every
part of the two counties, along the Border, the coast, the
lower valleys—everywhere, in fact, except the highest dales,
whose very inaccessibility was a defence: Piel (on an island
outside the harbour of Barrow-in-Furness), Howgill,
Sizergh (now the home of a religious community), Broughton-in-Furness, Millom, Dacre, Levens, Lammerside, Arnside, Burneside, Cliburn, Beetham, Workington, Denton
Foot, Scaleby, Yanwath, Ormside, Asby, Branthwaite,
Irton, Linstock, Hutton-in-Forest, Denton, Kentmere,
Naworth, Rose, Sockbridge, Randalholme.[1]

Some of these names will be unfamiliar even to those who
know the district well. They are spread over the whole area,
and it is notable that many of them belong to the valleys
round Morecambe Bay, where, one might have thought, the
people would have been comparatively safe from Scottish

[1] See *The Castles and Fortified Towers of Cumberland and Westmorland
and Lancashire, North-of-the-Sands*, by John F. Curwen. Cumberland and
Westmorland Antiquarian and Archæological Society.

raids. Only three of that list are total ruins—Piel, Lammer-side and Arnside. These Border defences have a way of adapting themselves to the centuries and still endure in a lively, practical way. Some of the castles have become man-sions—Sizergh, Naworth, Rose. Dalton Castle, which was not a fort but the manorial court of the Abbot of Furness, first became a court-house, and is now used as a Masonic temple. But the peles are usually farms, and indeed most of the old farmsteads have something of a pele tower built into them, though history and tradition may have forgotten. Even those typical farms of the dales, like Dalegarth Hall in Eskdale, and Coniston Old Hall on the bank of the lake, were once fortified. Now, with their comfortable slate walls, they look like the dalesman's equivalent of the Elizabethan manor house of the brick and timber country—even the large round chimneys like ship's funnels seem to be the dale version of the fantastic brick chimneys of Compton Wyn-yates and elsewhere. In these districts, being at a safe distance from the Border, the houses were less military in appearance and more care was given to comfort and convenience. Some-times, as at Millom, the old pele itself has been patched and propped and strengthened with glass and concrete, and still serves as a dwelling-house. More often, the farm-house is a new building, and the pele has become a barn or storehouse. But farm, barn, mansion or gaol, they still have the deter-mined purposeful look they always had, and give a gesture of rhetoric to the landscape.

As well as the peles and towers there were, particularly in the Solway district, several churches which were used as places of refuge from the raids. Burgh-by-Sands, Newton Arlosh and Great Salkeld are three of the most notable examples, each with narrow windows in the nave, set high from the ground, and each with a tower which might be used as a look-out. In some places, too, there were protective dykes.

Then in the fifteenth century was developed the great system of beacons. Cumberland seems a county specially suited to beacons, but, though "the red glow on Skiddaw warned the burghers of Carlisle," Skiddaw is not really a good place for a beacon. It is too high and remote. More suited for the purpose are accessible hills of 600 or 700 feet.

The beacons were linked together, more slowly, but nearly as thoroughly, as the A.R.P. warnings of the war. They covered the whole area from Bewcastle in the north to Black Combe in the south, with Rampside in Furness, and Farleton Fell in Westmorland; and from St. Bees Head on the coast to Stainmore on the edge of Yorkshire. In recent years they have been lit again for jubilees and like occasions, but while the relief map seems to promise a blaze along the skyline finer than the Northern Lights, mist and cloud have blotted out all but the nearest whenever I have been there. Indeed, the finest I have seen was one to the honour of George VI, which was lit by a crowd of mischievous boys on the day *before* his coronation. And the grimmest warning of all, shining across the sea in the blackout, was the fire of an American bomber which had crossed the Atlantic safely and then crashed on Lowscales above the Duddon Estuary.

The Border Raids

In the time of Henry VIII the Battle of Flodden, and later that of Solway Moss, put an end to the long years of continual warfare and large-scale raids. The southern part of the district now began to settle down, and the new castles and manors of the fifteenth and sixteenth centuries were more like houses and less like pillboxes. But it was a long time before the Border really became peaceful, and there now began the struggle for the Debatable Land, a struggle much more local but still fierce and protracted. This land lay between the Esk and the Sark, and on it the Armstrongs and Grahams and other families began to fortify farms and towers and to set up a law for themselves. All round this district raiding became the chief means of livelihood. Cattle, sheep, all transportable goods were stolen and carried off, snatched away again, and passed around and about in a game of beggar-my-neighbour till it was impossible to be sure of the real ownership. A lady of the house, when she was short of supplies, would serve for dinner a pair of spurs on a dish, for thieving of livestock ranked with hunting and fishing as a legitimate way of stocking the larder.

To this period belongs one of the best known of the Border exploits—the rescue of Kinmont Willie. At that time the Warden of the Western Marches on the English side was Lord Scrope, with Sir Walter Scott (known as the Buccleugh) on the Scottish side. They had sent their deputies to Dayholme of Kershope where, according to custom, a day of truce was proclaimed in which various matters could be discussed. William Armstrong, a notorious thief, was among the Scottish company, and on the way back he seems to have become involved in some sort of trouble with the English. At any rate, he was arrested and taken to Carlisle Castle. (This was in 1596, about thirty years after Mary, Queen of Scots, herself had been imprisoned there, following her flight from Scotland to Workington.) The Buccleugh at once demanded the release of Kinmont from the deputy-warden Salkeld, claiming that the arrest was a breach of the truce which should have lasted till sunrise of the next day.

He has ta'en the table wi' his hand,
    He garr'd the red wine spring on hie—
"Now Christ's curse on my head," he said,
    But avengèd of Lord Scroope I'll be.

"O is my basnet a widow's curch?
    Or my lance a wand of the willow-tree?
Or my arm a ladye's lilye hand,
    That an English lord should lightly me?

"And have they ta'en him, Kinmont Willie,
    Against the truce of Border tide?
And forgotten that the bauld Buccleugh
    Is Keeper here on the Scottish side?

"And have they ta'en him, Kinmont Willie,
    Withouten either dread or fear?
And forgotten that the bauld Buccleugh
    Can back a steed, or shake a spear?

"O were there war between the lands,
    As well I wot that there is nane,
I would slight Carlisle castell high,
    Though it were builded of marble stane.

"I would set that castell in a low,
    And sloken it with English blood!
There's never a man in Cumberland
    Should ken where Carlisle castell stood.

"But since nae war's between the lands,
    And there is peace, and peace should be;
I'll neither harm English lad or lass,
    And yet the Kinmont freed shall be!"

The ballad probably over-estimates the Scotsman's chivalrous respect of the observance of peace, but of his indignation there can be no doubt. The Buccleugh made various attempts to get Kinmont freed. Salkeld was approached direct, and the English ambassador at the Scottish court advised Lord Scrope to release the prisoner. When this failed both King James and Queen Elizabeth were approached, and then, finally, the Buccleugh decided to take it into his own hands. The ballad's account of the start of the expedition is no doubt romanticised, but it is too spirited to miss:

He has call'd him forty Marchmen bauld,
    Were kinsmen to the bauld Buccleugh;
With spur in heel, and splent on spauld,
    And gleuves of green and feathers blue.

There were five and five before them a',
    Wi' hunting-horns and bugles bright:
And five and five came wi' Buccleugh,
    Like Warden's men, array'd for fight.

And five and five, like a mason-gang,
    That carried the ladders lang and hie;
And five and five, like broken men;
    And so they reached the Woodhouselee.

And as we cross'd the Bateable Land,
    When to the English side we held,
The first o' men that we met wi',
    Whae sould it be but fause Sakelde?

"Where be ye gaun, ye hunters keen?"
　　Quo' fause Sakelde; "come tell to me!"—
"We go to hunt an English stag,
　　Has trespass'd on the Scots countrie."

"Where be ye gaun, ye marshall men?"
　　Quo' fause Sakelde; "come tell me true!"—
"We go to catch a rank reiver,
　　Has broken faith wi' the bauld Buccleugh."

"Where be ye gaun, ye mason lads,
　　Wi' a' your ladders, lang and hie?"—
"We gang to herry a corbie's nest,
　　That wons not far frae Woodhouselee."—

"Where be ye gaun, ye broken men?"
　　Quo' fause Sakelde; "come tell to me!"—
Now Dickie of Dryhope led that band,
　　And the never a word of lear had he.

"Why trespass ye on the English side?
　　Row-footed outlaws, stand!" quo' he;
The never a word had Dickie to say,
　　Sae he thrust his lance through his fause bodie.

For the actual rescue we may go to the more sober account of Lord Scrope himself:

". . . Yesternighte in the dead time thereof Buclughe's chief man with five hundred horsemen did come armed and appointed with gavlocks and crowes of iron, handpeckes, axes and skailinge lathers, unto an outewarde corner of the base courte of this castell and to the postern door of the same—which they undermyned speedily and quietlye and made themselves possessores of the base courte, brake into the chamber where Will of Kinmont was, carried him awaye, and in their discoverie by the watch, lefte for deade two of the watchmen, hurt a servante of myne and were issued againe oute of the posterne before they were descried by the watche of the inner warde and ere resistance could be made. The watch as yt shoulde seeme, by reason of the stormie night, wer either on sleepe, or gotten under some covert to defend themselves from the violence of the wether, by which meanes the Scots atchieved the enterprise with less difficultie."[1]

Anyway, Kinmont was rescued and King James resolutely refused to surrender him to Elizabeth. The Buccleugh, however, made another raid into England, and this time was given up to the deputy Warden of the East Marches at Berwick. "With ten thousand such men," said Elizabeth, "our brother in Scotland might shake the finest throne in Europe."

The Great Siege of Carlisle

When Elizabeth died and James VI of Scotland became James I of England, he rightly entered Carlisle as his first possession on the English side. From then onwards Border raiding ceased except as a sort of large-scale poaching, and the Border counties began to prepare themselves for peace. But Carlisle itself had not yet seen the end of war.

In 1524 the old castle had been unsuccessfully besieged in the rebellion known as the Pilgrimage of Grace. Now, in the Civil War between Charles I and the Puritan Parliament, the city was besieged again. Before the struggle broke out steps had been taken to increase the garrison at Carlisle, but in the early stages of the war Carlisle did not play a very active part. The Parliamentary forces made some attempt to take the castle in 1643, but this was easily repulsed and the town was held for the King. Then, after the Battle of Marston Moor, the Royal cause declined, and towards the end of the year began the famous siege of the city of which an account has been left in the diary of Isaac Tullie, a boy of eighteen. The Parliamentary forces were led by David Leslie and stationed at Newtown, Stanix and Harraby. At first there was little more than skirmishing, and the besieging forces tried to capture a few cows and other provisions. Then, as the winter went on, food began to get short in the city. The grain and the few cattle still left were rationed out. Coin was minted from the plate of the citizens. A fat horse was captured from the enemy and its flesh sold at a good price. Straw was taken from the roofs of thatched

[1] Quoted from *Castles and Towers of Cumberland and Westmorland.*

houses to provide fodder for their own horses. In June, hempseed, dogs and rats were being eaten. By the end of the month the citizens petitioned Sir Thomas Glenham, the Royal commander, that their horsemeat should not be taken from them to feed the garrison, as they could no longer face up to the famine. No reply was forthcoming for four days, and then "a few women of ye scalds and scum of the city mett at ye cross, braling against Sr. Henry Stradling there present who first threatened to fire upon them; and when they replyed they would take it as a favor, he left them with tears in his eyes."

After this, there was nothing to do but to seek for terms and the city was surrendered with honourable conditions for soldiers and citizens. The garrison marched out "with their arms, flying colours, drums beating, matches lighted at both ends, bullets in their mouths, with all their bag and baggage, and twelve charges of powder a piece."

The struggle went on in the rest of the county, however, and in 1648 Sir Philip Musgrave, coming down from Edinburgh, surprised and took the town on the night of the 29th of April. But the Royalist cause was crumbling, there was dissension among the troops and disagreement among the commanders, and before long Cromwell was able to demand and get the surrender of Carlisle and of Appleby, which also had been held for the King. Many other castles in the county had been held by the King's supporters. They had most of them reached a state of semi-ruin by the seventeenth century, at any rate in moats, walls, and outward defences, but the loyal landlords put up what resistance they could against Parliamentary forces. In most cases, however, the use of cannon not only overcame the defence, but started the decay from which they never recovered.

The Jacobite Invasions

After the Great Rebellion the north-western counties enjoyed nearly a hundred years of peace, and this, together with the belief that there was no longer any likelihood of war between England and Scotland, must have made the military authorities complacent about their security. For when danger did come, and from the same old quarter across the Border, the Cumberland defences were found incompetent.

When the Jacobites rose in Scotland in 1715, the local governors of Cumberland were thrown into a panic, Scarcely anything was done about mustering the militia. and when the small Scottish army advanced to Longtown it met with no opposition. The intruders then by-passed Carlisle and went on to Penrith, where 1,400 men had been gathered together by the Sheriff and the Bishop to block the way to the passes to the south. The local levies cannot have been a very formidable lot. Most of them were armed with scythes and pitchforks, and the rest only with such old swords and muskets as they could find in barns and chimney corners. They were quite untrained, had no idea of discipline, and very few of them had ever been in action before. It is hard to believe that these men had entirely lost the fighting qualities of their ancestors, but, in many cases, they got no chance to put them to the test, for as soon as scouts brought news of the approach of the rebels, the Cumbrian levies broke ranks and fled. The Jacobites proclaimed King James, spent the night at Penrith and passed on to Appleby the next day, without doing harm to the town.

The Jacobites did not get beyond Preston in this attempt, and the rebellion was put down fairly easily, but it should have given a clear warning that the defences of the Border were in a poor way. The warning was not taken, however, and when thirty years later, in 1745, Prince Charles Edward made another attempt to gain the throne for the Stuarts, he found the north-western gate left open once again.

The Young Pretender arrived at Stanix at the Martinmas Term-end, when Carlisle city was thronged with people from the farms and villages. The next day the investment of the city began, but after two days word came that Marshal Wade was approaching from Newcastle with the Government forces, and the rebels left Carlisle and went to Brampton to meet him. The deputy-mayor, Pattinson, immediately sent a despatch to the Government, saying that "the town of Carlisle had done His Majesty more service than the great city of Edinboro' or than all Scotland together." After two more days, however, when it seemed clear that Wade was not anxious to seek battle, the Jacobite army returned to the siege. Charles Edward lodged at Warwick, and preparations for the assault of the city were made under the direction of Lord George Murray. Trenches were dug to within eighty yards of the city wall, but before any attempt was made to scale it the white flag went up in the town, and soon the castle was surrendered. James III was proclaimed King in the market-place, and the mayor and corporation went to Brampton and there presented the keys of the city to Charles Edward. The rebel army went down to Lancaster and Preston as far as Derby. Then—for reasons we need not consider—it turned back. There was a long, disastrous retreat over the wintry Shap fells, with the Duke of Cumberland harrying them in the rear.

The country folk were more alarmed by the retreat than by the invasion, for it was feared that the Highlanders would loot and plunder in their exasperation and disappointment. The Duke's forces caught up with the rearguard of the rebels near Penrith and there was a small skirmish, but the Prince and the bulk of his forces managed to get across the Esk and into Scotland. The Duke now occupied the city of Carlisle, but the castle still held out. He built batteries and bombarded the fortress till further resistance was impossible, and then, after surrender, he treated the defenders with unparalleled ferocity. The leaders were hanged, drawn and quartered. Hundreds of followers were cooped in the dungeons during the hot months of summer, and afterwards hanged in batches. Among them was Major Macdonald (said to be the Fergus McIvor of Scott's *Waverley*), who was captured in Scotland and brought to Carlisle. The guide and tradition still point out the marks of his fingers worn into the sandstone cell as he looked back towards Scotland. Perhaps it was McIvor, too, who carved the wall with figures of naked women with enormous busts and sexual organs—queer signs of loneliness and longing which have outlasted the ache in the bone.

The Last Invasion

Most people would say that the Rebellion of the '45 was the last invasion of England. Yet there was another, a small one and that in Cumberland, and, most surprisingly, from the sea.

John Paul Jones, like the earlier invaders, was a Scot, born in Kirkcudbrightshire. As a lad he came to Whitehaven and was apprenticed there to shipbuilding. Whitehaven, in the mid-eighteenth century, was one of the most important ports in the country, and also a centre of the shipbuilding trade, but it can have had little of the elegance and culture which were found in other cities of that time. Wren's well-proportioned lay-out had been crammed with warehouses and slums, and the town must have known all the vices and horrors of eighteenth-century low life—drunkenness, brutality, rioting, poverty, disease. Foreign sailors would come there, mad for rum and women, and the colliers had their own fierce, defensive life. And over it all must have hung the cloud of coal dust, sign of the still greater horror which was soon to cover the working towns of England. The sea rolled up from Ireland and the Isle of Man, but even the sea was black on this coast, licking the quays with a grimy tongue.

Paul Jones, anyway, did not care for the place, and took his chance to sail for America in a slaver. There he became an American citizen, and in the War of Independence he was captain of a privateer, the *Ranger*, which was equipped at Nantes for the expedition against England. In the early morning of the 23rd of April, 1778, he sailed quietly into the harbour and began to set fire to the shipping there. The alarm was given, however, and the ship's crew had to pull away from the shore in two boats, and only through his knowledge of the harbour and its intricacies was Jones able to guide the ship out to sea before the guns of the battery (which had been spiked) could be brought to bear on him.

The inhabitants were greatly scared by this raid. The old batteries were repaired and new guns brought from Woolwich. From that day to this the Whitehaven people have never got over their suspicion of strangers. When the music stops in a Paul Jones the girls always grab at the nearest man out of sheer apprehension.

The Christians

The implied antithesis between the parts of this chapter is purely for convenience: it is not impossible for Scots to be Christians, and, in this case, many of the Christians were Scots—for the missions of the Celtic Church were the most charitable of all the Scottish invasions of England.

The Faith had been brought to the north first towards the end of the Roman occupation, when St. Ninian, who according to tradition was born on the shores of the Solway, evangelised among the Picts of south-west Scotland. Nothing is said about his having preached in Cumberland, but he must have passed through the county along the Roman roads on his way to and from Rome where he was instructed.[1]

St. Kentigern

After the collapse of the Roman Empire, religious or-ganisation decayed in England. The inhabitants of the northern mountains were left half or wholly pagan, such teachers as they had were ignorant or heretical, and there was not the slightest pastoral order. During that time the Celtic Church burned at its brightest, the Church of the holy islands, Iona, Mona, Lindisfarne. In the archipelagos of the west, in Ireland, in Scotland, and all down the western edge of the England-Wales mainland, was that strange civilisation which we can see now only as we see a sunken church through the tide. Little of it remains but memories, ornaments, illuminated manuscripts and carved stones; but, in those days—together with the Roman Church and the Byzantine Church—it was one of the three main branches of Christendom.

---

[1] Bede: *Ecclesiastical History* (*Everyman* translation), Book III, chapter 4: "In the year of our Lord 565 . . . there came into Britain a famous priest and abbot, a monk by habit and life, whose name was Columba, to preach the word of God to the provinces of the northern Picts, who are separated from the southern parts by steep and rugged mountains; for the southern Picts, who dwell on this side of those mountains, had long before, as is reported, forsaken the errors of idolatry, and embraced the truth, by the preaching of Ninias, a most reverend bishop and holy man of the British nation, who had been regularly instructed at Rome, in the faith and mysteries of the truth."

The church of St. Columba and St. Patrick had already
begun its mission to the English when St. Cuthbert took his
grasp on Northumberland and Durham. St. Patrick himself
may have visited Cumberland in the wild years towards the
end of the fifth century, but it was from Scotland, rather
than from Ireland or the north-east, that the renewed Faith
was to come. The leader of that movement was St. Kentigern, who is also known as Mungo, the patron saint of
Glasgow. His Life was written about 600 years later by
Jocelyn, a monk of Furness Abbey, and though legends
twine round the words like ivy round the capital letters of
the manuscripts, there is still a central thread of history.
Let us not despise the legends, in any case.

Kentigern's mother, then, was a girl called Thenew or
Thanet, belonging to one of the royal families of Scotland.
In imitation of the Blessed Virgin, she vowed herself to
maidenhood, and turned down Ewen, a chieftain, who loved
her. Her father, bitterly angry, cast her out and sent her as
a servant to a farm by the Solway or in the Lowland hills.
There not only her rank and wealth were taken from her,
but also her virginity, to save which she had given them up,
for Ewen followed her, and by treachery seduced or forced
her.

When it was discovered that she was with child she was
condemned to death, according to the laws of her tribe. She
was carried to the top of a hill in the Lammermuirs, tied to
a chariot, and sent rolling and bouncing down the steep
slopes. By some miracle the chariot was not dashed to pieces.
Perhaps the shafts stuck in the rock, perhaps the wheels
chose a safe path among the moss; she was not killed, and
it seemed afterwards that the angels must have borne her
up and saved her. But the justices were not satisfied. She
had saved herself by witchcraft, so now that the rocks had
spared her from a harlot's death she must die a witch's death
by water. She was taken down to the sea, put into a small
boat made of hides, and pushed into the tide without oars
or rudder. The coracle spun out into the sea, and at dawn
the girl was cast on the northern coast of the Firth of Forth,
and there, beside a shepherd's fire, gave birth to her child.
There was not even a manger to lay him in, nor straw to

wrap him in, but it was the shepherds who first found him, as once before they had found a child in a stable—the hagiologists did not miss the parallel. That is said to have been in the year 518.[1]

All this boisterous ante-natal treatment seems to have had no harmful effect on the child. He was brought up and instructed by St. Servanus, a hermit who lived nearby, and by the time he was twenty-five was made Bishop of Glasgow. He was already famed for his gentleness, courtesy and eloquence, and he lived a life of great asceticism, abstaining from wine, and sleeping in a coffin with ashes for a bolster. He also made a practice of reciting psalms while standing up to the neck in cold water. His favourite must have been *De Profundis*.

He continued his work with zeal until a time came when the Christians were persecuted in Scotland, and he had to flee to Wales, to his friend and fellow-bishop, St. David. Strathclyde, Cumbria and Wales were in close communion in those days, indeed the southern part of Cumbria was known as Wales and the people spoke Welsh. It was on this journey that he first passed through Cumberland. Jocelyn says that at Carlisle "he heard that many among the mountains were given to idolatry and ignorant of divine law; thither he turned aside, and, God helping him and confirming the word by signs following, he converted to the Christian religion many from a strange belief and others who were erroneous in the faith.

"Oh, how beautiful upon the mountains were the feet of him who brought good tidings, that published peace, that brought good tidings of good, that published salvation, that said unto Zion, thy God reigneth."[2]

The mountains, too, were beautiful, for Kentigern set up his cross at Crossfield, which must be Crosthwaite, where the old parish church of Keswick stands today. The present church dates mostly from the fifteenth century—a stubborn building with its squat Border tower, not a bit overawed by the bulk of Skiddaw. Southey is buried there and the river

---

[1] See *St. Kentigern and St. Herbert*, by H. D. Rawnsley, a rare pamphlet of much charm.

[2] Quoted from Rawnsley's *St. Kentigern*.

flows not far away, syphoning Derwentwater into Bassenthwaite.

Kentigern went on to Wales and there founded the
monastery which was to be named after his disciple, St.
Asaph. Then, in 573 a great battle took place at Arthuret
upon Esk, near the Solway, in which three British kings
defeated the Picts and Saxons. An old Welsh poem tells us
that it was fought over "a lark's nest." Such would not have
been more trivial than the cause of many other wars, but,
whatever the cause, the effects were great, for it gave
Strathclyde a Christian ruler and Kentigern was recalled to
Scotland.

Perhaps he was reluctant to go, for he was getting old,
but back he went to those hills above the Solway, and spent
the remaining years of his life at Hoddam near Dumfries
and at his cathedral of Glasgow. It was then that the miracles
began to spring up like flowers behind him, especially those
three which are commemorated on the arms of Glasgow:
the fish which had a queen's ring in its mouth, the robin
which was brought back to life, and the blackberries which
were in fruit at Epiphany.

St. Kentigern may have taken a special interest in the
mission he had begun in Cumberland, for the mountains
were not stony ground. Churches were founded in the path
of the saint, and today there remain eight dedicated to him.
Jocelyn of Furness says these are all at places where he
rested and preached and baptised. This may not be impossible, for they are all in the upper half of Cumberland,
and most have a well at hand except Crosthwaite, where
there is no shortage of water. Irthington and Grinsdale are
in the north, near the Roman road, the natural line of approach; Caldbeck, Castle Sowerby, Mungrisdale[1] and Crosthwaite are all around the Skiddaw-Saddleback group;
Aspatria and Bromfield lie between Keswick and the coast
and may be worked into the itinerary if you presume that
Kentigern went on to Wales by sea.

[1] The Rev. Thomas Lees thought that the first syllable is the name of
Mungo. See *Transactions of Cumberland and Westmorland Archæological
Society,* 1881-82.

St. Herbert of Derwentwater

Perhaps St. Kentigern stationed monks and priests in
Cumberland to minister to the people and carry on the work
he had started. Whether this is true or not we cannot tell,
but we do know that in the century after his death a holy
man lived on an island in Derwentwater, not far from the
place where Kentigern first set up his cross. St. Herbert's
Island is one of the largest in Derwentwater and is about
in the centre of the lake, with a smaller island, Rampsholme,
as a stepping-stone to the eastern shore. It is wooded now,
like the other islands, and has a little ruined chapel on it,
which may belong to the fourteenth century when the bishop
ordered that the vicar of Crosthwaite should say mass there
annually on St. Herbert's Day (13th of April). We can
imagine them walking from the parish church to the shores
of the lake and then rowing across—priests, acolytes and
country folk—for attendance at this festival carried an
indulgence of forty days.

From the island they had one of the finest views of all
Cumberland—indeed, not so much a view as an environment of mountain beauty. For if they looked anywhere but
at their boots there were vistas. Up lake to Borrowdale, peak
folded against peak as tight as a pineapple; east, Castlerigg;
west, the spike of Catbells, and behind it, beyond the dip of
Newlands, Causey Pike, Grisedale Pike, and the sprawling
muscular country around them; and down lake, the other
islands, the marshland that leads to Bassenthwaite, and, so
that there should not be any diminuendo in the landscape,
the great block of Skiddaw, which, more than any other
fell, makes you aware of itself by mass rather than by
height.

But St. Herbert did not choose his retreat for its beauty.
Mountains were welcome to saints not because they were
beautiful but because they seemed to have nothing attractive
about them, nothing which could distract the eye and the
mind. St. Cuthbert, on Lindisfarne, lived in a cell of which
"the wall on the outside is higher than a man, but within,
by excavating the rock, he made it much deeper, to prevent
the eyes and the thoughts from wandering, that the mind
might be wholly bent on heavenly things, and the pious

inhabitant might behold nothing from his residence but the heavens above him."[1]

St. Herbert no doubt had a similar un-Wordsworthian attitude to nature, for he and Cuthbert were friends, and their friendship has been recorded by Bede. From him we learn that the two used to meet every year, and that once, while Cuthbert was at Carlisle, the hermit of the lake went there to see him, and asked that he might pray that they should meet death in the same hour. "The event confirmed his promise and the truth of the prophecy; for they never met again, but their souls departed from their bodies at one and the same moment of time, and were joined together in a heavenly vision, and translated at the same time by angels to the heavenly kingdom."[2]

St. Bega

By then, Cuthbert was bishop of the Lakes, which had been absorbed into the diocese of Lindisfarne. Cuthbert and Herbert died in 687, and the Conference of Whitby had been held in 664. From that point it is generally understood that the English rites superseded the Celtic and that the Celtic Church was pushed back across the Border; but, in fact, the Church in Cumberland remained predominantly Celtic for a long time after this, and its pastoral system was that of the Celtic Church, monastic rather than parochial. The Irish saints are still remembered, especially along the coast. There are several dedications to St. Brigid, the cousin of St. Patrick, and even to St. Patrick himself. Santon Bridge in Wasdale, and Kirksanton farther south, commemorate the Irish St. Sancton, and best of all we have the legend of St. Bega.

Bega, according to the most colourful version, was an Irish princess who fled from home to avoid marrying a Norwegian suitor, and found herself in a ship caught in a storm off the Cumberland coast. She may have intended to land at Whitehaven, but the storm was driving her straight towards the headland to the south of it. She called on God,

---

[1] Bede: *Life and Miracles of St. Cuthbert* (*Everyman* translation), Chapter XVII.
[2] Bede: *Life of St. Cuthbert.*

and vowed that if she were saved she would live a life of prayer beneath the cliffs which threatened to kill her. The boat was cast ashore, perhaps at Whitehaven, perhaps at Fleswick, but she and her attendant women were unharmed. They crawled up the sandstone slabs and found a refuge in a cave or a hut. Then she went to the Lord of Egremont and asked him to grant her a plot of land on which to build a hermitage. The lord was scornful. But he would give her land, he said—as much as was covered by snow the next day and on Midsummer Day. To one who knows the Cumbrian weather it seems a rash promise. The snow fell right enough, three miles of it, around the headlands, and the Pow Beck, and Whitehaven. All trace of the nunnery has gone—it is even doubted by some if Bega ever existed—but the priory of St. Bees later rose on the lands which the snow chose for the church.

The Monasteries

From the time of the decay of the influence of the Celtic Church (in England) to the Norman Conquest, ecclesiastical affairs were very confused in the north-west. There was always doubt as to what diocese the district belonged to, and even what country. At one time it owed spiritual obedience to the Archbishop of York and civil obedience to the King of Scotland. Even after Cumberland was finally made part of the English kingdom, Scottish bishops continued to claim authority over it. At last, Henry I created the new bishopric of Carlisle, and set at its head a rich Yorkshire landowner, Adelulf. At first the bishop lacked funds to set up much organisation in the diocese. Throughout this time, in fact, the Church had carried out its spiritual and civilising work almost entirely through the monasteries. Eight larger religious houses were founded, mostly by Norman barons. The Austin Canons set up priories, at Carlisle and Lanercost; the Premonstratensians at Shap; the Cistercians an abbey at Holme Cultram; the Benedictines priories at St. Bees and Wetheral, both these being cells of St. Mary, York. Furness Abbey and its daughter house of Calder were also founded by Benedictines, though later they adopted the Cistercian rule.

Lanercost is the monastery of the Border. No other religious house suffered more from pillage and plunder, yet its west front is perhaps the most serene architectural composition in Cumberland. Holme Cultram, on the west, is the house of the Solway. It was founded when Cumberland was part of Scotland and King David was on the throne, and it continued to owe some allegiance to the abbot of Melrose. Much of its endowment was in Scotland, but this did not prevent the Scots from burning and robbing it, not even Robert Bruce, whose father was buried there. It was the wealthiest religious house in the county—the monastery of the fat marshlands, trading with Ireland and the Isle of Man. It was the church of the mists, the half-light, the shadowy sands of the Border. Michael Scott may have been a monk there before his magic studies earned him a place in Dante's hell.[1]

Little now remains of it: only part of the nave, with the aisles blocked up, which is used as the parish church of Abbeytown. The foundations of the monastery buildings lie about the churchyard among the graves and the "old man's baccy" or rough chervil.

There were also two houses of Benedictine nuns—at Armathwaite and Seaton, near Bootle. The Border, towards the end of the Middle Ages, was not the best of places for communities of virgins. Armathwaite, the handiest to the Border, seems frequently to have been plundered. Seaton, more out of the way, escaped the raiders, but the nuns were wretchedly poor, for they had few endowments and could hope for little help from the inhabitants of the half-barren lands around Corney and Waberthwaite. Above them was

---

[1] Quell'altro, che ne' fianchi è così poco,
  Michele Scotto fu, che veramente
  delle magiche frode seppe il gioco.
          (*Inferno*, Canto 20.)

How well he knew the game of magic frauds is shown in the stories told about him in Scott's notes to *The Lay of the Last Minstrel*.

We may notice here how often the Solway comes into the religious life of Cumberland—St. Ninian, St. Kentigern, the Battle of Arthuret, Michael Scott. It it interesting, too, that Father Gabriel Hebert, whose *Liturgy and Society* has had such a great influence on the life of many Church of England parishes today, was born at Silloth.

the desolate slope of Black Combe; below them, the sea. Their hearts must truly have been set on heaven, for there was nothing else to set them on.

Besides these main houses there were priories at Cartmel and Conishead, near Ulverston; settlements of friars at Carlisle, Penrith and Appleby; and a number of hospitals throughout the diocese.

Of the larger houses some are now in ruins and some still play their part in the religious life of today. Let us look at two examples of each.

Carlisle Cathedral

The Augustinian Priory of Carlisle was marked from the first to be the centre of the Church in the north-west. It was founded early in the twelfth century, and when, in 1133, the bishopric was created, the priory became the seat of the bishop, and its church, of St. Mary, became the cathedral. The priory has decayed, leaving stones for the antiquary to pick among, but the cathedral remains, the living heart of the diocese, offering its daily sacrifice and prayers for all the thousands who have never been inside a church since they were baptised.

The cathedral has suffered greatly from time to time. There were disastrous fires; then there was the Reformation; and finally the Civil War, when practically the whole of the nave was pulled down and the stones used to build defences for the city. What is left is really the bust of the church: head, shoulders and a few ribs—choir, transepts and the remaining bays of the nave. Once the nave must have been one of our most imposing churches, 140 feet or more of Norman arches. Now only two bays are left. Because of this the church seems hunched and bunched together. Its gables are too high for its length. It reminds you of those Romanesque monasteries, fitting the summit of a hill like an ice-cap, where the central roofs are lifted high above the others, not by their own walls, but by the slope of the rock. The new west end has buttresses strong enough for a sea-wall. The tower is sturdy, and must have often been a good look-out in the Border Wars. Indeed, when I saw it in war-time, there were ladders fixed against it, and it seemed to have been adapted to a modern use—in the way things always are at Carlisle—and was a post for roof-spotters.

When you go inside you think at once of the nave that has gone. The two bays still left have the strength and the solid peace of Norman architecture. They are bent and twisted a bit, for the foundations cannot have been good, but they belong to the age of Incarnation, when God came down, and men had not to fidget and strain. This part of the cathedral is almost completely blocked from the choir by the rood screen, and once was used as the church of the parish; now it is a sort of entrance hall, but the round arches above the transept, tall and narrow, are like aisles laid on end.

When you pass through the screen you pass to another age, the age of the Gothic, the age of search and growth, the "decadence" of the Middle Ages, which was finally to burst and flower into the Renaissance. The aisles still have something of the same dark patience of the Norman arches, blocked off as they are from the light by the high backs of the choir stalls. The floor of the aisles is lower than that of the choir, and you can walk up and down while a service is on. There are tombs about, and worn stones, and ancient painted panels of the lives of St. Anthony, St. Augustine of Hippo and St. Cuthbert. But when you step into the choir all the museum smell is left behind. You forget about the dates and styles and periods, and you realise that the cathedral is a very practical structure, "a machine for worshipping in," and a machine that is in good order, well oiled and polished, running smoothly in the grooves.

You notice first of all the light and colour. If it is morning, the sun pours through the great east window, a magnificent Decorated work, chiefly blue, a glowing, sky blue, cracked with angular, half-red clouds. There is blue elsewhere, too: the dark blue curtains behind the sanctuary, dawn-blue of the roof, each panel with a flaming sun in the middle, and a whole Milky Way of smaller stars. Then there is the gold reredos beneath the east window, the brass eagle, the white stone of the pulpit, the khaki stone of the pavement, all enclosed in the pink sandstone—it is a swirling pool of colour, with bright shafts of light and vivid seaweeds floating in the blue and gold.

The eye is dazzled, almost hurt: it winces and turns from the light; it seeks shadows and hollows and darkness, and the darkness is there in the canopies of the choir-stalls—the dark wood, black indeed, not the black of jet but the black of liquorice. They belong to the time of Henry IV, when architecture was still the major art and all carving and painting was related to it. The wood juts out above the heads of the singers, and spikes upward in a doll's-house cathedral of turrets, pinnacles, gables, buttresses and steeples—quite illogical, but of great charm.

The congregation sits on chairs between the choir stalls and the sanctuary. At the Eucharist, the voice of the celebrant and the responses of the choir swing backward and forward over the heads of the people like the surge and backwash of waves on a shingle coast.

St. Bees Priory

The old Benedictine Priory of St. Bees has adapted itself to modern life in quite another way.

We have heard of St. Bega and of the priory founded in the reign of Henry I on what may have been the site of her nunnery. It lies between the shore cliffs and the land which slopes to Copeland Forest. It became a wealthy house, though a small one, and at the Reformation all but the church was pulled down.

This, as with Holme Cultram, Wetheral and many other abbeys, became the parish church: that is to say, most of it became the parish church, for the choir was blocked off and allowed to fall into ruin.

I must say little about the building or else these pages will be filled with ecclesiastical description. It is one of the most interesting churches in the county, with a fine Norman door, three early English lights and a single gable window above it. The stone itself is beautiful—a deep red sandstone, red as cochineal. It is soft, too, so that the angular decorations of the recess of the doorway are being blurred away, as the face of the stone is re-carved by the weather in the smooth organic sculpture of natural forms, of bone, shell, rind and bark. It looks so soft, indeed, that you feel you could rub and shape it with your fingers. The rain soaks into it, and in wet weather it is as dark as coffee, and everywhere, on church, graveyard walls, and the old houses round about, there is a bright green weed with a tiny white flower.

When the church was restored the tower was given a new belfry, with a low slated steeple such as you see in Romanesque churches in France, or on the small towers of Southwell Cathedral. This is not only suited to the rest of the Norman building, it fits in very well with the landscape. St. Bees is not set among mountains, but whichever way you approach the village by road you come over a high hill and look down at the priory. This is always a difficult test for a building, yet the new steeple comes through very well, especially if you approach it from Whitehaven, and see it like a chip out of a round saucer from the bay between the headland and the Nethertown coast.

In 1817 a Theological College was established at St. Bees, and to house the students the old chancel of the church was roofed and restored. The college came to an end in the '90's and only the hall remains, a reconstruction of a very beautiful piece of transitional work. The hall is used for various parochial purposes, and I myself have lectured in it at a W.E.A. one-day school. It gives a grand echoing ring to the voice.

But this is not all that has happened to the old priory. Edmund Grindall, who succeeded Parker in 1575 as Archbishop of Canterbury, was born somewhere in the district (possibly at Hensingham) and almost certainly attended the priory school. He realised how much this would be missed after the dissolution, and, therefore, when he became a prelate he obtained from Queen Elizabeth Letters Patent to found a Free Grammar School at St. Bees. It was one of the last acts of his life, and he did not see the school set up, but set up it was and it still testifies to his memory, more, perhaps, than anything else that he did.

There was a gap between the dissolution of the priory and the founding of the school, and the latter did not inherit the priory buildings; nevertheless, it may naturally claim to carry on at least part of the monastic function. No doubt many of the stones of the old house went into the building of the new school, as they did also into farms round about, one of which is still called the Abbey.

The quadrangle, facing the road, with one Elizabethan wing, is rather pinched, but the school spreads sideways more generously, as if it were displaying itself to the railway line. All the buildings, new and old, are of the same sandstone, red above the turf of the playing field. Many generations of parsons' sons and sons of professional men have been educated there, and, while it draws a majority of its pupils from a wider area, it remains essentially the public school of Cumberland and Westmorland. It is not for one who has not attended there to speak of its achievements and traditions, but, even to an outsider, it seems evident that such a remarkable environment—the old priory, the dour little village, the wild coast and the wild fells—must have a lasting effect on any sensitive youth.

Furness Abbey

And now the two ruined abbeys. The monks of the northwest chose to build nearly all their larger houses on sandstone and of it. Furness Abbey is on one of the few outcrops of this rock in North Lonsdale. You have been travelling among limestone or Silurian slate, then suddenly between Dalton and Barrow the landscape changes. You enter the Vale of the (Deadly) Nightshade.[1] The soil is dark and rich, there are scarps of red rock, and the trees hang down the slopes, fat and heavy. After the cheerful limestone of the Kent Valley or even of the iron district of Dalton and Lindal, the dark red walls seem sullen and brooding. The stone is a passionate, introspective red, mahogany-coloured, almost brown, or greened with moss and mould.

When the abbey was founded in 1127, through the gift of Stephen, afterwards king of England, Furness was a wild and isolated part of the country, and its inhabitants were rough and independent, speaking a dialect still half-Norse. But the abbey prospered. Its possessions were almost as extensive as the Isle of Man. It owned farms and woodland, with wool trade and hunting; fishing in the Morecambe Bay estuaries and in Windermere and Coniston Water; mills,

---

[1] The flower still grows in the ruins.

iron-ore mines and shipping trade with the west. It remained isolated, a kingdom on its own, in the marches between England and Scotland, shut off on the one side by the mountains and on the other by the sea.

It is ironical, therefore, that Furness should now be one of the most accessible of our ruined abbeys. The main road to Barrow misses it by a few hundred yards, but the railway passes close; there is a station just outside the enclosure, and the old railway hotel is built on the foundations of the manor house put up by Thomas Preston, who bought the site when the monastery was suppressed. The town is not in sight from the abbey, though the mineral wagons go past, but the ruins have a special place in the affections of Barrovians. The suburbs spread near, along the edges of the fine Abbey Road, and every Easter the children used to come in hundreds to roll their pace[1] eggs on the turf nearby.

Because of all this it is not surprising that the ruins are neat and park-like. The hotel looks much more ramshackle, for a land-mine fell there during the blitz on Barrow, leaving the ruins unharmed. The lawns are cut and the paths are weeded. The Ministry of Works has taken charge and torn down ivy and tree, propped the walls with bolt and bar and scaffolding, and pumped cement into the cracks. All this was rightly done, for Furness is a textbook abbey, a large-scale model for the student, extensive, well preserved, and with all accessories—chapter house, cloisters, infirmary, even drains and sewage system. Its beauty lies in proportion and grandeur rather than in the romantic associations of decay. It is massive, bare and austere, with a long nave, and chancel arch, still intact, high and poised. There is not much decoration. In the chancel wall is a sedilia, with an elaborately carved stone canopy, Italianate in style. The cloisters have an arcade, with pillars and arches deeply recessed and fluted. The chapter house, too, was fairly richly ornamented, and the bases of the six pillars stand in it, slim and still, in the manner of classic ruins. The roof is entirely gone, but by looking at the roof of the infirmary chapel we can imagine how beautiful it must have been, ribbed and curved like bats' wings to the tops of those six pillars. Apart

[1] Really "pasche," or "paschal."

from this it is mostly plain, severe stone, as when it was quarried.

It does not need ornament, however; it does not need legends, nor ivy and hanging plants. It achieves dignity, solid and simple as Gregorian plainsong. It was built sternly for its purpose—as functional in design as a blast-furnace.

Calder Abbey

Calder Abbey, on the other hand, has all the qualities and associations which would have delighted the reader of Mrs. Anne Radcliffe. It is a place for ballads and ghost stories; a place for assignations and seductions. A figure of a monk occasionally appears on photographs, looking out of one of the windows, and the blood of the murdered Borderers still stains the stones.

The Calder Valley is one of those which make up the western cartwheel of the Lake District. It is small and unlike any of the others. The river rises very near to Ennerdale, but flows south-west, receiving the becks which come from Cawfell and the western edge of the Haycock, Steeple and Pillar group, most of whose streams find their way to Wastwater, the Liza or the Bleng. It is desolate, rather monotonous country, shapeless and flat in colour. The slopes of Cold Fell and the land around Worm Ghyll seem dead and dreary till you look at your feet, and see that the swamp is full of flowers—lousewort, bog-cotton, mountain pansies and speedwells. Then, a few miles above the abbey, the river cuts into the St. Bees sandstone, which here stretches as far as the hills. There is no instant change in the landscape, but the river flows in deep ravines, and, looking down, you see the red buttresses and slabs under the water, and grey and blue cobbles on the edge, washed down from the upper fells. The swamp dries up, the reddish drystone walls disappear; the river slices down into the tiny valley and the trees bubble up to meet it. Farms and walls, now, are of sandstone, like the village of Calder Bridge, and there is the green generosity of sandstone soil, dark green and dark red, the colours of autumn hawthorn leaf and berry. Below Sella Park the river gouges a gulley for itself, with red cliffs on the outward curve and on the other, pink, mauve and blue shingle of

Stone walls and drift—South Cumberland
Slater's Bridge, over the River Brathay
in Little Langdale

slate, granophyre and sandstone. There, in spring, the daffodils walk among the trees, making a gipsy scarf of colour, and in autumn the red rock flakes off and lies along the boughs of the trees, and, dropping, rots back to rock again. Below this, the land becomes flat and open. Sand blows across the fields and the hedges are of gorse, and the horizon, seawards, is only of low, bumping dunes. At its mouth the river loses itself. Just south of Sellafield it corrodes into a shallow, pebbly delta, with willows growing on little islands in midstream. It trickles among the stones, in a dozen runnels that flow beneath the railway line and finally rejoin and enter the sands. Here the channel of the river meets that of the Ehen (which comes from Ennerdale and Ennerdale Water), so that at low tide it might almost be called a tributary of the longer stream.

The spot where the Ehen and the Calder meet the sea was, until recently, one of the loneliest stretches of the coast. There was no road nearer than Sellafield Station, and that little more than a cart-track, and to get from one side of the river to the other you had to go miles inland to Calder Bridge. During the war, however, a factory was built on the wedge of the land between the two rivers, roads to carry bus-loads of workmen were laid down, a foot-and-cycle bridge was thrown across the Calder, and a cinder track was made past the golf course along the sands to Seascale. The factory is soon to become an atomic power plant, drawing its labour force from the half-derelict area around Egremont and Frizington. As they stand at present (1948), the factory buildings are not very conspicuous, but I am apprehensive of the town which may grow there, for nowhere could pimply-red bricks be less welcome than among the pale pinks, mauves, greens and lemon of the lower Calder.

As yet, however, the river remains much as the monks must have seen it. The abbey owes its origin, as do St. Bees and Wetheral, to the family of William de Meschin, the first Norman lord of Egremont, and was founded in 1134 by a colony of monks from Furness. This was a time of great distress in the Border counties, and the monks had been there only a few years when the Scots burned down their little church of wood and wattles, and they fled home to

Birks Bridge, Dunnerdale
Yew Tree Farm, near Coniston

Furness, and thence to Bylands in Yorkshire. Later the Abbot of Furness sent out another band of monks, and these rebuilt the abbey and restored the foundation.

Nothing even of this church remains, for the oldest part of the building, the west wall with a Norman doorway, dates from the late twelfth century. The nave was built in the next century, and one aisle remains, of five bays, leading to the tower with its high and graceful chancel arch. The chancel contains a sedilia, much less elaborate than that of Furness, but attractive in its way, and the north transept has a particularly lovely Early English doorway, the mouldings cut so deep that it looks like a series of arches, decreasing in size, each throwing a curve of shadow on the one behind. In the chapter house we find a still later style of architecture, with remains of a Decorated window, and one bay of a three-bay groined roof. This juxtaposition of styles, stepping up through the centuries, has a peculiar charm, though the periodical rebuilding was probably due to periodical destruction by raiding Scots.

The chief appeal of Calder is not architectural, but, as it were, literary. It is the sort of ruin that John Piper ought to paint. It would have made a setting for a ballad of Scott's or a stanza or two of Byron's; or better, perhaps, for the metrical tales of Mrs. Felicia Hemans. The ivy hangs over the arches like the shading of a Victorian engraving; the sun picks out a vignette or an end-piece—a trefoil here, a cracked moulding there. The shadows of the iron bars of the cell fall across the cresset stone, where burning wicks floated in oil to give light for midnight offices. Brambles are hooked about the columns, with dark berries dropping unpicked, and nettles and yellow weeds flood against the stone. When you walk through transepts you leave a little ghyll behind you in the long grass, which slowly closes as you go away.

This, I feel, is how a ruin should look, lying undisturbed in its rotting cerements of legend, instead of having every stone counted and noted, like the relics of a saint exposed to the faithful, as at Furness Abbey. But decay is not a state, it is a process, and unless something is done to check that process there will soon be no ruins left. A few sheets of lead or tarpaulin over the groined roofs are not enough to preserve the building. Ivy and creeper are picking its bones. Young sycamores high on the walls are growing into trees, and will split the stones with their roots. The ruins stand in the grounds of a private residence, so that you can view them (without trespassing) only on Fridays. How much the owners may be responsible for the upkeep I do not know, but unless they try, or someone else tries, to conserve what is still left, the dales' chief monument of the Middle Ages will soon be only a heap of stones.

Parish Churches

The time of the fall of the monasteries was the time of the rise of the parish church, but in Cumberland and Westmorland there is no local tradition of church building such as we find in other parts of the country, like the Cotswolds, or East Anglia, or the land around the Trent. The dales and the southern limestone country have each a style of their own, and of these I will speak. Around the Border, too, there is a number of fortified buildings, half church, half castle. For the rest there are only detached and individual churches, often of interest and beauty, but having little relation to each other.

Moreover, while we have many churches of twelfth- and thirteenth-century foundation, so much has been done in renovation and restoration, and in pulling down and rebuilding, that only a few of them remain in anything like their original state. This does not mean that they are not worth visiting. Few churches lose all their character even after the most brutal restoration. An aisle is left, or a chancel arch, a window, or a chapel. And even when the church is torn to the ground, the new building may hold an old font, or some glass, or a few slabs built into the wall. These are part of the common heritage of the parish church in England —there is no need to speak of them here.

A few churches of special interest come into mind: Over Denton and Isel, with their Norman remnants; Cartmel Priory, with its upper tower set diagonally on the lower; Kirkoswald and Greystock, the collegiate churches; Holy Trinity, Millom, where a particular curve is repeated and varied, fugally, in the tracery of the windows, one of which, a "fish window," a Gothic arch reflecting itself below, is unique in England for its size.

There is St. Mary's, Kirkby Lonsdale, by many thought to be the most beautiful church in the diocese. Outside it is square and dogmatic, and must have been still more so before the battlements were added at the restoration in 1866. The old Norman base of the tower has that rough rubbly look which you so often find in pale towers. A clock, set awry, gives it something of a squint, but it remains the comfortable church of prosperous wool merchants. Inside we meet at once the Norman west end, three pillars and three arches—the third arch resting against the wall. The arches above them are rather small, making the pillars come close together, but they have strength and stillness, and that understanding of rock form which is true to Romanesque architecture. These are shapes which would endure as gigantic fossils in the coal or sandstone grit which the next geological era will make of the surface of our world. There is good Jacobean carving in the woodwork, polished and brown as chocolate, and the stone is a warm, tasty-looking colour, like gingerbread or hazel-nuts. It is a church to make your mouth water.

Eighteenth-Century Churches

Of later churches the district has not much to show. The eighteenth century was the century of the towns, and there were few large centres of population in the dales. Nevertheless, Whitehaven was growing on the coast, and two of its three churches belong to that time. They are neither of them elegant, having unadventurous towers and plain walls, but they are sensible and courteous, they take their appointed place in the street, they are neighbourly and do not show off. The smoke and the coal-dust settles on them, and the sea-mists and the rain; dark leaves live long pauper years behind iron railings; but the churches remain as solid as Samuel Johnson. Inside, each has a gallery: that at Trinity supported on fat pillars painted like marble, reminding you in their shape and stance of the middle branch of the Church of England at the time of Paley,[1] confident, calm, and a little complacent. St. James's, on the other hand, is the high church, with iron pillars prettily designed and painted the green which is usually kept for pantries. There is also a pulpit, perched so high that the preacher must have felt like St. Simon Stylites. Whatever the bishops may decide, no woman is likely to preach from those steps. St. Cuthbert's, Carlisle, near the cathedral, while still rather plain, has more of the politeness and cosiness of the Georgian church as it is known in the south, but Penrith parish church is perhaps the most interesting eighteenth-century building in the Lake counties. To a medieval tower has been fitted a large, heavy-weight wrestler of a church. It is all in sandstone, blood-red, with a gallery held up by Samsons hewn each from a single block.

Nineteenth-Century Churches

I have spoken at some length about the eighteenth-century churches, for they seem to me well suited to the country of rock and fell. Their congregations are not always very proud of them—in the porch of Penrith Church there is a notice saying that the building isn't too bad considering that the architects of that time knew no better—but they have a sturdy, practical dignity and commonsense, which, I think, go well with the place and the people.

Gothic is rarely appropriate to the Lake District mountains. They are not huge enough to ignore its grotesqueness, nor small enough to need its fancy. Where it is most successful is in the Border churches, where the battlements and towers are intended as much for defence as decoration.

In the manufacturing towns of Lancashire and Yorkshire the Gothic was almost a necessity; but among the dales it was irrelevant. Moreover, the architects seemed to have drawn up their churches without a thought of the surroundings. Slate will not do very well for Gothic, so buff and red sandstone had to be carried to the slate country. Then they introduced spires. Nothing could have been more futile: the

---

[1] William Paley, author of the *Evidences*, lived much of his life in the diocese, being Archdeacon of Carlisle.

spires are insignificant and poky beside the fells. Amble-side, and St. John's, Keswick, are like a little boy's gesture of defiance. The only place where spires are effective is well away from the hills, as above the estuarine marshes on the coast.

The Dale Churches

Where attempts have been made to build large-ish Gothic-revival churches of slate—as at Burneside in West-morland—the result is disappointing. In the dales, there-fore, where transport of stone was difficult and expense had to be kept down, there developed a church which has little deliberate artistry, but is nevertheless very satisfying. Mardale Church—now slipping under the waters of Hawes-water reservoir—is such. Coniston Parish Church is another. They have a plain slate tower, with a doorway and porch in the base, and the roof of the body of the church sloping away from the tower, equally on either side, with no aisles. They are firm, simple and as indigenous as the oak.

Even simpler are the chapels in the smaller villages, where the tower becomes merely a turret to hang a bell in—like Seathwaite in Dunnerdale, Wonderful Walker's Church; or Whitbeck, which is reputed to have been a meeting-place for smugglers from Gutterby; or Wasdale Head, claimed, like others, as the "smallest church in England." In these there is scarcely an external decoration: a little freestone tracery in the windows, perhaps, that is all. They are usually not very old as they stand now, but they are quite them-selves, and belong to the landscape as completely and in-evitably as the stone walls and the old bridges.

The Churches of the Limestone Country

In one part of the Lake District, however, there has de-veloped a true, local type of Gothic—in the limestone region of South Westmorland. The stone alone distinguishes these churches, shining out white among the fields, or pale pink, like pink may, where it is mixed with sandstone.

Kendal Parish Church is the "cathedral" of this area—a fine spacious building, with five aisles (that is, a nave, and two aisles on either side). With its tall central tower, and the aisles spread out so far, it looks like a hen gathering her chickens under the wing.

Some of the chickens got away, however, and grew up by themselves—the parish churches of Burton-in-Kendal, Heversham, Beetham and the rest. Burton Church is bare and rather detached from the little town, which is otherwise so snug and friendly. Inside it is less cold but still dignified. Beetham Church, on the other hand, will ogle any passer-by. It has that sort of prettiness which at first seems to belong to a shilling calender, with a setting which might be copied for an antimacassar—road nearby, inn, big trees with the river behind, and a trellis-avenue up to the front porch, full of the red curly-hair of rambler roses. But you realise that the church has a deeper beauty which is not spoilt by this pretti-ness, just as a beautiful woman is not spoilt by ribbons and trinkets. The stone is so old that it has worn smooth, and the tower looks as if it had come off a wedding-cake, with a little sugary spike at each corner. Yet inside the air is grave and rich, like organ music. For a long time it was the only church in this part of the country. My grandmother was baptised there. Heversham, looking across the upper marshes of the Kent, is another ancient church, but it is not only the older buildings which belong to the tradition. Milnthorpe Church, tall and stiff as a schoolma'am, looking down her nose at the children playing in the square, is of the same breed, though the blood may be wearing a little thin. In Holme Church the blood is still thinner, yet even in this little mongrel-pup of a building the cocked ears of the tower have the genuine Beetham strain in them. The rock makes its own terms, and, however bad an architect may be, he cannot quite ignore them, unless he takes to brick.

PART III

Chapter VIII

THE SIGNATURE OF MAN

We have seen how man came to the district and we have noted the monuments he left of each separate invasion—monoliths, crosses, abbeys. Now let us look at the mark he has made in his everyday life—not the castles and churches, but the cottages and towns.

Roads

Many of the cottages before the eighteenth century were built of turf and nothing of them remains. Even the stone-built castles and abbeys fall into ruin; but roads have a way of going on living, whether they develop into motor high-ways or linger like a ghost-story as a right-of-way between fields and allotments. The present route over Hardknott and Wrynose cannot deviate very far from the road the Romans made from Ambleside to Ravenglass. The medieval roads, the roads that the monks followed and later the packhorse traders, are the same tracks we still use in the dales. They can have changed little: the surface is sometimes improved, the language of the inhabitants is more intelligible—that is about all. They are the special and loved possession of the walker. As you go up the dales, the road narrows and twists, the stone walls are covered with moss, looking more like dried-up waterfalls than the work of man. At last, the walls fall away, the road is free. It finds its own way through the last corridor of meadow between the fells. Then it bends left or right and begins to climb the pass, through water-splashes or over hump-backed bridges built of whatever happened to be lying nearby. In wet weather the rains find in the track a ready-made water-course; in dry weather the surface is like a gentle scree. The black-faced Herdwicks stand on the track and expect you to walk round them. But for once it is man and not the animal who has the first right, for the road was here before the sheep.

Pack-horse Bridges

After the Restoration traders came to the dales: wool-merchants and weavers, tin and copper miners, colliers, exporters and smugglers. They travelled in strings of ponies, up the west coast, and from Whitehaven inland to Keswick and thence over Dunmail Raise to Ambleside, or on to Penrith and south by Shap. It was for these traders that the pack-horse bridges were built. These are stone bridges, of one arch, usually with walls and a narrow track between. None of them is very old,[1] mostly about the eighteenth century, but they have the timeless look of rock. When they cross shallow becks they heave up from the flat fields, rather lonely and lost, Icelandic and ruminating. You feel that they may be buried deep in snow and forgotten for months of the year. But when they are flung over little chasms in rocky country (like Birk's Bridge in Dunnerdale, the Monks' Bridge above Calder Abbey, or High Sweden Bridge in Scandale, looking towards the head of Windermere), then they are virile and romantic. The rowans hang over them and the walls have a thick green pelt of maidenhair spleen-wort and wall-rue and rustybacks. The water scoops the rock like a woman kneading dough, and lies green as bile in the dubs, and froths under the chin of the arches at the floods.

There is nothing archaic about them. When carriages and heavier traffic came on the road, it was easy to develop a stronger and wider bridge of the same pattern—that by the mill over the Whelan Back at Boot in Eskdale shows the transition to the new type. Moreover, the single stone arch might well be considered by modern builders whenever a small bridge is needed in the dales. Just below the National Trust property round Wallabarrow Crag and the Duddon Gorge an ugly wooden bridge has been replaced by a single arch of local slate. It is still raw and new-looking, but this will soon wear off. From it there is a grand view of the rocky course of the river, the boulders where the weasels run, and the hazels, rowans and thorns which dribble down the sides

[1] There is a three-arch bridge near Furness Abbey which is thought to be of the late fifteenth or early sixteenth century, and a single-arch bridge (Souterhous Brigge) over the same Abbey beck which is probably fifty years older.

of the gully, changing greens like the water. It is also a thoroughly useful and practical piece of workmanship, giving needed access to the Cumberland side of the river, for the stepping-stones, some yards below it, are more attractive to mountaineers than farmers' wives.

Motor Roads

The new roads which carry motor traffic are not so very unlike the old. Arterial roads—with concrete kerbs, grass verges, and hedges clipped like convicts' heads—have to stay in the lowlands. The dales and the moorland still have twisting, hilly tracks. The surface is good, the corners are planed off, there are signposts and sometimes white lines, but the roads keep much of their old character. They often have their stone walls, for instance, and shave past the doors of cottages and farmhouses. Often the rock has to be blasted to make a turn, and you have the feeling of walking along the bottom of a quarry. Driving a car at night is an adventure, worse than a scenic railway at Blackpool South Shore, for always your headlights are shining on to a wall set square across your way.

Best of all the motor roads are those which run along the shores of lakes. Not the bare lakes, like Wastwater, where the road is only a sort of promenade, but the wooded lakes, Ullswater, Windermere (especially on the Finsthwaite side), Thirlmere (on the west side, looking across the lake to Helvellyn) and Coniston (on the Brantwood side, looking across to the Old Man). In most of these the road does not run along the water-edge, but dodges round knolls and through copses, approaches the water and runs away from it, noses up, pauses, sniffs and bounds away like a courting bitch. The road and the lake are in league with one another, yet the road is not assertive, you never see much of it at a time, and from above it is scarcely to be noticed.

Quite different are the main roads over the passes, Kirkstone, Honister, Whinlatter and Dunmail Raise. Here the road is bare and obvious, a long curling rope of tarmac laid across the grass and the rock. Here the country changes from ballad to epic, from *Willie Drowned in Yarrow* to *Beowulf*, and the road has the plainness of a chronicle, though not without its digressions and circumlocutions. Proudest of all the roads, perhaps, are those like that from Ulpha to Eskdale over Birker Moor,[1] where the moor rolls broad and dark, and the groove of the road is the only line on which the eye can steady itself and measure the landscape. The road then is like a tonic note to a scale, giving pitch and perspective to all around it.

On these roads, too, I find that the telegraph poles and wires are likewise welcome to the eye. Indeed, as well as line, they add rhythm to the scene, the unbroken rhythm of repeated posts over which the waves of the fells can billow and splash in syncopations and counterpoints. Looking from my window early one September morning, when the level sunlight caught every tree and chimney, I saw Black Combe striped with vertical spokes of light, the poles which carried guiding lights for an aerodrome on the coast. Since then I have seen them again when I have looked at sunrise, but at other times of the day they were invisible.[2]

And on a misty day, when distance is lost and the moor floats like an island, and the curlew's call comes from no recognisable direction, neither behind nor before, nor from the sky, nor out of the earth: on such days the telegraph wires are like a life-line to civilisation, and help to give human dimensions to the landscape.

Coastal Roads

It is strange that on all the Cumberland coast there is scarcely a road more than a few miles long. In Furness, from Barrow to Ulverston, there is a delightful stretch of road, through Rampside and Bardsea along the limestone shore, looking across Morecambe Bay, and there is the fine road running beside the Solway from Iver north of Maryport to Silloth; but mostly the roads make great scallops inland, side-stepping the estuaries and joining towns and villages.

For a long time the Cumberland Development Council, together with public authorities in North Lonsdale, have

[1] This offers one of the most extensive views of the Cumberland mountains to be had from any motor road.

[2] They have since been taken down.

been calling for a new road along the coast from Lancaster to Whitehaven. Such a route is surely necessary if prosperity is to be restored to the industrial area of West Cumberland. Moreover, it would take heavy traffic away from the villages where it ought never to be—as it is, all lorries coming from the south to Barrow or West Cumberland have to go hopping round the estuaries as far as Levens Bridge and Newby Bridge.[1]

All the coast schemes include a new road from Whitehaven to Barrow, bridging the Esk-Irt Estuary, and bridging or damming the Duddon. The Morecambe Bay part of the project presents greater difficulties. The most ambitious scheme involves the building of a huge embankment from Lancaster to a point somewhere near Aldingham on the Furness coast. This would reclaim an enormous area of land, and leave Grange and other places stranded on the edge of acres of flat farmland. A less costly scheme is to build two embankments, from Hest Bank to Humphrey Head and again across the Leven Estuary. This would leave the southern tip of Cartmel still on the coast, but it would cut off Westmorland entirely from the sea.

The scheme is not new—it was brought forward as early as the eighteenth century—and in 1837 George Stephenson made an "Oracular Survey" for two routes for a railway between Lancaster and Carlisle, one over the fells and one along the coast. The next year came John Hague's "Most Magnificent Project" of reclaiming Morecambe Bay and the Duddon Estuary, which was taken up with some enthusiasm, but had to be dropped because it was altogether too vague and costly. Later John Abel Smith had a plan for a railway ferry from Fleetwood to Furness, with a railway across the Duddon to Whitehaven and Carlisle. This scheme, too, was dropped, though he got as far as building a pier at Roa Island.[2] In the '60's a start was really made to bridge

---

[1] To avoid confusion it might be pointed out that Levens Bridge is on the River Kent which comes from Kendal, while Newby Bridge is on the River Leven which comes from Windermere.

[2] I am indebted for much of this information to Mr. J. L. Hobbs and Mr. J. Melville, who had made a special study of the history of the Furness railway for its centenary in 1946.

the Duddon. Power was obtained from Parliament, tenders were invited, and building material was accumulated at Askam. Then the scheme was dropped. No reason was given, but it is generally thought that the promoters feared the development of the port of Whitehaven to the detriment of Barrow.

The obligations incurred by the approach to Parliament still remained, however, and this was settled by an agreement that the fare from Millom to Askam (a distance of ten miles round the head of the estuary at Foxfield) should be charged on the distance by the bridge that was not built—about four miles. The fare remains (July, 1948) at 11*d.* (single) for the ten miles—the cheapest railway journey in England.

Railways

I have already outlined the main railway routes in the district, and I want now to think of them only as part of the scene. The railway does not enter into the real dale country. Except for the Eskdale narrow-gauge line it approaches nearest at Coniston and Windermere, and in the Cockermouth-Penrith and the Shap lines. One can understand how indignant Ruskin was at the proposal for the Coniston line, as a railway, when it is first built, must be an ugly and glaring scar, especially in country which needs continual blastings and cuttings, embankments and bridges. But the English countryside has taken the railway to its heart. The embankments are soon covered with grass and many flowers, strings of bunting colours, white, yellow and red, dog-daisy, primrose, hawkweeds, ragged robin. In the ditches at the side there are bog plants and rarer flowers, and where cuttings let light into the woods, foxgloves and rose-bay. Ferns and lichens are soon acclimatised on the broken rock, and even the cinders have their particular weeds.

The trains themselves look more at home in the fells than many tourists, whether they run along the express lines over Shap like prehistoric pachyderms, or pant up the hill from Penruddock to Troutbeck, puffing smoke among the birches. I know the children of a poet whose favourite picnic place was a bridge on that line, where they could watch the water below and the trains above.

In the lowlands, of course, the railway is already a familiar and traditional part of the scene. Here and there it may draw too straight and defiant a line—as along the shores of Bassenthwaite, and in stretches of the coast—but on the whole it is friendly, adaptable and good-mannered. The view down the lower reaches of many of the western rivers (the Mite, the Esk, the Leven, the Kent) is given a dramatic curtain by the railway viaduct.

Moreover, the builders of the railway have shown much sense in their stations. Almost all of them are quiet, modest buildings, humdrum admittedly, but rarely obtrusive. Most, too, are of local stone—slate in the fells, sandstone or limestone in the lowlands, Eskdale granite along the coast. The architects had a fondness for the round arch supported by freestone, which at Ulverston comes out in full fancy-dress rather like a casino on the Italian Riviera. The rebuilding of Barrow Station, badly blitzed, may give us our first modern station, and it is to be hoped that room will be found in it for Copper Nob, the old furnace engine, which used to stand in a conservatory-like glass case at the entrance. When a Railway Exhibition was held in London some time before the war, Copper Nob went there, and moved on his own steam from the case to the wagon that was to take him.

Canals

We have only one canal of any length—the Lancaster-Kendal canal. This passes through the limestone country from Carnforth by Burton into the Bela valley and thence to Kendal. It runs in a sort of terrace at the foot of the Hutton Roof hills, which are bare as teeth above it, but the fields round about are green and gentle. Nevertheless, the canal is very unlike those of Hertfordshire. Here are no wooden bridges and locks and willows and white paint. The water is clear, not muddy; the sides are bare but for reeds and water dropwort and ragwort. Very frequently there are limestone bridges, humped and tubby, like a fat boy with legs apart making a back for leapfrog. Sometimes, from the top of one of the bridges, you can see half a dozen others, above and below. Here and there, planted beside the water, are rows of firs or larches, dark green against the grey of the bridges. Across the valley are the low furry hills around Beetham and Milnthorpe, and the sky is wider here than anywhere else in the dales, and the clouds are the colour of the stone.

A canal is more personal than a road, and this one is like a family link between the villages and houses that it passes through. The children play under the bridges, often wetting and occasionally drowning themselves; and during the war Italians from the Bela camp wandered along the banks, kicking stones in the water and hoping that a girl would speak to them. The canal is not much used now, and might have been demolished had it not been of value to farmers for draining and irrigating their land. It is strange but pleasing to find such a quiet stretch of water in a land where streams usually dash and splash and gurgle and growl, and I think that most people in lower Kendal would be sorry to lose it, except, perhaps, the mothers of young children.

Cottages and Farms

The cottages and farms of the dale scarcely seem to be the work of man at all. It is rather that the rock itself, the green, blue, purple and grey slate, has shaped itself into these halls and houses, so that the people are still, in a way, cave-dwellers. The walls are thick, doorways and windows low, square and deep-set. On the roof, too, is slate—perhaps rough slabs from the local quarries, or the green slate of Honister, or dark grey Kirkby Roundheads. There are porches in front of the doors, a wall on either side of the house with a peaked roof, and perhaps one flagstone laid level across.

The cottages usually stand toeing the road, with not even a plot or flowers to border them. Often, indeed, at corners, where the road has been widened, the cottage juts out like a bus which has got jammed. There is rough plaster on the walls, which are whitewashed, white as starched linen, or sometimes colour-washed with pink or green or blue. In the Coniston districts there is a popular dark orange shade of autumn oak.

Farms are of any shape. The house may be set and angular, three windows up, two and a door down, with chimneys at either side like a dog pricking its ears. But the group of house and outhouses composes itself in cubist shapes, with oblongs and parallelograms of sun-wash and shadow, and unexpected planes of yellow, brown or red where hay or bracken is stacked in a barn.

The village inns are very like cottages, whitewashed and with porches, or like farms, square and set back from the road. Indeed they often *are* farms, for there is not enough custom to make a living for the landlord, who therefore has a few fields, keeps hens and a cow or two, and sends his sheep on the fells. There are many small inns, like *The Fox and Goose* in the Whicham Valley, with scarcely a house within a quarter of a mile. Some, like the inn at the top of Kirkstone Pass, have become prosperous stopping places for the modern traveller. Others—*The Angler's* (Ennerdale), *The Royal Oak* (Keswick), *The Salutation* (Ambleside) and *Wasdale Head*—have developed into large hotels, each with its own type of customer. The *Wasdale Head Hotel* is the headquarters of the rock-climbers, and you risk breaking your neck there, not so much on the rocks, as by falling over the ropes and boots which lie about the hall. Practically all the country inns now cater for visitors, if they have the room, but there still remain many, like *The Woolpack* (Eskdale) and *The Traveller's Rest* (Ulpha), where the shepherds meet and the dialect clicks at the white tables, and wrestling trophies hang beside the dart-board. These places have a way of making and moulding their owners to the true type. It is told how three young students visiting *The Traveller's Rest* in the early nineteenth century tried to mock the landlord by sending him a note in Latin asking for their bill. They got the bill in Latin, Greek and Hebrew, with an appendix pointing out the mistakes in their own Latin, for the landlord, whose speech was as rough as any farmer's, was a retired Cambridge don. The dale villages are lined up along the roads. There is no room for them to widen it, with the cliffs at their back gardens and the beck running down the front, and in this they are unlike the traditional English village, with winding lanes and a green or common.

Farm, Tilberthwaite (bequeathed to National Trust by Beatrix Potter)

The Small Towns

Many of the same characteristics can be seen in the small towns which are everywhere found at the foot of the dales. Here, no doubt, the community can ease itself like a fat woman sitting in a bigger chair, and there will be a square in front of the market, perhaps a green and a market cross. Here, too, there are other colours besides the slate. There is the freestone of the old church and of the lintels of the village school; there are stucco fronts above the shops and certainly a few brick villas and bungalows. But the "almshouse" Tudor which is so typical of the valleys of the Midlands and the South is not much seen, and there is no black and white timber at all.[1] Here, though, we find smithies and garages, grocers and chemists and doctors; and here there is a regular bus service, and perhaps even a station.

When you move northward into the Cumberland plain, you move into the sandstone country, and the villages are red and lichenous, like a Christmas pudding gone mouldy. Here there is more sign of Tudor, but it is the stout, practical Tudor of the Border. Sometimes you do come upon a village or a district which, at first glance, might belong to another part of the island: such as that very odd peninsula between the coast and the main road from St. Bees to Whitehaven. It is cut off from all trade traffic and the tourists have never heard of it. Girls from Whitehaven sometimes cycle through it on their way to bathe at St. Bees; otherwise it keeps itself to itself. And here, Sandwith and Rottington, and Beckermet,[2] a little farther south, have the drowsy look of a Shropshire village, with little Gothic arches pushing themselves into the walls and the sort of bars on the windows that suggest Perpendicular. The streams sidle under the red bridges. Yet at Sandwith there is also a different look, wary and grimy with a salt tang, too. The village street is a real street; there are more pubs than you would expect; and some of the houses have those small square windows you often find in old warehouses by the quayside. When you go

[1] Except where wealthy strangers have bought country houses and had imitation timbering *painted* on the cement or plaster!

[2] This village, at present unspoilt, may perhaps suffer from the nearness of the atomic power plant at Sellafield.

Watendlath

a few hundred yards out of the village you see the reason. The trees dwindle, the hedges open, and there on the headland which drops to the unseen harbour of Whitehaven is the colliery, with black sheds and pithead wheels leading up to the two tall chimney-stacks. It jumps clean out of the fields as if it were the work of fairies. There is scarcely a house to be seen, nor a railway line, nor any sign of the town. Even the smoke looks as if it were drawn in charcoal on the clear sky, hundreds of feet above the shore. Five minutes later you are among the suburbs and you feel the downward drag of the streets, but in Sandwith you are still in the country, still in Cowper's England, or at least in Crabbe's, though the miner and the quarryman have set up house beside the farmer.

The Coastal Towns

The towns and villages on the coast are different again. Here the stone may be sandstone or slate or limestone, according to the part of the coast, or it may be cobbleducks from the shore, but in each case the identity of the stone is lost in the stucco or concrete which the sea winds make necessary.

From Whitehaven to Workington we have the colliery coast. North of that is the Solway, and Allonby and the other villages have a bare Scottish look; south are Ravenglass, Bootle, Haverigg, and small stranded groups of farms at places like Drigg, Annaside, Layriggs, where you feel that the statesman has wandered from the dale, but is clinging to his old way of life, trying to graze sheep on the very sand. Farther south still is Morecambe Bay, which is not so much the coast as an indeterminate country of sand, marsh and water.

There is not much shipping now, but Ravenglass, the port of the Romans, continued to dock small cargo vessels until the middle of the last century. Before the building of the Furness Railway, Ravenglass was the main supply port for Gosforth and the other west coast villages, importing mostly coal, timber, wheat (for Gosforth mill), oatmeal, bacon, potatoes and other foodstuffs. These were discharged into carts and so carried through the district. The harbour was always rather difficult, owing to the three channels of the Irt, the Mite, and the Esk, and the sandbanks which form and shift between them, and in 1823 a tower was built on Newtown Knott (now part of Muncaster Park) as a guide to the mariners.

There are popular holiday resorts among the seaside towns—Silloth, Seascale, Grange and Arnside. Carlisle has its afternoon playgrounds on the Solway; Whitehaven at St. Bees; Barrow on Walney Island. There are golf-courses and hotels. In parts (Braystones, Silecroft, the Rampside coast road) there are bungalows and beach-huts. Some of these are shacks built of corrugated iron, old doors, asbestos, and empty petrol drums. You carry a bucket across the shingle to get water from a tap.

The sea is cosmopolitan. It does not learn the dialects. The waves that break off St. Bees Head are the same as those off Wales, or Cornwall, or the Hartlepools. It casts up the same sort of wrecks everywhere. So along the Cumberland coast the local and the universal meet. Languages, habits and ways of life are mixed. The farm lad, going to the sands to find straying cattle, stumbles across visitors lying half-naked in the dunes; bathing costumes are spread to dry on the gorse bushes beside coarse aprons; commercial travellers have holiday affairs with local girls. War washed up even more strangers than the sea: thousands of airmen at the aerodromes on dunes and marshes; sailors and W.R.N.S. at training centres; Americans and Colonials at dispersal camps; soldiers at anti-aircraft and searchlight stations; munition workers at the new factories in the villages. But the rock and the sea remain the same. The rock is Cumberland, and the sea is everywhere.

Village Economy

In all our area we find little signs of the Feudalism which has ordained the social development in the rest of the country. In the villages, of dale, of lowlands and of the coast, there is a marked freedom from the influence of the hereditary landowner and the Great House. Influence there certainly is, but often it is of an industrialist or brewer who has bought up land and farms and houses, or, more particularly, controls the local labour market.

Not only is the influence of the Great House absent, but the Great House itself. There are castles in the Lake District and old halls with funnelled chimneys, but there are few of those Georgian buildings which are the centre of life of the country gentry. Instead we get a type of country house peculiar to the district. It was built in the nineteenth century, when the Lakes were becoming fashionable, and rich men from Manchester were wanting to retire there. It came out of the suburban Gothic which is to be found on the edge of south-coast holiday resorts. It still keeps something of the style in the many gables, steep roofs, and sometimes attempts at bay-windows, but it has put on Cumberland clothes. The stone is not brick but slate again, and the window-frames and the beading on the gables are all painted dark green. There are no conservatories now, nor flowering urns, nor parterres, but gravel paths and fir trees and enormous dark rhododendrons. It is one of the first signs of the Romantic movement in the Lakes.

Such houses, however, remain the homes of strangers, of settlers, of permanent visitors; not those of the old squires. As you look around the villages you will be surprised to find how many of them are centred, not around farming and marketing, but around some industry. The mountains are poor agricultural land; the Norsemen came and settled in isolated farms in small groups, and they probably got as much out of the land as anyone. Since then the population has grown, but it has been largely an industrial population, even in the remote dales. Mining and quarrying have been the main source of livelihood since the time of Elizabeth. Mining has now shifted to the coast, but villages like Coniston grew up essentially as mining villages, and Keswick was the market town for the rich mining area of lower Borrowdale. Worked-out mines are to be found in nearly all the dales, and the remains of bloomeries are scattered through High Furness and in Eskdale and Wasdale.

Then there are the wood industries—saw-mills and bobbin-mills—the latter to be found all over the place, evidently to serve the great wool trade of South Westmor-

land, which now has its centre in Kendal. As a child I found
something strange in the idea of bobbin-mills—they might
have been worked by gnomes or dwarfs—so that when I
heard of them at Ulpha I was quite ready to believe of
treacle mines there too. Those who fear that afforestation
and its accompanying industries will ruin the Lake District
should go and see Tarn Hows[1] near Hawkshead. Here, the
centre of an afforested area, is a little lake which has become
very popular with cyclists and motor tourists. It is certainly
a gem, almost a trinket, almost too pretty and not quite in
character. It is a double lake, figure-eight-shaped with
islands, and fir trees all round it and on the islands, spiky
or feathery. It is tiny, but to scale: many of the trees are
dwarf as yet, so that you have the impression of looking
down from a great height on a large Swiss or Canadian
lake. Yet across Tom Heights are Coniston Old Man and
Wetherlam, and, farther round, Langdale Pikes, familiar
and homely, and, still further, Helvellyn and the Ullswater Fells. If you climb to the top of the rise above the
tarn you see Windermere and Esthwaite Water, and in the
distance the sea, and there is one exciting view, through a
conifer wood, of Coniston Water, end-on like a long curved
knife.

Yet not only are the trees due to the forest industry, but
so is the tarn itself, for it was formed by damming a stream
in a swamp to give water-power to the saw-mill in Yewdale
below. The overflow from the reservoir skidaddles down
Tom Ghyll[2] in a long string of Skeltonics that include at
least one waterfall poised like a champion diver.

Then there is the wool trade. All over the area, not only
in Westmorland, you will find small wool factories for spin-
ning or carding or weaving. Many of them have closed
down during the time of the last generation or so, but many
still remain. In the Cumberland Plain the main centre is
Wigton, where "John Peel" tweed is woven. Milk and
dairy factories have been set up at Aspatria and Milnthorpe,

[1] This is really the name of the farmhouse nearby. Strictly speaking, the
tarn has no name.
[2] Ruskin, showing a bad ear for the local language, renamed it Glen
Mary, and the phrase has unfortunately caught on.

and it has been proposed to open another at Egremont. All these—minerals, stone, wood, wool, milk—are industries which you might expect, but there are some surprising ones as well: Burton and Holme make carpets; Burneside and even the delectable Beetham make paper. At Backbarrow near Greenodd the landscape comes from an early picture of Picasso's—blue walls, trees dripping ink and the road a sheet of sapphire, for they make "ultramarine" there.

Many of the local industries are dying out as the tourist trade takes their place. The old factories are mostly converted into cottages, but many fall into ruin. The Lakes, indeed, are a country of ruins—not the romantic ruins of castles and abbeys, but small ageless ruins of factory, farm and cottage. The walls bulge and collapse; soil blows over the stones; nettles and ground-ivy take root; some half-wild garden flower—lungwort, large red dead-nettle, periwinkle or feverfew—haunting the hedge like a lost tom-cat, is the only sign that a cottage once stood there.

The Mining Villages

I shall deal later with the history of mining in the Lakes, but now let us consider those villages and towns which owed their existence primarily to mining and see how they have adapted themselves to the new tourist trade.

The two most important are Coniston and Keswick. The Coniston copper mines are very ancient. As late as the last century they employed about 900 men and boys, and the railway from Foxfield was built for them. The mines are closed, but the fell still gives work in its slate quarries. The main livelihood of the villagers, however, comes from the visitors, but Coniston has managed to absorb them without rolling down its shirtsleeves. There is one row of brick villas, and, rather hidden away, there is a putting green and the Ruskin Museum, but it remains still a stone village, plain and not fussy, turning its back on the lake. The fell gives not only wealth but light, for water-power was harnessed and the village had electricity long before the industrial towns on the coast. You can see the pipes which bring the water down the fellside—running near the beck in the larchwood behind *The Sun Inn*.

Keswick has much the same history as Coniston, except that the mines are not in the town but in the hamlets round about. Keswick and Coniston were closely connected, and, when the German miners were there, the copper ore from Coniston was smelted at Keswick. Later it was shipped down the lake, carted to Ulverston or Greenodd, and thence went by sea to Wales.

At one time Keswick was the centre of a small wool trade. Then came the most prosperous period of mining during the Elizabethan age, and later the manufacture of black-lead pencils from the Borrowdale graphite. Round the market-place there are still the courts where the workers lived, packed tight as the pencils, and there also the Moot Hall, a very attractive, slim building, painted green and white, with a tower and a little steeple like the lid of an ink-well.

But this older Keswick is being driven into the side streets. It is the shopkeepers and boarding-house keepers and hotel keepers who own the main roads now. Let us admit that they have not done all they might. The worst type of modern shop-front is absent, and the local council has made a meritorious attempt to control and restrict building. You will not find red-tiled roofs and ugly bungalows at Keswick. Indeed it suffers from too little vulgarity rather than from too much. There is a blur of damp good taste over the town, like a mist risen from the lake. There are art and craft shops, and local carvings, and water colours of scenes of the Lakes. Streets are named after the Lake poets, and there are stacks of their poems in the shops; you feel that every Keswick child who wins a school prize asks for a leather-bound copy of Wordsworth or Southey—more probably Southey, for he was a much better husband and had no illegitimate child in France, and if his poetry isn't so good, what does it matter, for nobody's going to read it.

Let me try to be fair to Keswick, however. Its situation is magnificent—no other town in the district can compare with it. The lake, the valley and the fells are laid before you so that you can see without any effort the sort of views which elsewhere you have to walk or climb for hours to find. The town is quiet and not without beauty. There is nothing strident or flamboyant there. Visitors are thought about and looked after and not made to feel strangers, and the town can even accommodate the large crowds who go to the summer convention for an evangelical week-end among the mountains. It is tasteful, cultured, almost, in its way, cosmopolitan, but I find it very hard to believe that it has anything to do with Cumberland.

The Wool Towns

The manufacture of woollen goods started in Kendal some 600 years ago. John Kempe, of Flanders, came over to England in 1331 to set up weaving by improved methods, but though Cornelius Nicholson[1] says he settled in Kendal, there is no real proof of this. Nevertheless other Flemish weavers may have come to the town, and certainly Kendal cloth is mentioned in enactments before the end of the fourteenth century. By Tudor times the town was supplying London with much of its cloth for everyday, knock-about wear—not fine or fancy stuffs, but good, hard-wearing woollen cloth, rather coarse, and known as Kendal "cottons."

The wool was spun by housewives and woven by their husbands on cottage looms—not till then did it go to the town, to the fulling mill and the dyer. It was particularly for its dyes that Kendal was famous. Its "spotted cottons"—white spotted with red, green or blue—were probably the dress of the English bowmen at Flodden Field; but better known still was the Kendal green that was worn by Falstaff's "three misbegotten knaves."[2] This colour was obtained by dyeing the cloth first with the yellow of dyer's greenweed (*Genista tinctoria*), which grew wild on the marshes, and then with a blue extracted from woad.

[1] *Annals of Kendal*, by Cornelius Nicholson (1861).
[2] *Falstaff*. But, as the devil would have it, three misbegotten knaves in Kendal green came at my back, and let drive at me;—for it was so dark, Hal, that thou couldst not see thy hand.
Prince Henry. These lies are like the father that begets them,—gross as a mountain, open, palpable. Why, thou clay-brained guts, thou nott-pated fool, thou whoreson, obscene, greasy tallow-keech,—
Falstaff. What, art thou mad? art thou mad? is not truth the truth?
Prince Henry. Why, how couldst thou know these men in Kendal green, when it was so dark thou couldst not see thy hand? come, tell us your reason: what sayest thou to this? (*Henry IV*, Part I, Act II, Sc. iv.)

The trade began to expand during the reign of Edward IV, encouraged by the Parr family of Kendal Castle, and reached its height under Henry VIII. By this time it had spread into the neighbouring towns and villages—up the Kent to Staveley, down the valley to the Milnthorpe district, over the low hills to Windermere, and along the Rothay and the Brathay. Miss M. L. Armitt estimated that there were at least eighteen walk-mills or fulling-mills in the parish of Grasmere in the fifteenth and early sixteenth centuries.[1]

By the time of Elizabeth the trade began to decline. Kendal cloth went out of fashion in London, and the plague, which came to the district at the end of the sixteenth century, carried off many of the workers, particularly the cottage weavers—tradition says it was very severe in Langdale. The merchants of Kendal itself were able to keep in business by diverting their goods to America to clothe the negro slaves; but the trade disappeared from the villages.

These villages fall into two groups—those built on slate[2] and those built on limestone. The slate villages include most of the best-known centres for visitors on the Westmorland side of the Lakes: Ambleside, Grasmere, Skelwith, Langdale and Hawkshead. When the trade declined these valleys were left derelict. The population was greater than the land could support,[3] and there are signs of desperate attempts to plough stony patches of fellside for the sake of a handful of oats.[4] Wool was still woven in the cottages and carried to Hawkshead market to be sold, but the towns adapted themselves as well as they could to the new conditions. Fulling-mills became tanneries or carding-mills; and bark-mills, saw-mills, bobbin-mills were set up in the old buildings.

[1] M. L. Armitt: *Fullers and Freeholders of the Parish of Grasmere—Transactions of the Cumberland and Westmorland Archæological Society*, Vol. VIII, New Series (1908).

[2] This includes the Borrowdale Volcanic Series as well as the Silurian rocks.

[3] "Here is cold comfort from nature, but somewhat of warmth from industry. That the land is barren, is God's pleasure; the people painful, their praise. That thereby they grow wealthy, shows God's goodness, and calls for their gratefulness." (Fuller: *Worthies of Westmoreland*.)

[4] See Miss Armitt, *opus cit.*

Most of these, too, have closed down and the buildings have disappeared or been so altered that they are no longer recognisable, but I believe that the sturdy manufacturing spirit has not gone from the villages. It accounts for the slight oddness of the buildings, an oddness which is not always obvious at first. Ambleside has its old mill and the house on a bridge, and it has also a solidness about it—buildings bigger than you would have expected, with angular gables, and alleys and archways. It has not nearly so fine a site as Keswick—there are none of the higher fells very near it, and it is some distance from the head of the lake, with a rather dull, alluvial flat in between. Nevertheless it lies in what is perhaps the busiest part of the district, full of day visitors from Lancashire, who come up the lake on the steamer; but it copes with them as Trafalgar Square copes with foreigners without being the less London. The hotels, cafés, art-shops and map-shops are there, of course; but you don't feel that they own the place. They seem rather to have rented their places like stall-holders in a market. Yet they are quite at home, and I, for one, am thankful to them, and have bought good books and eaten good meals there.

Ambleside is fortunate in that, though it is in the middle of the Wordsworthian country, it has no spectacular associations with the poet. Wordsworth, like Shakespeare and Burns, gives rise to frantic pilgrimages on the part of non-readers. They drive up to Grasmere in charabanc loads—many Americans among them—pay their duties to Dove Cottage and try to get a glimpse of Rydal Mount so that they can marvel how the man worked his way up in the world out of nothing but poetry. Surprisingly, the Wordsworth Museum, at Grasmere, opened some years before the war, holds a collection of really valuable manuscripts instead of old slippers and second-best milking-stools.

The other main centre of pilgrimage is Hawkshead, with the Grammar School that Wordsworth attended as a boy, and Anne Tyson's cottage where he lodged. Hawkshead, indeed, is the centre of the country which most influenced the boy—the land around Esthwaite Water, with Windermere on the one side and Coniston on the other, and with the Old Man, Wetherlam and the Langdales overlooking it. This is the country of the first two books of the *Prelude*.

Hawkshead presents a problem which is unusual in the Lakes, and we must face it frankly. It is, then, quaint, picturesque, old-world. It deserves all those adjectives which I've tried to keep out of this book, and, moreover, it deserves them in a quite deliberate sense. It is not just quaintly quaint; it is genuinely quaint. It has to be ranked with other villages which have been put under a glass case for the sake of their beauty, their historical associations, or more often for their oddity. As a result, there is that smell in the air which you find in a parlour, which is swept and polished and has fires once a week, but where the windows are never opened and the children never allowed to play.

Yet it is hard to see what else the town could have done, for Hawkshead's oddness is not the sort which could easily be adapted to present-day life. It had to preserve itself as it was or else change beyond all knowing. Its beauty—it has great beauty—is not of the practical kind. It is not clearly related to everyday life, nor even to art. It is the beauty of accident—of narrow lanes and whitewashed walls, of houses where you have to go *outside* to climb upstairs to bed, of Flag Street, Pillar House, the *Red Lion* yard, and the *Old King's Arms*. The town did not shape itself with any clear idea of what it was doing, but we admire now not ingenuity or architectural skill, but rather the angles and slopes of wall, roof and loft, and the shapes of shadows on the whitewash. Straight lines, here, are so diverse and unconventional that they take on the subtlety and homeliness of curves. In this rather abstract world Hawkshead exists and is justified; it has had to pay a great price. The town attracts me and I like to visit it, but I feel a twinge of conscience whenever I do.

The way from the slate to the limestone is by the Windermere ferry, Bowness, and Kendal. Windermere is a strange town in that it owes its existence almost entirely to the visitors. It is not really a native town at all, but it manages to achieve an unexpected dignity, with its slate boarding-houses and bay-windows. Here, as elsewhere on the way to Kendal, the nearness of the limestone has led the builders to use rough blocks of it for window-sills instead of sand-stone. So we have houses in two shades of grey, or rather, in gray and grey, for one vowel seems darker to me than the other.

Of Bowness it is better to say nowt. At least it gives me one pleasant memory, when I went in a garage and saw a hose-rack on the wall with a notice beside it painted in good-sized lettering:

THIS HOSE-RACK IS PURELY ORNAMENTAL.

Such humour is, I think, typical of the North. It reminds me of an advertisement which appeared fairly recently in *The Workington and Harrington Guardian:*

"The person who took a refuse bin from ——— may have the lid if he or she calls at this address."

The district of the lower Kent is not so full of old mills as the Windermere district. Here, you feel, the sheep were bred and the wool spun and woven before it was sent to Kendal. Today it is as gentle and quiet and rural an area as you will find in the two counties—though many of the villages have their own small factory of some kind.

Milnthorpe is the metropolis. It is a small market-town with good-mannered houses of white and yellowish stone, and terraces of low cottages. The village school stands in the middle of a square below the church. There is no schoolyard and the children run in the street at playtime, where a break-water of stone discourages the traffic. Coming round the corner in a bus one April morning I found the children playing in one half of the street and a travelling fair set up in the other. The driver tried to skirt round the fair and got himself jammed between the wagons and the wall, and had to spend ten minutes or more backing his way out.

Yet Milnthorpe is no moth-ball model. The twentieth century rattles through it along the main road to Levens Bridge, which is one of the chief motor routes of the north-west, and Milnthorpe accepts it as casually as a cigarette. It can even absorb the nineteenth century into the family circle: opposite *The Black Bull* you will see Kitchen's Memorial Reading Rooms, 1880, with dormer windows and painted gables all of limestone and khaki freestone, and with delightful drainpipes, twisted spirally like a stick of barley sugar. Inside you can sit by a round table and read the newspapers. A notice tells you that the use of the room is free to residents, but that visitors are requested to place one penny in the box provided. You drop in your penny as loudly as possible when you hear someone coming, and you hope that they'll be impressed with your honesty.

Burton-in-Kendal, on the other side of the lower valley, is of one street, beside one of the two main Carnforth-Kendal roads. Small as it is, it is nevertheless a highly organised village. It does not seem just to have grown, but to have been planned by an artist. Because of its proportions, the sense of scale and neighbourliness in its houses, you are scarcely aware of its smallness. Even the square with a market-cross is intimate and formal, a half-sized set which might easily be transported whole to a London stage for an opera. There is a box of a cobbler's shop at the corner, so small that it would all go—upstairs and downstairs, back and front—into a fair-sized room. The eyebrows of history hang over the village like the upper rooms of the old house held up by pillars on the pavement, and there is a slight taint of quaintness in backyards and cobble side-streets; but try to diddle any of the Burton people and you'll soon find whether they are living in the seventeenth century or the present day. Shiny Virginia creeper dawdles over the yel-lowish-grey walls.

There are other villages, too. Beetham is the Sweet Auburn of the plain, but the more ordinary villages are attractive too; Heversham is rather suburban, terraced above the upper stretches of the Kent estuary, where the white marsh mists are clotted on the white stone walls. In the heavy days of August, when the sun scarcely oozes through, the light sometimes catches the limestone scars on the Meathop side of the valley, otherwise invisible, and the stone shines white in the haze. Other villages, like Holme, are more serviceable, with shops, pubs, garages, a dance in the Institute on Saturday night, and sometimes a travelling cinema show for the old folk who can't get to Kendal or Lancaster in the bus. Most of them have oldish houses which are worth looking at, but their attraction does not lie in things like that. It lies rather in the feel and smell of the place. You can sit for hours on a wall at the back of a kitchen garden, with the whitewashed apple-trees standing in the long grass. You lean against the shed, tuck your heels under your skirt if you are a woman, and talk about quarries and Original Sin. Over the wall is a field, green as Ireland, with a cart or two and corrugated iron lying about, and an old Ford truck used as a fowl-house, rusted red as sorrel. The chickens stray across the field like stones wandering from the wall; at the side are the houses of the village, back-end-on, with the church tower above them; and farther away, the railway line and the low, juniper-blue hills—it is a landscape as satisfying as baked potatoes and as tasty as kippers.

Kirkby Lonsdale is the old market-town of the sheep-rearing fells. When you cross over the Hutton hills you pass into a new kind of country. This is no longer the dales, the craggy land of the little sagas; this is a broader, wider country, the "backbone," stretching across to Yorkshire and the North Sea. The town stands on the steep western slopes of the valley; over the Lune are limestone moors, and Ingleborough, like a great marquee with one end higher than the other. Much more than any other town in the two counties, it belongs to Tudor England—not black and white Tudor, but the Tudor of the Cotswolds. The stone, too, is very like the chamois-leather yellow of Cotswold stone. It is a gravely beautiful yet busy town. Along the main street there is scarcely a house or a shop which does not give pleasure in its shape and companionship. Many of the houses are of the eighteenth century or a little later, with the outlying streets sturdy and strong, whether they consist of tiny cottages, two rooms up and two down, or big, double-fronted houses of three storeys. In the centre of the town some of the buildings are more consciously elegant, like *The Royal Hotel* and the Vicarage, but many are still bluff and chubby, accommodating their shops as an oak-tree accommodates squirrels. There are brushes and buckets, grocery and children's clothes on sale. You can find post-cards and teashops if you want them, but the town is more concerned with the farmers and their wives who come in by cart and car and bus. They are a practical, cheerful, almost garrulous folk: no longer dalesmen but next-door to Yorkshiremen, men who look out upon broader fields. There is so little sign of frivolity in the streets that it is rather a shock to come upon the Market Cross in the square. It was set up in 1905, and is octagonal, with wooden seats set in every other arch, the whole shaped like a crown. No doubt when the Rev. J. Ll.-Davies, D.D., presented it to the town he did not intend it for a joke, but it is hard to see it as anything else. Nevertheless, the inhabitants are probably very fond of it, though when last I saw it one of them had played hoopla on the turrets with a bicycle tyre. I would have liked to decorate it with still ruder objects, and to resist the temptation I made off down Jingling Lane, where the walls have a lovely rind, rich as an orange. How different is the old cross in the Swine Market opposite Abbot's Hall—a drowsy pillar, set on steps, with a stone globe in place of its original cross-head.

Kendal

Such are the towns which once were apprenticed to Kendal. Now only the master-town retains its old trade, to which it has added others, in particular the production of boots and shoes. Kendal (once called Kirkby Kendal in distinction from Kirkby Lonsdale and Kirkby Stephen) is a surprising town to find in Westmorland. Those who have seen it only from the train passing through Oxenholme on the way to Scotland can have little idea of its character. To begin with it is so tight. Though there is all the Kent valley to spread in, it is piled closely on its group of hills, the streets almost overlapping like slates on a roof. When you leave the main street, you find a great cliff of houses rising above you, as if space were as precious as on New York island.

It does not reveal itself at once to the visitor. Its main street has a deceptive and artificial smile of shop-fronts and offices which, on the whole, might be found anywhere. The Town Hall, which must rank among the most comic public buildings of the north-west, disproves the axiom that the whole must equal the sum of the parts, since its decoration, which is in every possible style of architecture, adds up only to Gothic.

It is when you move off into the side-alleys or wynds[1] that you find the real Kendal. Here you walk in deep ghylls between flat walls of stone, the walls of warehouses or factories, or the sides of shops and hotels. Sometimes as you penetrate farther from the street and the light, you find a whole row of houses, opening on a cobbled pavement and a street only a few yards wide, with the doors broken down and boarded up as the houses are deserted or turned into store-rooms. The walls are bare and bony, without ornament or trimming, yet they are not uncouth. The windows, contracting in size as they ladder up the side of the walls, are straight and determined. Narrow and sunless as the courtyards are, they are never dirty. There are too many winds from the fells to let the smoke hang over Kendal, and the old limewash is still white, and the painted signs still legible. These are not the murky, foggy alleys of the East End of London: these are like rock-dwellings on the coast, where a thousand old women have set up house in the caves, instead of in shoes, and have scrubbed the steps, whitewashed the sills, and hung little muslin curtains across the crannies. Some of the alleys contain surprises: off Finkle Street there is a canyon with enormous dark walls, but from it you enter into the most bland and tasteful public conveniences I have seen anywhere—without joking, they are a fine example of interior design and decorating. Everyone who goes to Kendal ought to pay a visit.

As an industrial town Kendal is unusual in that it is the centre of a large *rural* area, and has next to no relationship with any other industrial town. Although it is not the capital of Westmorland, it is the administrative centre, and it has the bustle and buzz and combine-harvester hum which is typical of large country towns. It is the cultural centre too, claiming the oldest musical festival in the country, which is visited regularly by the Hallé Orchestra and which has

[1] "And the system of wynds is a Scottish or North-country contrivance. It is even to be seen in its beginnings in towns like Leeds or Sheffield, where, in their older parts, an infinity of courts and obscure passages lead off from the street." (*Edinburgh*, by Sacheverell Sitwell and Francis Bamford.) To Leeds, Sheffield and Kendal you might add Carlisle and Whitehaven.

Seatoller, Borrowdale

produced singers and instrumentalists known throughout England.

Kendal seems to have been fruitful ground for the early botanists. John Wilson, or "Black Jack," was a shoemaker there, and William Hudson was born at *The White Lion Inn*. George Romney, who we may presume to have been interested in natural forms, was apprenticed to a portrait painter in the town. Moreover, John Gough, "The Blind Philosopher," was also in his way a botanist. He was born in Kendal in 1757, and at the age of two lost his sight as the result of smallpox. In spite of this he set himself to study, and acquired a good knowledge of zoology, music, the classics, and more particularly of mathematics, of which he eventually became a teacher, counting many distinguished mathematicians among his pupils. Of all his accomplishments, however, the recognition of plants and flowers by touch seems to me the most astonishing.

"The plant to be examined was held by the root or base in one hand, while the fingers of the other travelled slowly upwards, over the stem, branches, and leaves, till they reached the flower. If the species had been already met with, this procedure was sufficient for its recognition; if it proved to be a novelty, its class was first determined by the insertion of the elongated tip of his tongue within the flower; thus he discovered the number and arrangement of the stamens and pistils. When the flower was small, he requested his reader to ascertain these points with a lens. The class and order being determined, the genus was next worked out, word by word of the description, so far at least as the state of the specimen would allow. But his perceptive power over form was most conspicuous in the analysis of species. It was truly wonderful to witness the rapidity with which his fingers ran among the leaves, taking cognisance of their divisions, shape, serratures, and of the presence or absence of hairs. The finest down was detected by a stem or leaf being drawn gently across the border of his lower lip: so fine, indeed, that a young eye often required a lens to verify the truth of the perception."[1]

[1] Cornelius Nicholson: *Annals of Kendal*. The character of John Gough is drawn by Wordsworth in *The Excursion*, Book VII, lines 482-515.

Hawkshead, Flag Street

The Market Towns

The towns we have mentioned have mostly been those of the dales. There remain the market towns scattered all over the two counties, among the hills and in the lowlands. Their main characteristics are not dissimilar from the dale towns. They are built of the local stone (whatever it may be); they are solid, practical and never pretty or archaic. On the whole they have more in common with the small manufacturing towns you find in the Yorkshire Pennines than with the Tudor and splash towns of the Midlands and the South.

There is Appleby, the capital of Westmorland; Brough, with its horse-fair; Kirkby Stephen; Ulverston; Whitehaven, which is now a coal-mining town; Cockermouth, a quiet town, looking as if it were made of plastics, with the fells on one side and the iron and coal country on the other; Wigton, a comfortable, red-tweed town; Brampton, on the Roman Wall; and Penrith.

Yet each of these, and of others I have not mentioned, has its own personality, and it would be tempting, if there were space, to compare and contrast them. To consider, for instance, two which lie on opposite sides of the district: Penrith and Ulverston. Penrith is the chief of the sandstone towns—red, solid and comfortable, and it opens from lower Patterdale to the farming country around the Eden. Ulverston, on the other hand, is grey and white, on the junction of the slate and limestone, and lies between the Morecambe Bay valleys and the mining district of Furness. Both owe much to the eighteenth century—Penrith its church, its many nonconformist chapels and meeting houses, and the square houses behind them; Ulverston its more elegant streets on the outskirts, for Ulverston was the fashionable resort of North Lonsdale in the eighteenth century, and the country gentry came to it for the theatre and dances. Moreover, each town is dominated by a small hill. At Penrith it is the Beacon. The houses are stepping up the side of it now, the dead are buried there among Van Gogh cypresses, but the Beacon still retains something of its old grimness, as when the boy Wordsworth saw the remains of the gibbet, where had hung in chains the body of Thomas Nicholson, executed at Carlisle for the murder of Thomas Parker, a butcher.[1] At Ulverston it is the Hoad, rather more detached than the Beacon but no more rugged. It looks across the salt marshes of the Bay, and very rightly carries a monument shaped like a lighthouse. From the top of the lighthouse you look up to the Windermere Fells, but outwards too, to the sea and the giant cranes of Barrow shipyard and even to Blackpool Tower. I remember that as a lad I climbed the steps to fulfil a holiday task, which, so far as I can remember, was to see which way the wind was blowing.

Before the Victorian era these towns must have been isolated and even rather primitive. Roads were very bad, and communications lay through wild and marshy country. They were far from the metropolis, from a university, and from any fashionable centre like Bath or Scarborough, yet they managed to produce a reasonable number of remarkable people. William and Dorothy Wordsworth were born at Cockermouth; Thomas Tickell nearby at Bridekirk, whence he went to Egremont, where his father was rector, and to school at St. Bees. John Dalton, the chemist, came from the same district, Eaglesfield near Cockermouth, and George Romney from Dalton-in-Furness. Apart from Romney, who is no great boast, the Lakes have been poor in painters, although they have attracted so many. "Warwick" Smith, the friend of Francis Towne,[2] was born in Cumberland and left many topographical drawings, and there have been crowds of sketches and water-colourists whose work hangs in every teashop in the district. But of our native artists, none, I think, catches the glint and glance of the air more truly than Beatrix Potter. Hartley Coleridge is our best poet since Wordsworth.

It should be said, too, that the district has been served by many excellent local newspapers, most of which still survive with all their old sturdiness and independence.

---

[1] *The Prelude* (Book XII). See *Wordsworthshire*, by Eric Robertson, for the reasons why this incident should be associated with Penrith Beacon.

[2] Towne himself made some very remarkable drawings of the district, and so, of course, did Turner. Constable left some early water-colours of Langdale and Borrowdale, and Ruskin's work should not be forgotten.

The Quakers

We ought not to leave the market towns without at least a reference to the Quakers who have played such a part in their development.

According to Burn and Nicolson they first appeared in the district at Kirkby Stephen, where the vicar, Francis Higginson, incited the magistrates against them in the time of Oliver Cromwell.[1] It is extremely unlikely that these revivalists of Kirkby Stephen were indeed Quakers, but the incident shows that the Westmorland fold were ready to listen to the unorthodox travelling preacher.

The first real evidence of the appearance of the Quakers in the district concerns George Fox's visit to Sedbergh in 1652. From Sedbergh he passed on to Firbank and preached a famous sermon on the rock outside the chapel, where he gained many followers, including Francis Howgill. From Westmorland he drew many of his first missionaries— George Whitehead, Edward Burrough, John Audland and others.

The next year he came into Cumberland. He went first to Bootle on the coast, where he was set on by a gang of toughs, and after staying a day or so in Millom, he went to Brigham near Cockermouth; from Cockermouth through

---

[1] "Mr. Higginson produceth instances of these people running about the streets, foaming and bellowing out such like expressions as these: 'Repent, repent! Wo, wo! The Judge of the world is come!' Some of them stood naked upon the market cross, on the market days, preaching from thence to the people. Particularly, he mentions the wife of one Edmund Adlington, of Kendal, who went naked through the streets there; and two others of the Society, a man and a woman, who called themselves Adam and Eve, went publicly naked, and when concerning the same at the assizes, the man affirmed that the power of God was upon him, and he was commanded so to do.

"Many of them in their assemblies, sometimes men, but more frequently women and children, or they who had long fasted, would fall down suddenly, as in an epileptic fit, and there lie grovelling upon the ground, struggling as it were for life, and sometimes more quietly as if they were just expiring. Whilst the agony of the fit was upon them, they would foam at the mouth, their lips would quiver, their flesh and joints would tremble, and their bellies swell like a bladder. In such fit they continued sometimes an hour or two; and when it left them they roared out with a voice loud and horrible.

"All which easily accounts for the name of Quakers being given to them."

(Burn and Nicolson: *History of Westmorland.*)

Caldbeck to Carlisle, where he was imprisoned "in the dungeon amongst the mosstroopers, thieves and murderers."[1]

When Fox was released he went to Caldbeck again, and from thence visited Wigton, which was to be a strong centre of the Quaker community. Fox also had many followers in North Lancashire, and in particular was sheltered at Swarthmoor Hall, near Ulverston, by Judge Fell, whose widow he married later. Near Swarthmoor, just off the road between Ulverston and Urswick, is a seventeenth-century Quaker meeting-house of particularly attractive appearance, with its own small burial ground. Earlier Quaker burial grounds are to be found elsewhere in the district.

Of the many other distinguished Quakers[2] I need not speak, but there was one, George Moore, whom I should not forget, for scholarships and exhibitions have been set up in his memory, and I in my time won one of each. I sat the examination for the exhibition in a little school in the grounds of Carlisle Cathedral. The choirboys were practising in the next room, the bellringers were practising in the tower, the trains were rattling out of the station on the way to Scotland: I tried to write my essay on The Roman Wall and thought enviably of the Quaker habit of silence.

Carlisle

And so it is the Quakers who have led us to Carlisle. We were bound to get there in the end, for the city dominates the north-west of England just as its castle once dominated the way to Scotland. All Cumberland owes allegiance to Carlisle, yet it is not really Cumbrian. I have lived all my life in Cumberland, but when I go to Carlisle I feel as if I were in a foreign country, for it belongs neither to England

[1] Fox's *Journal*. He goes on: "A filthy, nasty place it was, where men and women were put together in very uncivil manner, and never a house of office to it; and the prisoners so lousy that one woman was almost eaten to death by lice. Yet, bad as the place was, the prisoners were all made very loving and subject to me; and some of them were convinced of the truth, as the publicans and harlots were of old."

[2] See *Early Cumberland and Westmorland Friends*, by Richard Ferguson, 1871.

nor to Scotland, but to the Border. It is the capital of a strange Debatable Land, unmapped, undefined, which stretches along the Solway Marshes and the lower Eden, around the Roman Wall, up Liddlesdale and Annandale, and especially around Carlisle railway station. The platforms there are always in a state of insecure Border truce.

When you come out of the station you are aware of Border Gothic everywhere—massive in red sandstone. But all this belongs to the nineteenth century—there are scarcely any medieval buildings in Carlisle except the cathedral, the castle, the citadel and what remains of the walls. You go towards the railway viaduct to the old part of the city, and enter it between two hotels. This is West Walls. Behind you is the cathedral close, the eighteenth-century houses and the cathedral itself. In front the walls drop steeply down a sort of rampart. There are trees in autumn dribbling red leaves on the red stone. The walls are moist and warm, and below, like a moat or the surge and sweep of a river, is the railway, with a great flow and ebb of life towards Scotland and back. Beyond the railway is the new town, the roofs soaking up the evening sun like pink blotting paper. There are spires and towers breaking the roof-line, and everywhere among the slates and tiles little bursts of dark green or yellow or brown as the trees thrust up from gardens. Farther, heaved against the south, are the Skiddaw fells. It is all such as you might expect from a Midland city, or, say, the Welsh Border, and then, as your eyes get used to the glow of the sun, you notice that the spires and towers are not those of churches or clocks, they are chimney-stacks and the turrets above factories, for Carlisle is now an industrial town, and a busy one.

It is hard to find the peace which you expect in a cathedral city. Yet I do think you can find it, on a Sunday afternoon, in the nineteenth-century residential streets that branch off Warwick Road, not far from the centre of the city. The houses are of red and cream bricks, with cream chimney pots and sandstone sills. The footwalks are paved with slabs of sandstone, worn into hollows, smooth or rather rough-smooth like pumice-stone. There are trees at the edge of the pavement, all cut back tight to bunches of branches at the top of the trunk. The dead leaves go bouncing and scratching along the road in autumn and the sun is bright on one side of the street, and people come from the Methodist chapels, from Harvest Thanskgiving or a Pleasant Sunday Afternoon. I have sat on the steps to listen to the organ through the doors, and no one troubled me, but a dog came out of a front door to make friends with the stranger.

I walked along a side street, marvelling that this could be in Cumberland, and came across the still more surprising Portland Square, with its heavy, ornate Victorian houses. Yet here works the staff which appointed the men who taught me to read and write; and here, too, is the County Library, from which I borrow the books I need to write this one. All the threads of the county are gathered together at Carlisle and knotted. Sometimes they seem to be in a tangle.

Chapter IX

THE HERITAGE OF THE DALESMAN

THE chief heritage of the dalesman is the dales—the country, the villages, and the dale way of life. But let us look for a moment at certain practices, customs, habits, which he has inherited from his ancestors. I do not mean the folk dances and ceremonies which are preserved with desperate enthusiasm in the way that ornithologists protect a bird that is nearly extinct. Such survivals, like the Grasmere Rush-bearing service, are interesting and charming, but I am thinking rather of the trades and sports which are still a vital part of the life of the people, and no more need to be preserved than love-making.

It is tempting to look for survivals of the Northmen in the dale customs. If there are any such they are not to be found among the industries, except that of Herdwick sheep farming. Apart from farming, the traditional industry of the dales is mining, and there are only a few local crafts, such as basket-making, especially the making of swills. The swill is large and oval, shaped like a coracle, and made entirely by hand. There is an upper rim formed of the branch of a tree, about a thumb's thickness, and usually with the bark left on. The body of the basket is made of strips of wood, two inches wide at the centre, plaited in a pattern of elliptical curves. The whole is not nearly so heavy as might be expected, and gaps are left as handles at either end of the rim. It is, however, very strong. If you threw it out of a second-floor window the road would more likely be damaged than the swill. You can lift heavy weights in it—potatoes, logs, coal—and the farmers use it to carry turnips to the sheep in winter. Their wives use it for washing, and there can be no more serviceable clothes-basket than a swill, for whichever way you put it down it swings on its round bottom and rights itself like a loaded chessman. It stands up to wet and wear and has the beauty of simple shape which you find in toadstools and stones. Its sheer practical value is so obvious that there is no sign of its giving way to mass-produced baskets imported from outside the district. Some of the swill-makers work single-handed, others are the heads of small firms. They are to be found at Broughton-in-Furness, Woodland, Milnthorpe, Ravenglass and elsewhere.[1]

Fox-Hunting

It is to the sports, then, that we must look for the legacy of the Northmen, and perhaps we can find it in hunting and in the dale meetings.

Fox-hunting is particularly associated with Cumberland on account of John Peel, and it is true that most dalesmen love the hunt better than marriage. I cannot pretend to speak about it with enthusiasm, for I do not like to think of dogs biting foxes. If only we could believe of the fox, as Docetism held of our Lord—that He did not *really* live and suffer on the earth but only appeared to do so for the edification of the faithful—then it would be possible to see the hunt as one of the most exhilarating sports in the world, played on a superb ground. But that is not so, and when the hounds fly across an open fellside, or run up and down outside a larchwood with a flurry of terriers behind them, I cannot forget a wretched animal half-dead of burst lungs and heart before the teeth get at him.

Nevertheless, hunting in Cumberland is not just a fashionable display of cruelty. The job of killing foxes is a necessary one, and its followers have to take it in the rough. It is now generally known that red-coated huntsmen riding to hounds have no part in the dale hunts.[2] All the hunting has to be done on foot, and as the fell foxes mostly lie well above the arable line, and nearly always make for the tops when pursued, the followers must be prepared to climb the highest fells and cover the roughest country in the course of their run. They must be ready to face wind and rain and bitter cold, to cross slopes shin-deep in bog or snow, to go for hours through mist, guessing where the hounds are only

[1] Those who saw Mr. Martin Browne's production of my play *The Old Man of the Mountains* at the *Mercury Theatre*, London, September 1945, may remember that the widow (Miss Henzie Raeburn) carried on the washing in a swill at the beginning of the first act. The swill was made by Mr. Airey of Milnthorpe.

[2] I do not speak of the lowland hunts, of which there are several.

from their voices. The country includes such dangerous drops as the screes in Wasdale, Pavey Ark in Langdale, Dow Crags on Coniston Old Man, and other places where both fox and hounds have been known to fall to death.

The fox, wherever it can, makes for an earth or borran. Some of these are terrifying spots: chimneys or caves, plugged with chock-stones and rubble; or places where crumblings of rock have weathered away from the cliffs and fallen, making a heap riddled with holes and tunnels; or the working of old mines and quarries, where the roof and sides are still insecure and may collapse. This is where the terriers are used. Their job is to make the fox bolt, but often in the dark cracks of the crag it is a fight to death. Now and again neither fox nor dog reappears, and no amount of searching with crowbar or even with dynamite can find the one nor save the other.

At other times the fox takes shelter on a benk, a narrow ledge, or a cliff-face, where the hounds cannot reach it without falling. Sometimes it cannot get back again from its refuge, and must stay there till it starves or falls. I have heard of a man lowered on a rope to shift a fox from such a perch. He succeeded—so well indeed that the rest of the hunt went excitedly after the fox and left the man dangling in mid-air.[1]

The best way to watch a hunt is to get well up in the fells before it begins. The fox is almost certain to make uphill, so that with any luck you can view the first part of the hunt without more than running along the level and scrambling over a few walls. From a well-chosen point it may be possible to watch the hounds nearly all day, but if the fox gets well away you have to be ready to cross country, and even then you should not lose more height than you can help. It is usually easier to skirt round the head of a valley than to descend one side and climb the other. The hounds often leave the majority of the followers miles behind. A run is recorded in which the fox started on Skiddaw in the afternoon, passed through Portinscale, up Borrowdale and over the mountains to Westmorland, and then got away in the

[1] See Richard Clapham: *Foxhunting on the Lakeland Fells.* (Longmans, 1920.)

darkness towards Broughton in Lancashire. The hounds, who also had got away from the huntsmen, were found the next morning asleep on Coniston Crag.[1]

Where the change from fell to lowland is sharp and bluff, as often along the coast, and there are roads and lanes skirting the base of the upland, it is possible to view a hunt quite well from below. I have even followed one by car. It was at the *John Bull Inn* at the foot of Black Combe. The hounds were working at a height of between 500 and 1,000 feet, and kept climbing the paws of the hill and disappearing into the next gulley or combe. Five or six car-loads of us managed to keep them in sight for a long time by speeding along Whicham Valley, and on the Silecroft-Whitbeck-Bootle road as far as Stangrah. There are five fell-packs—the Ullswater (hunting Patterdale and Mardale), the Blencathra (Skiddaw and Borrowdale), the Melbrake (Cockermouth, Buttermere, Loweswater), the Eskdale and Ennerdale (the western dales), and the Coniston (Old Man, Langdale, Windermere). Of these, the Eskdale and Ennerdale probably hunts the wildest and roughest country, as its district includes the Pillar and Scafell groups. If the fox takes to the lowlands from here, it faces country of adventurous variety—the mosses and sands of the Duddon and the Esk, the dunes of the coast, or the iron-ore mines of Hodbarrow or the Cleator Moor-Egremont district, where the going is every bit as rough as on the fells.

Through *D'ye ken John Peel* Cumberland is thought of by many people as the typical hunting country, and a film has been made showing Peel as the master of a fashionable hunt. In fact he was a Cumbrian statesman living at Caldbeck, where he hunted the western part of the fells with his own small pack of hounds. This was good rough work, out every morning at 5 or 6 o'clock on foot, no horses, no red coats.[2] He died in 1854, but it was not until after his death that the song became popular and made him famous. Woodcock

---

[1] *Victoria County History.* Article on Foxhunting.

[2] It is scarcely necessary to say once again that the original version of the "coat so gay" was a "coat so gray." If it is objected that grayness is not the sort of quality one qualifies by degrees, I would reply that it is exactly the sort of thing which is done regularly by unpractised versifiers.

Graves, who wrote the words of the song, liked Cumberland so little that he was glad to get away from it, and emigrated to Tasmania in 1833. Followers of the Eskdale and Ennerdale swear that John Peel wasn't to be compared with Tommy Dobson, the Eskdale huntsman.

Hound-Trailing

Fox-hunting is certainly a democratic sport in the dales, but the sport which has developed from it, hound-trailing, has a still wider appeal. Hound-trailing is a remarkable example of the way the heritage of the dales has passed in many cases into the hands of the miners, changing somewhat in the process, but keeping its true character. Trails first became popular at the dale sports and agricultural meetings, and every flower or stock show still has one. Then trails began to be held in the small towns on the borders of the district, and now it is a highly organised sport under the council of the Hound-Trailing Association founded in 1906. During summer and autumn there are trails nearly every day in one part of the district or another, and the more popular dogs may go out two or three times a week. Form is followed very closely, with trailing-notes each week in the local papers, and the leading hounds are listed in a championship table according to the number of wins and places. It ranges into Yorkshire and as far south as Kendal and Lancashire, but the chief centres of the sport are the industrial areas of West Cumberland and Furness. Here the miners turn out by the hundred to the track, travelling from town to town by train and bus. In the 1944 season £425 was raised for charities from four meetings at Barrow. The leading hounds are no doubt valuable animals, but it is not beyond the means of a working man to buy a pup and rear it, and the dog, if it is successful, becomes the pet and mascot of the local supporters. In this way, the followers of trailing feel that it is a sport which is near to them—not remote like horse-racing or Association football. Greed and the itch for gambling have no doubt much to do with its popularity, and there are heartbreaking tales from the past of miners who starved their children to feed their dogs on cream and eggs. But it is probable, too, that the trailing appeals also to a hidden, scarcely understood desire for freedom and even beauty. The delicious names alone suggest this—Starlight, Lonning Lass, Lawless, Randale, Dowcrag, Briery, Fibre Mills.

Certainly a trail is often charming to watch—the hounds slipped in a field on the outskirts of the town, perhaps a grubby little patch of grass among the cinders and allotments, to make their way across the farmland to the rock or moorland, bracken or heather, which is almost always near. Up they go along the tops, perhaps out of sight, and back again in thirty-five minutes or so. They have a curious leisurely style of running most of the time, taking wall and dyke in an easy-going way, casting about a friendly eye as they run. The track is laid by two men with aniseed in old stockings. They start together from a point half-way round the course, and each goes by a different route to the starting-point. Many tricks were no doubt played in the past. False tracks were laid; hounds were lured off the course and fed or drugged; others were seized, carried off by car, and put on the trail at another point well ahead of the others. There are even stories of judges who moved the flags which marked the winning posts, so that the leading dog, following the trail, was disqualified, and another dog, running wide, won. But now there is much closer supervision and the tracks are watched and guarded.

Nevertheless, the hound, running a trail, does seem to lead an independent life. It has no jockey, no man wagging a flag before it or driving an electric hare. It goes off on its own, has a look round the country, and comes back again, and the winning hounds seem to have a real idea of what they are doing. Sometimes, of course, they don't come back. The puppy Wistful disappeared from a trail at Lindal, in 1944. For some days there was no sign of it and then it was seen several times at Ulverston near the Hoad Hill, but it was a week or more before it was caught, no worse for its wanderings, having lived apparently on scraps picked up here and there. Occasionally there are accidents. Very occasionally a hound takes to sheep worrying.

For many, however, the main interest in the trails is not the dogs but the men. Here bookie, miner, shipyard- and steel-worker, shopkeeper and clerk mix with farmer, farm-labourer and squire. The unnatural antagonism between town and country, industry and agriculture is forgotten, and both acknowledge what they owe to the same tradition.

The Dale Sports

The hound trails are now one of the chief attractions of the dale sports. These may vary from the fashionable meetings at places like Grasmere, to village celebrations where a fruit and vegetable show joins with a baby show, where the ice-cream man cycles out from the nearest town, and where the brass band parades from the Institute to the Mission Room and back to the sports field. Heard from the tops, a brass band smells of hay and lemonade, and swells and fades with the wind like a cheap wireless on the medium wave. Looking down you see the crowd like wood-lice round the ring, and the marquee with its red pennons and the cars lined up on each side of the road. The sky is blue as smoke and the bracken thigh-deep. Here again the town-folk go to the show and have a few bob on the trail and perhaps a drink at the pub. The town lads, in particular, are able to find a way into the field behind the gate-keeper's back, and like to help to drive the animals from any spot to any other. When I was a boy the local schools were given a holiday for Green Show, held three miles away. Some of the mining towns have their own sports, like Egremont Crab Fair, with dancing in the streets and a gurning competition.

Gurning consists of putting your head through a horse-collar and pulling the ugliest face possible. It has been my privilege to know for a good many years one of the champion gurners of West Cumberland, of whom it is rumoured that the first time he won the prize he did not really enter but was merely following the efforts of the other competitors with interest and sympathy. Having once been made aware of his latent talent, he has made good use of it.

At these small sports meetings there is often horse-jumping and musical chairs, but at the larger gatherings the only performers are men. Grasmere is the greatest of them all, in the cup-like valley from which there seems no outlet, with the dark summer leaves on the lower hills and the crags all round. It is held on the Thursday nearest the 20th of August

—one of the wettest times of year in the Lakes. Sometimes the valley is swimming with water for days before, and then, on the morning of the sports, the sky clears and the sun clamps down on the meadows like a red-hot plate. Or perhaps there is that warm, pewter-like weather, when the clouds are low, and fells flat as prints, and there are scarcely any shadows. Then, suddenly, a wet wind spirals out of the lake, the rain comes down steady as a steel grill, and the gentry shelter in the stands and tents, or in their own cars. They do not mind terribly, for they have luncheon baskets and cups of tea, and they came to meet each other as much as anything, though some of them, like the late Lord Lonsdale, certainly have their hearts in the sports.

But the dale folk are not to be consoled with sandwiches and umbrellas. They sit with their coat collars turned up, and huddle beneath shelter, watching the clouds. The sports are a banked-up, slow-burning passion with them, like cricket to the man who sits in a pavilion waiting for the rain to stop to let the *A* team play. I know one old man who as a boy and youth in the 1870's lived just below Boot in Eskdale. He worked on the Irton estates, and at the time of which he told me he was hauling timber Wasdale way. After his day's work he would meet his friends at the *Woolpack Inn*, which is a mile or so above the village. It was the evening before Grasmere Sports, and half a dozen of them decided to go. They each went home to tell his family, get some supper and pack a few slices of bread, and then met again at the *Woolpack*. They set off on foot over Hardknott to Cockley Beck and over Wrynose into Little Langdale. It was midnight before they got to the inn in the lower dale, but one of them knew the landlord and they knocked him up and spent the night on the kitchen floor. After an early breakfast, they went by Elterwater and Red Bank to Grasmere, saw the sports, came back the same twelve or fourteen miles overnight, and were at work the next morning. My friend remembered every yard of the journey and every fall that he had seen at the wrestling. Yet, in spite of his love for the dales, the need for work and money had gradually taken him away from them. First of all he got a job on the railway, helping to build the line which runs from

Ravenglass to the quarries on Muncaster Fell. He would tell how the men made use of the gangers' wagon to have a night out at Ravenglass—free-wheeling downhill, and pumping themselves slowly back again. Then he became a miner, first at the Eskdale mines, then at the little mines at Kirksanton below Black Combe, and finally at the large and wealthy Hodbarrow mines. He was very old when I knew him, and would walk slowly along the asphalted embankment at the side of the Duddon Estuary, with the mountains, beneath which he was born, standing on the skyline.

There is much jumping at the sports—long-jump, high-jump and pole-jump—but, after the wrestling the chief interest is the Guides Race. The route is always out of the field to the steepest fellside nearby, up for 1,500 feet or so, and down again. Grasmere and Coniston are both well placed for such a race, especially Coniston, with the Yewdale Crags just above the village—a beautiful, scrubby face of rock, screes, patches of grass, rowans, birches and juniper, beside which the obstacles of *Noah's Ark* at Blackpool Pleasure Beach are just baby play. The competitors walk, run, climb, scramble up as well as they can, but once they are at the top, the race changes. They come down in a great chain of leaps, jumping from crag to crag, crashing through the bushes, skating down the screes. A man who reaches the turn with a lead of 20 yards is likely to be nearly 100 yards ahead a minute later. The strain on the heart is immense, and a man must be in the best of condition, be used to hours on the fells, and must know without thinking exactly where to put his feet.

Wrestling

Then comes the wrestling.

I would like to think that here is a direct relic of the games and tourneys of the old Norsemen, but the early history of the sport is too confused to be sure.

Wrestling, in the Cumberland and Westmorland style, is the most good-natured of all forms of physical combat. It needs a calm concentration and watchfulness which has no place in it for malice or anger. If you lose your temper you will lose the fall. Often you see men smiling quietly to them-

198

Burton-in-Kendal
Beetham Bridge and River
Bela

selves as they waltz round each other, waiting for a chance to attack, and when they fall they get up with the look of surprise that you see on the face of a very young child, who knows that it cannot walk without falling, yet is never quite ready for the fall when it comes.

The men stand face to face, breast to breast, locked closer than lovers, each clasping hands behind the other's back, one arm above the shoulder and one below. If a man breaks hold, except when throwing his opponent, he loses the fall. The round ends when a man is on the ground—there is no need for both shoulders to be down as in some forms of wrestling. Usually, of course, both men fall together, and the loser is the one who is below. Sometimes, a skilful and agile wrestler can twist in the arms of an opponent even while he is being thrown and so end the fall uppermost. Physical strength alone is not so important as may be thought. A man who is much the stronger of the two can always win by forcing in his opponent's back, but granted that there is reasonable equality of weight and stature, the fall will go to the more skilful or more enterprising wrestler.

Of the methods of attack—hipeing, inside striking, in and out, the chip, haming, hankering the heel, haunching, cross-buttocking, grandy stepping and the like—I shall not speak here. They would mean little to those who have never wrestled, not even as lads at school, and, indeed, it is probable that the majority of modern spectators at the big meetings know nothing of the technique by which their favourite wins. Dale wrestling is a sport for the wrestler, not the spectator. It is a standard joke that if you want to see the wrestling at Grasmere you have to enter. This is because of the size of the crowds, of course, but it is true in another sense, for the spectator sees only two men staggering round each other like a couple of drunken policemen trying to dance. The real contest that is going on is lost to him. It is not to be *seen* at all. To appreciate wrestling the mind must move in imagery which is almost entirely tactile. The wrestler must fix his hold, keep his balance, try to judge the mind of his opponent entirely by touch. Muscles and joints must learn to think in their own dimensions.

It is a sport, then, for individualists; for men who want to

Kendal—a yard
Penrith

be in it, for men who like a lyle furtle. It is admirable for farmers' sons and shepherds, who form village teams and enter for the village championships. (Wrestling meetings are arranged like knock-outs—the winner working his way through one round after another to the final. A wrestler must win many matches to gain a belt—but if he loses one, he is out.)

We hear of wrestling being condemned in the counties as early as the seventeenth century,[1] but the first organised meetings seem to have been at the villages of Langwathby and Melmerby in East Cumberland. Melmerby Rounds on Midsummer Day and Langwathby Rounds on New Year's Day (when the ground must have been hard for the loser to fall on) were well established by the second half of the eighteenth century. Another meeting was held in July at the top of High Street, in the Ullswater fells, where, presumably, the wrestlers would need to wait for their second wind before beginning their contests. In the early nineteenth century, Professor Wilson ("Christopher North") helped to establish the sport at Ambleside, which began to rank with the Penrith and Alston districts. Keswick then rose in importance as a centre for wrestling, and finally the great "metropolitan" competitions were organised at Carlisle, the winner of which might reasonably call himself world champion wrestler, Cumberland and Westmorland style.

We now come to a magnificent list of names which have in them the very bone and breed of the dales: William Richardson of Caldbeck, Thos. Nicholson of Threlkeld, Miles and James Dixon, Harry Graham of Brigham, Robert Rowantree, William Dickinson, Tom Todd, the Rev. Abraham Brown, and half-forgotten names like those given by Litt: "his last four opponents being A. Armstrong, J.

---

[1] "All scandalous persons hereafter mentioned are to be suspended from the sacrament of the Lord's Supper, this is to say—any person that shall upon the Lord's Day use any dancing, playing at dice, or cards, or any other game, masking, wakes, shooting, playing, playing at football, stool ball, wrestling. . . . These Counties of Cumberland and Westmorland have been hitherto as a Proverb and a by-word in respect of ignorance and prophaneness: Men were ready to say to them as the Jews of Nazareth, Can any good thing come out of them?"—*The Agreement of the Associated Ministers and Churches of the Counties of Cumberland and Westmorland* (1656).

Frears, T. Richardson, and T. Lock, all of them good wrestlers."[1]

And, of course, William Litt himself. Litt was born at Bowthorn near Whitehaven in 1785. "His parents held a highly respectable position in society, and he received a liberal education, with the object of fitting him for a clergyman in the Church of England."[2] Study did not greatly appeal to young William, however, and he took to farming for a while, but his heart was really in wrestling. Soon he became one of the most famous wrestlers in West Cumberland, fighting his way through the ring, year after year, between 1805 and 1815. In 1811 he met Harry Graham on Arlecdon Moor, below the Ennerdale fells, for a purse of sixty guineas—the largest sum wrestled for up to that date. Litt was in poor health at the time and wanted to postpone the match, but Graham's supporters insisted that it should be carried out, and Litt, after losing the first three falls, won seven out of the next eight. During these years in which he was winning great honour as a wrestler, farming and business were neglected. He tried to recover his fortunes as a brewer, and when this failed he went to live at Hensingham, and finally emigrated to Canada, where he died in 1847, broken down in body and mind.

Fine wrestler though he was, we remember him more for the fame he gave to others. When he started to write the history of the beginnings of wrestling in Cumberland and Westmorland, some people seem to have doubted whether he had the literary ability to tackle his subject. He himself had no doubt. He argues with such a critic in his preface:

" 'Does not the subject require a *practical* man?' 'Yes.' 'Thinkest thou there is one man in the kingdom who has won as many prizes as I have and can write better?' "

His confidence was justified, for *Wrestliana* is one of the classics of English sport—to go beside John Nyren on cricket. Moreover, it is one of the best books which has come out of Cumberland. It has the true Cumbrian tang in

---

[1] William Litt: *Wrestliana*. (Gibson, Whitehaven, 1823.)
[2] Jacob Robinson and Sidney Gilpin: *Wrestling and Wrestlers*, to which is added Notes on Bull and Badger Baiting (1893).

it; and the prose, in spite of some stiffness of phrase, has the physical, tactile strength of a wrestler.

Litt claims an honourable descent for wrestling, pointing to *Genesis* for the first recorded match—that between Jacob and the Angel. He argues that there is no sport which more deserves encouragement from educationalists and moralists, and is anxious to assure the reader of its propriety: "In preparing themselves for the contest, our modern wrestlers never encroach upon decorum so much, but that any lady may witness it without feeling her delicacy in the least danger of being wounded by it." In fact, it is not so much her delicacy which is in danger of being wounded as her sense of the ridiculous. The traditional dress is that of white singlet, long white underpants, and a dark pair of drawers. Wrestlers in the minor contests usually wear socks and *suspenders* outside the underpants, so that, when they pose with belt or cup, they look like characters from an early comedy film; but the champions of the last century used to dress themselves like gladiators, wearing vests and drawers embroidered in silk. Most men wrestle in stockinged feet, though Litt is supposed to have worn top-boots.

The history and philosophy are only the preliminaries of Litt's book. The real substance is in his biographies of the wrestlers and his descriptions of the matches he has seen.

Here he is writing to a fellow West Cumbrian:

"Taking leave for the present of the eastern side of Derwent, we must go westward as far as Gosforth before we find another wrestler of such celebrity as to entitle him to notice in these Memoirs. In that place we find one of the most distinguished characters at that period between Derwent and Duddon, in the person of John Woodall, who was brought up as a husbandman, and succeeded his father as proprietor of a small estate in Gosforth. Woodall though not the tallest, was, we believe, the strongest man we have yet noticed. His person was symmetry itself; he stood about five feet eleven inches high, weighed upwards of sixteen stones, and all who knew him agree in considering that he was the strongest man in the west of Cumberland. As a Wrestler, Woodall was more indebted to strength than science; but he possessed the former requisite to such an uncommon degree, that he was considered no unequal opponent for the powerful and scientific curate of Egremont (Parson Brown). At the *King's Arms*, in that place, Woodall exhibited a remarkable and rather extraordinary specimen of his prodigious strength. Having been thrown for a prize by a shoemaker of the name of Carr, a well-known Wrestler, the latter, flushed with his victory, began to ridicule Woodall on the circumstance; Woodall, though a very peaceable man, yet wishing to turn the laugh against Carr, caught him up in his arms as if he had been an infant, and hung him by his breeches waistband upon one of the hooks in the ceiling."

And here he is describing, with obvious relish, how Philip Stephenson, the trained and fancied champion of the regiment of Westmorland militia, then stationed at Whitehaven, was beaten by William Ponsonby, a butcher, "at Saint Bees Moor during the annual races":

"Stephenson's officers were somewhat noisy respecting his great capabilities, when a friendly wager was offered them to produce a man on the ground to wrestle him a single fall. The offer was immediately accepted, and Philip eager to be at work soon appeared in the ring fully prepared for action, and anxiously expecting his opponent. After waiting some time, Ponsonby, the man selected for the trial, entered to him, rather the worse, or probably the better, for the 'water of life' which had been plentifully administered to him, but no solicitations could prevail upon him to strip. Fully satisfied that if he won the fall it must be without loss of time, he chose to decide the business with his clothes on. The quickness and impetuosity of Ponsonby's attack carried all before it. Notwithstanding the boasted guard of the soldier, his neck and shoulders instantly exchanged situations with his feet. Philip was up in a moment and anxious for another trial, but Ponsonby was not to be had, his friends had carried him off in triumph, and Philip was obliged to wait for another opportunity of balancing accounts with him."

After Litt's time wrestling grew in popularity, until in 1851 a championship match was held at Flan How, Ulverston, for a purse of £300. Ten thousand people saw the match, in which Robert Atkinson beat William Jackson by the best out of five falls.

In the second half of the last century the wrestling at Grasmere grew in importance, dominated by the figure of George Steadman, who held the world championship for over thirty years. His last appearance at Grasmere was in 1900, and he died four years later at Brough. Older people still remember him: for the rest of us he lives in the records and in photographs—a massive man, weighing over eighteen stone at the age of 46, yet muscular and agile. He had a way of standing before the crowds, head and shoulders well back, paunch forward, and his half-smile, his great forehead and his white side-whiskers gave him a look of pride, almost of condescension. I have in front of me as I write a photograph[1] of Hexham Clarke and Steadman in the ring at Grasmere. They are not wrestling, but have taken their stance ready for the word to go. Steadman has rather a remote look in his eyes, and his whiskers are as benevolent as an archdeacon's, but his mouth is set and the power of the man is shown in the waves of muscles along his forearm and in the link-like lock of fingers in fingers. Clarke has the half-moon moustache and the straight gaze of a Victorian cricketer. He was not so big a man as Steadman, but he was another bonny wrestler. Steadman's son was also a well-known wrestler and once broke the collar-bone of an uncle of mine—not, however, at wrestling, but at Rugby.

Since those days interest has declined: partly because, as I have said, wrestling is not really a sport for the spectator; partly because it does not lend itself to regular and systematic betting—you can't expect wrestlers to turn out three times a week like hounds. Today, though the big meetings still draw crowds, champions are no longer household names in the Cumbrian towns. I do not know that this is generally to be regretted—wrestling is a countryman's sport, not a profession—but it would be a pity if it disappeared altogether from the district. It is an excellent, healthy, amiable sport, and I would like to see it practised and taught in every school throughout the two counties. Every secondary school

---

[1] In *Some Records of the Annual Grasmere Sports*. Compiled by Hugh W. Machell. (Chas. Thurnam, Carlisle, 1911.)

—most of them with a good proportion of country pupils— should be a wrestling academy. In some schools this is the case; in others the sport is forgotten, largely because the control of the school, or at least of games and physical training, is in the hands of a stranger, unacquainted with the traditions of the place where he teaches. Appointments to the teaching staff should never be made on purely academic qualifications. Too often that means that important positions are held by men and women who are quite out of touch with the special needs of the locality. The result tends to be schools which try to turn all their pupils into second-hand suburbanites. They will never succeed completely, but they already succeed too much.

Chapter X

THE LAKES TODAY

The Changing View

U P to about the middle of the eighteenth century the Lakes belonged to the people who lived there. It was they who made the dale villages and towns and the dale way of life. They were obviously fond of their home, but it is doubtful if they ever considered whether it was beautiful or not. Perhaps some did and some didn't, but certainly they never expected anyone to admire the mountains. To us nowadays this seems a lack of perception, but to the countryman, the country is his home and his livelihood. Mountains are barren blocks which grow nothing and hinder communication. It was only when there developed a large urban population that people got into the habit of seeing the country not as an environment but as a spectacle. Today, in the minds of many, production seems to belong to industry and the country is largely a collection of pretty scenes, or an inhabited park. Such people will often carry to absurd lengths their preference for barren scenery, and will sign petitions that ploughland or forest be let return to waste, and drained fields to swamp. In the eighteenth century the dales folk noticed with surprise that people were coming from London and other parts to look at the lakes and fells. The first travellers never went far from the main road, kept as much as they could to lake level, and clearly preferred the gentler scenes—Derwentwater, Grasmere, Rydal and Windermere. "Beauty lying in the lap of horror" expressed their usual reactions.

The most famous of them was Gray. The *Journal* of his tour in 1769 to Patterdale, Keswick, Grasmere and Kendal is not nearly so full of shudders as many think. He noted the scenes with much greater precision than you might expect, and kept his prose free from superlatives and generalisations. Yet he was as ready as a child at a pantomime to believe any story about the hills, where ". . . all farther access is here barred to prying mortals, only there is a little path winding over the fells, and for some weeks in the year passable to the dalesmen; but the mountains know well that these innocent people will not reveal the mysteries of their ancient kingdom, 'the reign of Chaos and Old Night.'" I wonder which of the innocent people told him that one!

Moreover, whenever he was among crag, in Borrowdale or on Dunmail Raise, he seemed to get the idea that the rocks were likely to fall on him. Such was the common impression among the early travellers, and the first topographical prints reflect this feeling. Huge cliffs overhang like the upper storeys of a Jacobean house; trees are long and bare as snakes; cloaked figures from Salvator Rosa lurk on donkeys among caves and grottos. These pictures have often great charm, but they entirely ignore the texture and form of the mountains, and usually they are so imaginative in their landscape that it is difficult to recognise the scenes. It wasn't long before the visitors lost their first tittering terrors and began to regard the mountains, as some people regard music, as a stimulus to romantic emotion. In less than ten years after Gray's tour, Richard Cumberland expressed the feelings which would occur to all travellers of taste:

> Trembling now with giddy tread,
> Press the moss on Gowdar's head;
> But lo, where sits the bird of Jove,
> Couch'd in his eyrie far above;
> Oh, lend thine eye, thy pinion lend,
> Higher, yet higher let me still ascend;
> 'Tis done; my forehead smites the skies,
> To the last summit of the cliff I rise;
> I touch the sacred ground,
> Where step of man was never found;
> I see all Nature's rude domain around.[1]

Mountains now became the symbols of freedom, liberty, progress, the Natural Law and everything else which the Romantics believed in. The greatest literary men of the time, Wordsworth, Coleridge and Southey, lived in the dales, which therefore became a place of pilgrimage. Young Shelley and young Keats visited Keswick; De Quincey went

[1] *Ode to the Sun.*

to live at Dove Cottage when its previous tenant moved to Rydal Mount. There was also a large circle of minor figures, poets, naturalists, philosophers—Professor Wilson at Windermere, John Gough at Kendal, Elizabeth Smith at Tent Lodge on Coniston. Then came the romantic extravagance. The Lakes cannot claim any of the more spectacular follies, but huge castles were built, bristling with turrets and battlements. At Conishead Priory (now a Miners' Convalescent Home) near Ulverston, a little chapel was built in the grounds (or possibly restored from a ruin), and an old man was paid to be a hermit. At Penrith the picturesque was cultivated on a larger scale. Walking one day on the slopes of Penrith Beacon, I came across a farm some of whose buildings looked odd and gawky. When I went up to them, I found that the walls on the south side had been built above the level of the roof and fitted with castellations and little towers. It was as if a piece of theatrical scenery had been left propped against the side of the farm—and, indeed, that was really the case, for it was designed to give a Border grandeur to the view from Lowther Castle. Connoisseurs of the mock-Gothic will appreciate still more the inventiveness of the mining company at Wellington Pit, Whitehaven, who fashioned the pit buildings like forts to match the early nineteenth-century castle, now a hospital. Soon more tourists began to come to the lakes, and the Rev. William Gilpin showed them what to look for and how to look. They were to scrutinise every landscape as if it were a work of art, and if they felt they could improve the view, they were not to hesitate to reorganise the scene mentally, and perhaps to throw down a cottage or plant a dead tree.[1] Wordsworth, like William Gilpin, had an artist's eye for a scene, but he had also a deep respect for the land for its own sake. He and his lovable sister brought a new understanding to the dales. He belonged there; his approach to the mountains was not a fashionable literary one. His mysticism never blurred his eyes to the *fact* of Nature—a primrose by a river's brim never ceased to be a yellow primrose however much more it may have been. He worshipped the general, but he loved the

[1] In *Observations Relative chiefly to Picturesque Beauty on the Mountains and Lakes of Cumberland and Westmorland* (1786).

particular. Wordsworth was followed by many others who, often in rather humble ways, added to our knowledge and understanding of the fells—William Green with his sketches, Jonathan Otley with his *Guide*, and all the archæologists, geologists, naturalists, country parsons and poets of the last hundred years, to whom this book owes everything that it has.

In spite of all their painstaking and affectionate work (and, to some extent, because of it) a change has come on people's minds about the Lakes. They exist no longer just as a place—they are now something to be admired, to be enjoyed, to be held sacred, to be protected, according to the temperament of the visitors, or perhaps even to be exploited, to be shown off, to be made the most of. They are now a "beauty spot," a "shrine," a "national heritage," a curiosity, even a prodigy to be exhibited like a fat woman in a circus. This is surely regrettable, but it is also inevitable; it is a heresy, but one which no one can avoid—I certainly can't. But it has made the mountains self-conscious, and I fear that to attempt to preserve them from industrialism will, in fact, turn them into beautiful invalids. Such schemes as that under discussion for Ennerdale would mean that the Lakes would take a proper part in the economy of the nation, and might not this, at a cost of some destruction of natural beauty, restore to them independence and self-respect? No one wants to see the dales covered with unnecessary dams, girders and pylons, and the Friends of the Lake District are right to be wary, but they must be careful that they do not change without knowing it from friends to nurses, and from nurses to embalmers.

If, however, the Friends are ready to acknowledge industrial needs, their advice can be of great help. In the case of Ennerdale it was not the dam which was going to do much harm (the lake, in fact, had been Whitehaven's reservoir for many years), but the rise and fall of the water which would leave a rim of dead rock and mud round the edge. I do not think the Lakes have much to fear from honest industry. Let us watch out instead for umbrella tea-gardens, Tudor cafés, red-tiled hotels, unnecessary motor-roads over the passes, speedboats on the lakes and motor-cycle tracks on the hills.

The Tourist Trade

Nevertheless, the tourist trade has come to stay in the dales, and there is no need to be ashamed of it. To give health and rest to thousands is an honourable work, and the dales can accommodate them and welcome them, and, indeed, can benefit from the change of company. It is important, however, that the dales should not be dependent on the tourists; that they should go on living their own life and become neither a museum on the one hand nor a little Blackpool on the other.

The main signs of the tourist trade are obvious—the hotels, the youth hostels, the boarding-house towns—all of which form a link between the dales, the towns of the lowlands and the rest of England. During the lean years before the war, many girls from the coastal towns worked at the hotels during the summer, saved up their tips, and went home for the winter to live on the dole. There is also a more immediate contact between the dalesmen and the tourist, and one which seems to me much more interesting. Most of the dale farms take visitors and serve ham-and-egg and rum-butter teas—it may be that there is room only for two or three, but in some cases catering becomes the main source of income. I am thinking of a typical case, a farm on one of the lakes. The shore here is private and the farmer has boats for hire. You look across the lake to a magnificent mountain view, and in the morning the dew is on the window-ledge and the mists lie among the gooseberry bushes. The farm is of some 60 or 80 acres, nearly half of it fellside, and the rest running steeply along the edge of the lake, so that ploughing is a navvy's job. There were once cottages attached to the farm, but these have been converted into one house to make a building, which, if the family are crammed into one end, will now house twenty or more guests. It is on these that the household really depends. The farmer's wife and his daughter work like slaves all the summer, with perhaps a woman from the village to help to make the beds, or a girl to wait at table. The farmer and his son do not bother much with the guests—they work on the land. They plough what the Agricultural Committee makes them plough, but their chief aim is to grow fodder for the horses and cattle and mangolds for the sheep. The rest of the farm produce is directed more towards the kitchen than the market: milk, cream, eggs, poultry, bacon and hams, and vegetables, for prosperity depends on the food they give to the guests.

Such is a way of life very different from that of the old statesman, and it inevitably leads to a sharp awareness of town life. Indeed, though the dalesmen are more isolated from towns than are country folk of many parts of England, they seem to me to look to the town more than many. For the younger people, the cinema, the car or bus trip to the town, and especially the dance hall, create an horizon which differs from the town horizon more in scale than in detail. In October when the Lakes season is over they go to Blackpool for their holidays (a very sensible thing to do when you have been cooped in a narrow valley all the summer), and, in return, a surprising number of Blackpool people go to the Lakes. Much of this is natural and healthy, but when a young man or girl, living on a farm, gets his or her mind set on the town, the vista shrinks, and he or she loses *touch*—something comes like a film between the hand and the soil. I have known a young woman living within two miles of one of the most visited spots in the Lakes whose curiosity had never been roused enough to make her go to see what it was like.

The Future

The problem of education is particularly difficult in the dales. The cost of upkeep of tiny village schools is immense per head of the scholars, and neither Cumberland nor Westmorland is a rich county. In many of the schools there are only two teachers to serve a mixed crowd of boys and girls from 7 to 14, and at Wasdale Head there was once a famous school of four scholars. Some of these difficulties are being overcome by closing the smaller schools and taking the children by bus into the towns. But this turns the mind of the child away from the countryside. He begins to think of education as something which is needed only in the towns. We do not want to go back to the old schools—they were often dark, smelly caves, with narrow windows copied from almshouses and monasteries, with rotting wooden floors, no light, little sanitation. What we must do is to build larger central schools in *the more accessible villages*, not in the towns. This is particularly necessary in the case of secondary schools, which otherwise draw the best brains out of the countryside and never send them back. At Whitehaven, for instance, the secondary school, which already has enough to do to serve its own town, has to receive children from a huge area of villages and small mining towns. The boy who comes into a centre like this naturally directs his thoughts to the town, and his studies usually fit him for clerical, professional or technical work for which there is no opening at home. Country secondary schools are very necessary if the scholarship boy or girl is not to be tapped away; and not only schools, but rural industries, where there are interesting jobs with a reasonable amount of leisure and opportunity for advancement.

I like better those attempts to take education to the villages themselves. W.E.A., which has rather exacting requirements of registers and attendance, is able to function freely mostly in the larger villages, but the education authorities send occasional lecturers even to the most remote villages. The lectures, of course, are hit-and-miss affairs. I have known a lecturer with an apparently unattractive subject find a full hall and an enthusiastic audience; I have known another find only the vicar and the man who was going to work the magic-lantern. This must be accepted by the authorities as quite likely to happen. It is no good trying to assess the value of the classes by numbers. So much depends on accident—on the weather, or the moon, or whether or not there's a dance or a fair on the same night.

The work of the Women's Institutes is well known all over England. I don't know if village drama classes are equally widespread, but they are certainly very active in the dales, especially in the Furness and Cartmel areas. The education authorities usually provide a coach and producer, and each group not only performs in its own village, but enters for a drama festival. The standard reached is often surprisingly high, and that it makes a genuine interest in drama is shown by the welcome given to the travelling companies of the Arts Council in any village that is lucky enough to have a public hall. Mr. Martin Browne, touring with his *Pilgrim Players*, tells me that rarely has he known any audience be so appreciative of *Murder in the Cathedral* as in one of the limestone villages of lower Kendal. The drama group has also a social use. It brings together people differing in age, sex, and class. There is always a danger, of course, that it will fall into the hands of one particular clique—the vicarage clique, the educated maiden ladies, or the retired business people—but the organiser should see that this does not happen. When it is really well run it combines class and club, and mixes education with the pleasures of showing-off, dressing, making-up, and even of music and dancing. There can be no better counter to the cinema.

If, then, the drift from the country to the towns can be stopped, if the country folk are given their own industries, and further opportunities for leisure, recreation and social life, we can be sure that some of the amenities of town life will be ready to go to them. Water and sanitation are still great problems in the villages, but electricity is now arriving. Cars and buses make shopping easier, and many villages and farms are visited regularly by baker, butcher and fish vans, and perhaps by the greengrocer. I was walking through a village on the coast at about midday when a man drove up with a motor-cycle and side-car van. He blew a whistle, and immediately all the cottage doors opened and women came out with plates. I went over to see what they were buying. It was fish and chips, kept warm on little tanks of hot water.

PART IV

Chapter XI

THE MINING SCENE

Mining in the Fells

M INING, as I have stressed frequently, is one of the main industries of the Lake District. Today, it has declined in the District proper, and passed to the surrounding lowlands, but the extent to which it was carried on in the past among the fells will surprise many people. The Romans certainly knew of the presence of lead, zinc, iron and silver, and before them the Celtic tribes dug for copper. In the sixteenth century a company was formed to work mines in the Keswick district, the works being carried on chiefly by Germans, who were brought there by Elizabeth and whose contribution to the local tradition can be traced for centuries later. By 1567 the furnaces were at work near Keswick, smelting ore mostly from the Newlands mines, but also from Caldbeck and Coniston. Elizabethan Keswick was a busy, cosmopolitan, industrial town, enlivened, no doubt, by much suspicion of the foreign workers, until gradually these intermarried with Cumberland families and became themselves Cumbrians—their anglicised names can often be found in the farm records.

Before the invention of gunpowder mining was a very difficult operation. The workers of those times—almost mythically known as the "Old Men"—used "stope and feather"—"implements consisting of two thin pieces of iron, called feathers, about six inches long and half an inch broad, flat on one side and round on the other, and a thin tapering wedge or stope of the same length and width. A hole was bored in the rock and the feathers placed in it, with their flat sides together and parallel with the cleavage of the rock; the point of the stope was then introduced between them, and driven in with a hammer until the rock was rent."[1]

---

[1] John Postlethwaite: *Mines and Mining in the Lake District* (Moss and Son, Whitehaven). This fascinating book is one of the classics of Lake District literature.

214

Alston : glimpse of valley of South Tyne on Left
Wrestling at Bootle—typical village sports

The Old Men worked like explorers in the dark, cutting openings just big enough to get through, prospecting for themselves, and in some cases raising ore on their own account and paying only a "tribute" to the owners. Local folk-lore is full of stories of miners who found rich deposits of ore—sometimes shown to them by the fairies or the devil—and kept it secret from the others. Sometimes they made their own little hoards in a cave or abandoned tunnel, saving up for their old age, and then perhaps died before they drew out the balance, leaving it for later generations to find.

Even after the introduction of gunpowder, mining among the fells reminds you of the enterprises of the Merchant Adventurers. Methods were so crude that any mine was a gamble. One after another failed, changed hands, was let go derelict, then opened again. More recent miners have found valuable ores in the rubble left by the Old Men, and even today there is speculation about the practicability of re-opening some of the mines.

Mining among the fells falls roughly into four districts—the Caldbeck district, the Keswick district (including mines in Borrowdale, Newlands, Thornthwaite above Bassenthwaite, and Thelkeld below Saddleback), the Helvellyn and Ullswater district, and the Coniston district. The main ores are galena (producing lead and silver), blende (sulphide of zinc), hæmatite (iron), and copper. Of these, lead alone is now regarded as of practical working value, and the Greenside mine at Helvellyn is the only one where there has been recent development on a large scale, though it is possible that barytes[1] may become more important in the future. In the bed of the former lake at Kentmere there is a large deposit of diatomite which is composed of the remains of the minute water-plants called diatoms.

The galena found in the district is usually rich in silver, yielding up to 25 ounces a ton when smelted. £4,000 of silver was extracted for lead in Cumberland and Westmorland in 1909. The Goldscope Mine in the Vale of Newlands has also produced some gold as well as silver.

The chief source of lead in Cumberland has been not the

---

[1] This is used in the paper and paint trades. Abandoned lead mines are now being reopened for the sake of the barytes ignored by the old miners.

Tarn Hows—an artificial reservoir
Keswick

fells but the district round Alston, in the east of the county, on the Northumberland border. These mines were certainly worked in the twelfth century and were known then as the Carlisle Silver Mines. They were so important that the miners were given special privileges (such as the right to cut as much wood as they liked for smelting), which they claimed with great tenacity. The Alston mining field has remained important to the present day, when it is mostly owned by Greenwich Hospital. Lead is also reported from the Cross Fell area.

Besides these fairly widely distributed ores, there is tungsten in the Caldbeck Fells, and the famous graphite or plumbago mine, near Seathwaite, in Borrowdale. This, before it was worked out, was one of the wonders visited by tourists (including Gray). The wad, or blacklead, is a black shining earth, found in sops or pipes of various sizes. A deposit found in 1803 yielded $31\frac{3}{4}$ tons, worth then about £100,000.[1] It was used in the eighteenth century for casting "bombshells, round-shot and cannon-balls," and was so valuable that guards were set round the mine, and the miners were stripped and searched when they left work. Later it was used for the lead pencils manufactured at Keswick.

Besides these ores in the fells proper, the surrounding lowlands offer gypsum, magnesium limestone, fireclay, shales and clay for brick-making, and, of course, iron and coal.

Of the fell mines Coniston is probably the oldest, having been worked, it is thought, on and off for about two thousand years. In the middle of the last century it employed hundreds of men and boys, but then declined and was closed down before 1890. What remains of the building has now been made into a youth hostel. The choice is a happy one, for the hostel lies in a sort of combe or scoop between the Old Man and Wetherlam, looking down to the lake. Wise walkers will approach it over the shoulders of the fells from Dunnerdale or Langdale or Tilberthwaite, instead of making for the village and then having to face a 1,000-foot climb at the end of the day. The choice is happy, too, because the old mines of the Lake District have become romantic. Whatever

[1] Postlethwaite: work quoted.

dangers and handicaps the Old Man may have had to face, we now feel a great attraction to these little tunnels and caves, where the wounds are already healing and the bones knitting together. The old buildings, always of slate, are sliding back to scree again, the underground springs are finding new runnels in the empty levels, and lichen and gorse, or, lower down, blackberry and rowan, are closing the mouths of the shafts.

Even when they were working the mines must still have been attractive, sometimes with great water-wheels driven by an aqueduct like Brandley Mine. Postlethwaite tells of one mine with a chimney a mile and a half high (or long) carried up the mountain-side, so that when the ore was smelted the condensed lead might be swept out of the flue from manholes made at intervals.

The Iron Mines

Of the fell minerals I have left iron to the last, because, though it is certainly found in the fells, it is in the carboniferous limestone of the lowlands that it exists in such quantities as to be one of the main foundations of life in modern Cumberland.

Oddly enough, it was among the fells that it seems first to have been found: in Ennerdale (Knock Murton), Eskdale, Dunnerdale and in High Furness. The Romans mined and smelted it, and so did the early British tribes. There are patches of slag or cinders in Eskdale, Wasdale, and Furness, particularly round Coniston Lake. That at Wasdale—at the foot of the lake, between the screes and the River Irt—is thought to have been almost certainly Roman, the ore coming from a little vein near the top of the screes which was used later to give ruddle for marking sheep.[1]

In the Middle Ages the mining of iron ore increased considerably, especially around Egremont, where it has gone on continuously ever since. The first lords of Egremont, always benefactors to the Church, gave mining rights to the monks of both St. Bees and Holme Cultram. It was in Lancashire,

[1] *The Archæology of the West Cumberland Iron Trade*, by H. A. Fletcher, *Transactions of the Cumberland and Westmorland Antiquarian and Archæological Society*, Vol. V, 1879-1880.

however, among the Furness Fells, that the industry first developed on a larger scale. Up to the time of the dissolution of the monasteries, smelting was by means of open hearths, and remains of these small bloomeries can be found scattered all over High Furness. Charcoal was used for the firing, and in this district we had iron and wood close together, as later we had iron and coal round Whitehaven. Often the bloomery was set up in a narrow gorge beside a beck (that mentioned at Strands in Wasdale is a typical example), where the wind would sweep down and supply blast without bellows. Coniston and Hawkshead during the early sixteenth century must have been in a little Black Country, with charcoal-burners living in their huts among the woods, and the smoke of the furnaces trickling among the trees. Finally, the destruction of the woods became so great that the tenants petitioned to the Crown that they were deprived of their "proper fewell," and the permanent furnaces were closed down in 1564, though small itinerant bloomeries came into being to supply local needs.[1] Some of the Furness trade crossed the Duddon to Millom, where the Huddlestons of Millom Castle had set up a blast furnace to smelt the ore which they mined at Water Blean nearby. When the Water Blean supply failed, they seem to have imported a certain amount, quite unaware that at Hodbarrow, the Mains, or outlying part of their estate, there was one of the richest deposits of ore in the whole of England.

The early eighteenth century brought the cold blast furnace which led the way to the modern period. In 1711 the first of these furnaces in Great Britain was built at Backbarrow, near Greenodd. It is still producing iron and may be the oldest in operation in Europe. This was followed by about half a dozen in Furness, one at Leighton in Westmorland, one at Duddon Bridge, just over the Cumberland border, and a group at Maryport, Frizington and other places round the Cumberland coalfield. Charging of the furnaces was done by swills.[2] The Duddon Bridge furnace, which was working until 1880 and still stands, looking

---

[1] See Dr. Fawcitt: *The Early History of Local Iron Ore Mining*, printed in *The Barrow News*, September 30, 1945.

[2] Dr. Fawcitt, to whom I am indebted throughout this section of the book.

rather like a barn, is only fifty or a hundred yards away from the river, with the birches, bluebells and daffodils all round it. Just below the bridge, at the side of the river, you can see traces of the wharves to which the barges came up the estuary with the ore. Of this stream Wordsworth wrote:

> Remote from every taint
> Of sordid industry thy lot is cast;[1]

and if he were there today he might well write the same again, so quickly do the wounds heal.

We come now to the beginning of the development which was to create the great iron industry of the nineteenth century. There are two main ore-producing areas in the district, both of them in the western curve of the limestone which rings the fells. The larger of the two lies in a narrow bend between the Skiddaw Slates of Ennerdale and the coal measures of Whitehaven-Workington. It starts about Egremont,[2] and continues by Woodend and Beckermet, Cleator, Cleator Moor, Frizington, Salter and Eskett, Rowrah, to about Lamplugh.[3] At one of the mines at Montreal, Cleator Moor, iron and coal were once raised from the same shaft.[4] The other area is in Furness, around Dalton, Lindal and Askam, and it appears the other side of the Duddon at Millom and Whicham. The total production of the West Cumberland district is the greater of the two, but Hodbarrow Mine, Millom, much exceeded every other single mine during the years of its maximum output. The prosperity of the mines increased enormously because of the development of blast furnaces, but it began to decline in West Cumberland after 1890, though at Millom it lasted longer, the Hodbarrow Mine averaging over half a million tons a year in the early 1890's. Since then the output has

---

[1] *The River Duddon,* Sonnet II.

[2] It continues farther south to an indefinite extent as a *concealed* ore-bearing limestone. At Egremont the limestone is at the surface.

[3] Around Lamplugh the ore occurs in workable quantities in the Skiddaw Slates.

[4] The shaft was sunk close to the "Main Coal Fault." It produced ore from the limestone on the one side and went through the fault to the coal measures on the other.

steadily declined, though new shafts have been sunk and new mines opened, and though reserves are estimated to be still considerable. Such is inevitable, for mining exhausts and does not replace. All the mines in Furness are now closed down, and in Cumberland production is restricted to six or seven of the larger mines, mostly in the Egremont district. Not only do these districts feel most severely the strain and shock of slump, but the very life is drained out of the land beneath them. Young men and women who grew up in the dole years of the 1920's and 1930's find it hard to believe that the towns where they live were once busy as anthills and wealthy as the mint.

When we consider the Cumberland and Furness iron mines within the landscape we must first of all realise their scale. They do not spread over large tracts of the country like the industries of the Midlands or South Yorkshire. The smaller mines are contained in a few acres, and the larger fields are narrow; in every case there is wild mountain near at hand, and in several cases the sea also. Here are none of the spectacular industrial views—nothing like the black, sultry miles of the greater collieries, or the evening sky around Sheffield, where every hill is a volcano and pylons grow as thick as pines.

Mining, except that it exhausts, is more akin to agriculture than to manufacture, and iron mining, in particular, remains a sort of rural industry. Unlike coal, iron ore does not blight grass and tree with black dust; instead, the limestone soils seem unusually fertile, and bushes and herbs grow luxuriantly. But most surprising of all is the absence of the feeling of dirt. The ore spreads a fat red soil over the land, the red dust soaks into the wood of sleepers and fences, staining them to mahogany, and pools, drains and rivers run red long after they have left the mines, sopping round the stems of rushes or oozing through the gravel. The ore varies in colour, but at Hodbarrow it is purplish, like a pickle-cabbage, and rubble tips and refuse heaps are bright red, as if the earth had been coughing up its lungs. Soon the scabs are half-hidden as the grass grows, and weeds and long green horse-tails.

A mine is always moribund, bleeding to death at the

height of its vigour, so it is the derelict mine rather than the working mine which becomes permanent in the landscape. We can study them best, therefore, by looking first at the Furness mines, between Lindal and Askam, some of which have been closed[1] for so long that they have already been assimilated into the pastoral scene. The soil here is very fertile, and nowhere are there such fresh fruit colours, reds and greens of raspberries and gooseberries. At Millom, though the mines are in limestone, the town is of slate, and in West Cumberland the people seem to have preferred to build of the easily obtained red sandstone; but here in Furness walls are all of limestone, though in the towns themselves there is much brick and stucco. The old pit buildings are broken down, and often the land has caved in beneath them; there are great feather-boas of ivy flopping round the windows, and rowans and thorns are rooted in the floors. Spleenworts shine on the limestone, and bracken and buckler fern block steps and skirting and hide the broken soil and blastings and splinters of rock. Rabbits burrow in the old rubble tips, and the birds fizz in the thickets of willow and elder which grow around the sumps. In the valley between Askam and Dalton, where the land is well wooded, the old tips are like red screes, with the birches and chestnuts padded round them.

Farther north, in West Cumberland, where some mines are still at work, the scars are fresh, and instead of the heavy romanticism of Furness, we have a living industrial landscape. Here the ground is by nature rough and knobbly, and this has been emphasised and exaggerated by the artificial hills of tips and slag-banks and the artificial combes of subsidences. The chimneys and pithead wheels group themselves against the sky, sometimes with quite self-assured artistry, and the little engines fuss up and down the lines. The waste patches are covered with willow-herb now, and there are rarer flowers if you look for them, but here, the limestone strip is so constricted that you are much aware of the contrast of the coalfield on the one side and the fells on the other. It is not a rich landscape like Furness. Instead, Dent bulges up, bare as a bald head, above Cleator Moor,

---

[1] Newton Mines at Dalton were not closed until the end of 1944. Roanhead and Anticross were also working until fairly recently.

and farther inland are shoulders of the Ennerdale Fells, amplifying the shapes of the slag-banks in a hard, sleety green.

Florence Mine at Egremont is dapper and productive. Even the ore looks specially clean, like heaps of bright red tooth-paste squeezed out of the earth; but farther north you come on the land of many tiny derelict mines, with no trees but with villages hiding behind the hedges. The mines and the villages are not far apart. You pass one, there is a turn and a dip in the road, you cross a stream, and you are in a copse with a splatter of green, then the next tip-heap, like an old sand-pit of very red sand, half dug away and overgrown. Nature is fighting back, but as yet you feel that the country is derelict—the corpse of a countryside, with the bowels cut out and left drying in the air. Yet it is a landscape, too, of surprising views—pollard willows around works reservoirs, the red alpine scenery of the tips, the great brick viaduct at Kekle, and weirs running dark as burgundy.

At the southern tip of the county, at Millom, and across the Duddon at Askam, the iron comes out on the coast. Here the landscape has an extra salty taste, and to the red, green and white is added the yellow of sand. The magnificent Hodbarrow Mines[1] are part of my boyhood. The town where I was born is set on the mines, like a house set on a rock—but a rock which unfortunately was hollow. After school I would walk past the mines seeing a friend home; we played among the thorns and railways in the winter dusk, with the smoke freezing on the sky. In holidays we would picnic on the heath nearby; some learned to swim from the sea wall, and later we took our first girls there. Yet though they are so important in our lives, the Hodbarrow Mines are rather aloof from the town, creating a small continent of their own in what was neither land nor sea.

The first shaft sunk there was at Hodbarrow Point, where the limestone rocks grapple into the estuary. It is still there, choked with bramble and thorn. When I was a child my dog chased a rabbit and fell down the shaft, to climb up again,

---

[1] It was largely through the ore from these mines that local furnaces were able to produce the special West Coast Pig-iron, with its very small percentage of phosphorus and sulphur.

cut and bruised but otherwise uninjured. Nearby the bloody crane's-bill grows as if the ore wagons had been dripping. The present workings have moved away from the shaft, leaving the limestone cottages and the old lighthouse like pele towers on the rocks. The new mines grew up on the dune coast, but when it was found that they lay beneath high-water level, a wall was built to keep out the tide. Later more ore was discovered, and another wall was built, a great arc a mile and a quarter long, from Hodbarrow Point to near Haverigg. The land caved in beneath the old wall, which stands now, archaic as the Wall of China, cracked in the middle, slowly curtseying out of sight into the sand.

Between the inner and the outer barriers lie the new acres. The old swash channel is a map of sand, where terns and gulls nest, and in the swamps grow marsh cinquefoil, Dutch rush and orchises. You stand in a hollow. Above the dune-cliffs are the pitheads, dribbling ore into the sand; on the other side, the rim of the barrier makes an horizon clean as that of the sea. Far away, between the chimneys and pit-wheels you get glimpses of the town; farther still of the fells, but they do not belong to the real world any more: the real world is just this desert of sand, blossoming with pink iron flowers.

Blast Furnaces

It is possible to find signs of the smelting of iron ore from a very early date, but the modern hæmatite pig-iron industry did not begin in Cumberland till about the middle of the last century. In 1841 blast furnaces were opened at Cleator Moor, a strange town which sprang into prosperity out of the bare rock, and now stands with the dead bones of that prosperity lying all round it. In the next decade furnaces were set up at Seaton, Harrington and Workington, and (in Furness) at Barrow. The trade grew in the 60's and 70's; in the West Cumberland area Distington and Maryport joined, with Millom in the south and Ulverston and Askam in Furness. Now only Workington and Millom and Barrow are still working, but the production is much higher per furnace than it used to be. At Workington and Barrow there are also important steel works.

Most of the coke needed for the furnaces used to be imported from Durham, but today a great deal of it is produced in coke-ovens in the West Cumberland coalfield. Most of the limestone used is also from local quarries.

No one who has any feeling for architecture will deny that blast furnaces are often splendid and exciting structures. Seen broadside they have a fine rhythm, each single furnace repeating the pattern, with a criss-cross of girders and derricks tangling the eye, and the chimneys drawing tall irregular bar-lines down the staves. Seen end-on at an angle they are like a ship, a battle-ship, long and narrow, iron-clad, with the chimneys like masts. They are among the few industrial plants which are not ugly or insignificant from the air—the Millom Ironworks, for instance, seen from the top of Black Combe or Coniston Old Man have shape and dignity, and the smoke flies from the chimneys in parallel streams up the estuary. Moreover, they *belong*. They are not foreign, like some shambling mass-production factory. They are made of iron and they work in iron; they are on the rock, of it and for it.

The chimneys need to be very tall to draw the enormous blast, and are often slender as larches and varied in design. There is a whole book to be written and illustrated about the chimney-stacks of the North. Askam Ironworks had the second highest chimney in the country—327 feet, with a million and a half bricks in it, built in 1865. It was felled about a dozen years ago, and the sands seemed to have lost a neighbour.

One ironworks I know on the coast. The sea half-circles it like a comma, and at high spring-tides the furnaces run down to the edge of the water, reflected below like the double pipes of an organ. The oyster-catchers spit and pipe in the air, and gulls settle on the water, sending an earthquake along the inverted chimneys. Here, too, and elsewhere there are reservoirs where swans, ducks and moorhens nest, and the fountains spread a trellis of spray across the cooling beds. In the spray rainbows hover, dipping and waving like carpets being shaken, and the works are seen through a moving wash of colour.

There is also a continuous buzz about an ironworks—not

the clang of a factory, but the drone of a beehive or a dynamo. It hangs for days at a time over the town when the wind is blowing in the right way, but you never notice it, except when the furnaces are tapped. There is often little sign of movement and few people about, yet the whole place seems to be humming with power.

Beside the ironworks are the slag-heaps which seem to many the most typical signs of the devastation of industry. Except possibly for Barrow and Workington, the Cumberland and Furness slag-banks do not, as those of South Lancashire, sprawl over the towns like the carcases of grey mammals. Our slag-banks are smaller, more companionable. Yet one must admit that there is something repulsive about a slag-bank, at any rate as a neighbour. It is not the colour—for they are the colour of stone; it is not the shape—for they are more or less the shape of tumuli or alluvial hills; it is not even the dirt—for though there is some dust around a slag-bank, they are cleaner and freer from fumes than the average city street. No, I think it is rather that slag is so *dead*. It is like frozen sputum or fæces cast up out of the earth. It is empty of birds and even of rats. It does not alter with the seasons nor with the years. The darkest back-yard puts out a fern or a creeper in spring, the most deserted street shows sometimes a new speck of paint, but the slag-bank remains the same year after year, generation after generation. It does not even decay.

For all that, anyone who has played among the slag-banks as a child would be sorry to lose them. Whatever the psychologists may say there can be no planned playground quite so satisfying as a slag-bank. There is nothing at all you can damage, nothing that you should treat carefully. If trespassing is forbidden it is a purely technical ban which any boy would feel honour bound to break. There are scars, slopes, screes, dips, hollows, caves, sometimes tunnels. It is full of places for ambushes and secret parleyings. It is mysterious, even terrifying, especially at night with the mist over it and the light from the street lamps reaching scarcely above its flanks. Then the gang game is necessary—you need the comfort of knowing that others are doing as you do, that you are all banded together, whether against Redskins, or a still more malicious neighbour-gang. Then, too, is the time for those complicated games of hide-and-seek, where each goes away into his little gulley of darkness, not knowing what is going to happen to him, and at length surrenders, or rushes wildly to the Base along the top of the bank. After that, the wail of "All-in-all-in-all-in-all-in-all-in-all-in-all-in," the hands cupped round the mouth, sounds as mournfully as a bagpipe lament.

The smaller slag-banks, too, are rarely far from the countryside. Often they slope into meadows, where buttercups grow among the fragments of slag, or (if the weight of the bank has broken the drains) into ponds full of rushes and lesser spearwort. At Askam the bank stretches straight out into the sands like a pier or a mole. The high tide washes round it, and there is a tunnel near the dunes so that people can pass up and down the shore. Here the sand is beginning to cover the slag, and the lower slopes are already green with horse-tails. At Cleator Moor, too, where the slag is particularly crumbly, weeds are getting a hold. No doubt even the barest slag-banks will be covered in time and grassed and weeded, but wherever practicable the process should be hurried up by tipping soil or iron-ore rubble. Rain and wind and dandelion seeds will do the rest.

At a distance, however, the slag-banks sometimes fit more happily into the landscape. They can be gravely beautiful under snow, and I remember, too, winter evenings on marshy fields near the coast, when the sky is purple and wires and thorns are black and cold, and the slag-banks slant out of the mist, lonely as icebergs and the faint mauve of an uncooked white of egg.

It is at night, however, that the slag flares into beauty— the living slag of the working furnaces. Tipping is like no other night scene. You watch the little engine climbing the bank, with the shapes of the ladles behind it, dim in the lights. Then the engine stops, waits, and runs forward again. The ladle swings over. For a moment the slag remains tilted, a burning moon looking straight at you—you can feel the heat on your face a hundred yards away. Then the crust breaks, the red-hot syrup pours down the side of the bank, and the whole sky is alight. The light does not flash, but spreads as if a packet of red dye has been dipped in the night, and then ebbs away again, till there are just glowing trickles down the slope of the bank.

The whole industrial area is alive at night. The furnace chimneys have the ground lights on them and soil among the dark clouds; the railways and shunting yards are hung with rocking lanterns; colliery pit-heaps have distant jets like naphthalene flares. And in the estuaries at high tide the lights float out on the water, dipping and splintering as the waves shake, and unheard engines drag little trollies of light after them.

The Coal Mines

Coal was known to the early Britons in Cumberland and to the Romans, but in those days wood and peat were preferred as fuel, and it was not until the sixteenth century that we know of coal being used for smelting at Keswick. This coal came from Bolton, and early in the next century, outcrops began to be worked at Whitehaven. About that time there passed into the hands of the Lowther family the lands which had belonged to St. Bees Priory before the dissolution of the monasteries. Sir Christopher Lowther, the second son of the purchaser, settled in Whitehaven and began to work the coal and to make a harbour in the creek. He was succeeded in 1644 by his son, Sir John, who gave all his energies to the exploitation of the wealth under his feet. The colliery now began to expand rapidly. By 1700 the Lowther pits[1] at Whitehaven were producing 27,000 tons of coal a year. Meanwhile other landowners were looking for coal farther along the coast. The Curwens began on a small scale at Workington, and attempts were made to develop Parton as a colliery port. Whitehaven by mid-eighteenth century was the third or fourth most important port in England, shipping large quantities of coal to Ireland, and for a while it seemed likely that it would be one of the great centres for English trade with the New World, but the barren land behind it

---

[1] I do not know if the practice is general throughout the country, but in Cumberland only iron mines are called "mines"—coal mines being called "pits."

and the difficulty of land communication handicapped it greatly in competition with towns like Liverpool and Bristol.

The coal trade grew nevertheless. More shafts were sunk and deeper ones, and it was realised that huge stocks of coal lay beneath the sea. Today the greater amount of the coal in West Cumberland comes from under the sea, and at White-haven the workings stretch about four miles from the shore at the farthest point, and it is estimated that the coal may extend twelve miles under the sea, though whether it will ever be practicable to mine it cannot be told. An imaginative Bevin-boy claims to have heard the trains running at Douglas, I.O.M.

The sea added another great danger to those which always attend mining for coal. In the accounts of the collieries we read of one accident after another:

1737: "5th Friday, Fire Damp Killed 22 at 4 o'clock in ye M."[1]

At other times men, boys and horses, and even women and girls, were killed in explosions, trapped by falls of the roof or drowned by inrush of water. In 1837 the sea broke into three of the Workington collieries, causing great loss of life, and in recent times the danger has not gone altogether. In 1910 one hundred and thirty-six lives were lost in an explosion at Whitehaven, and, in 1947, one hundred and four at William Pit in the same town.

Coal is not found in veins or pipes but in seams, like layers of jam in a sandwich cake, varying in thickness from an inch to ten feet or more, each seam representing a period of geological deposition. A seam may stretch over a large area, and can be met with and recognised wherever a shaft is sunk. The same seams are worked at many different collieries, and have been given attractive names like Main Band, Bannock Band, Lickbank, Cannel Band, Crow Coal and Ten-Quarters. The seams do not lie flat but bend and buckle like an old gramophone record, so that at times they

[1] In the pay-bill for Corpsill Pit, quoted from *The Archæology of West Cumberland Coal Trade*, by Isaac Fletcher, *Transactions of Cumberland and Westmorland Archæological Society*.

are close to the surface and at times deep down. The miner
divides the coalfield into three sections—the area in which
the coal measures are exposed or covered only by boulder
clay; the area of under-sea coal; and the area, to the north
and south, where the coal dips under the Permian sandstone
of St. Bees and the Cumberland Plain. But to those who view
the coalfield from above it seems to fall into three different
sections, according to the character of the country and the
towns. First, and by far the most important, the colliery
coast, stretching from Whitehaven through Parton and
Harrington to Workington, and on again through Flimby
to Maryport, overlapping some way inland; secondly, the
area of scattered colliery villages, mostly fairly high above
sea level, bordering the iron-ore country, including Moor
Row, Cleator Moor, Kekle, Moresby, Pica, Lowca and
Arlecdon; and thirdly the narrow whip of coal which curls
north-east of Maryport, through Dearham, Bulgill and
Aspatria almost to Wigton.

Let us look first at the inland coalfield around the banks
of the River Kekle. Those who know only the coalfields of
Durham and South Yorkshire must forget about them, for
here is no landscape blighted and blackened to a heap of
ashes. It belongs, really, to the skirts of the fells. As you
mount the hill from Whitehaven, above Hensingham, you
come out on a high table-land looking east to Ennerdale,
west to the sea, and farther ahead to Scotland. The land is
farmed but it has the look of moorland. Plovers settle in the
ploughed fields, and in the meadows there are patches of
swamp and rushes. It is bare, open, lifted towards the sky,
with scarcely a town to be seen except in the dip towards the
coast. Out of this landscape rises the pit-heap of a colliery,
black, double-peaked, looking at a distance like the mountains of the Isle of Man. It grows bigger as you approach it,
a great Coolin of cinder, jutting out of the fields without
warning. The grass and hedges have the soiled look which
you always find near collieries, but they are still moorland;
the curlews have not left them. You pass on to the village of
Moresby Parks, looking down the cliffs to the Solway. Its
houses are small and sullen, brooding inward, dark and
neurotic. The stone is sandstone, and when the sun breathes

on it there are geranium colours under the grime. Below, the coal haze is heavy over the coast, blurred and purple. In the clefts of the cliff the sun lies like a gilt lacquer on the black sea. You follow on, curving inland, losing sight of the coast now in the hollows of the road. You climb the ridge and come suddenly to Pica, an incredible village. The sour, open moor is all round it, but the houses are shunted together like trains, jammed close as if the slums pressed in on every side. This is where the nineteenth-century industrialists stalled their workmen. The twentieth century had hardly been able to mount the hill to Pica, and sanitation, there, belongs to another society; yet the women look happy enough at the doors, and the children red-faced and energetic, for there is money now at Pica, as at all the West Cumberland towns, and the wide moor stretches round them. You pass through the village, turn the corner by the little sandstone quarry, down a hill, and soon you are in a hamlet, cosy as a teapot-cover, with chestnut trees and young larches, and strawberry plants spreading wild over the garden hedge. Here the collieries are forgotten, but when you come out into the open again, there is Pica, stranded on the top of the hill, ugly, and soon to be unwanted, but not without courage.

The colliery coast contains scenery more completely ravaged by industry than any other in Cumberland, and also more dramatic. You get a splendid view of it from Kells, the hill above Whitehaven. Looking north beyond the harbour, you see the cliffs looping in and out in a link of small bays and promontories as far as Workington. One great colliery stands on the cliff top, the screes of coal sliding almost over the edge. The railway line runs on an embankment at the foot of the cliffs; there is no road, but you can go along the shore at low tide or by a path through William Pit. The cliffs are of purple sandstone, dark with coal-dust, and with patches of grass and gorse and primroses among them, with here and there buttresses of brick so that landslides will not block the line. The shore below is a geological rubbish heap —great fragments of sandstone, battered from the cliffs, flung everywhere about, and savage seaweed and the black crumbs of coal and cinder. In the time of depression when hills of coal stood unsold beside the pits, the miners and

Furnace and Fell (Black Combe from Borwick Rails)
Across the Duddon Estuary to Low Furness

their wives would wander up and down the shore, filling buckets and sacks with drift-coal for their fires. Yet in sunshine the sea can be blue, the sea breeze blows the smoke back from the sky, and the hills of Scotland float along the horizon anchored to Criffel.

But often the sky does not seem to matter, and we are in an underworld landscape of Miltonic horror. There are magnificent shapes and gestures, fine swinging chords of rock, but it is all dark and damned. There are old coke-ovens grown over with weeds, columns of slag left stacked in the sea like strange Hebridean rocks, old run-ways and mineral railways jutting out into the air like the prongs of broken forks. At Harrington a slag-bank makes a huge grey headland on which, during the war, Home Guards had a lookout reached by steps cut in the slag. Then there are the old buildings of pits and workings—enormous sandstone halls, now roofless and windowless, shells that fire might have left or time stripped and riddled. They stand like ruined abbeys in the scoops that run down through the cliffs. Beside these are the miners' houses, many of them empty also, with whole blocks crumbled in on themselves, a heap of plaster and sandstone rubble at the doors of the other streets. Here the black blood of the pits has congealed to scabs which cry out for pity. The houses crouch against the cliff; the rocks hang over them like a thundercloud; the coal dust is their only air. Yet in the evenings the men turn their backs on the cliffs, and walk on to the shore in their shirt-sleeves, and sit among clumps of yellow bird's-foot trefoil and pink stork's-bill. The little children paddle in the pools, wiping the coal-dust off their ankles as they dry their feet, and the boys play cricket on the sandy pitch between the railway line and the slag.

Workington offers the usual steelworks and blast furnaces, but beyond the town the landscape changes. First there are the flats at the north of Wordsworth's Derwent, where it seems that all the pits and middens of the district have been tipped on the land. Then, on the way to Flimby, the cliffs drop away, and there is a dune coast, with shingle half of coal, and conical tips, sometimes smoking like volcanoes, each with its small funicular to carry tubs to the summit.

Maryport Harbour
Holborn Hill, South Cumberland

Already, however, we are returning to rural Cumberland. The woods begin to close in. Farther north, around Brayton, there is heath, remnant of the old forest, with little clumps of birches where the trees grow so close that the trunks stand up tall and bare as a bunch of sticks, with brushes of leaves at the top. It is sandstone country, rich in vegetation, and the only strange sight is that of the Ellen, flowing black under the bridges towards Maryport.[1] Suddenly you see the miners, black as niggers, walking home through the bracken, and between Bulgill and Dearham Bridge you come across the colliery, hidden like a gipsy encampment in the wood. The black rubble heaps slope into the red soil, the pithead gear stands up among the tree-trunks, and the heavy leaves smother the wagons. Farther inland, in the Workington district, a colliery appears just as unexpectedly at Camerton, on the lower Derwent. Here, out of a green and silvery landscape, the pitheaps jerk up from the riverside. The river itself tries to sneak past, creeping and twisting like a whipped sheep-dog, and a little church stands in the peninsula which it makes. The gravestones are small and dejected, almost islanded in the water, and overshadowed by the ink-blue cliffs on the other side of the stream.

[1] Formerly called Ellenborough.

CHAPTER XII

THE MINING TOWNS

THE industrial area of West Cumberland and Furness has three larger towns, all on the coast: Whitehaven, Workington, and Barrow-in-Furness. Whitehaven and Workington are both primarily colliery towns, though Workington has important steel and iron works. Barrow, too, has steelworks, but it depends mostly on shipbuilding, so that it is less local and more like the general run of industrial towns. It has come into being almost entirely within the last hundred years and its buildings are typical of the nineteenth century, with a town hall of Balmoral Gothic and many side streets with bow-windows and apron gardens. Yet Barrow must be one of the cleanest towns in the North. It is on a peninsula between Morecambe Bay and the Duddon Estuary, so that the sea is round it on three sides, and, indeed, part of the town has spread over to Walney Island, where it is round it on all sides. In the Channel between the island and the mainland are the docks, so that the sea licks its tongue almost to the back steps of the town hall. Yet, because it is not a port, there is little flavour of the sea in the town itself, and its broad streets remind you more of a Midland city, combining manufacture with marketing. Especially is this so of the fine Abbey Road, which leads from nearly Dalton to the centre of the town, with trees at the edge of the pavement, and with schools, cricket-grounds and parks at the side. All this helps to detach Barrow from the country behind, and it is probably better considered with the rest of Lancashire. It is even cosmopolitan with its foreign sailors and submarine crews. But the newer suburbs, on the hills outside the town, look across the Duddon to Black Combe, or up Morecambe Bay to the Westmorland fells, and the old allegiance is not entirely forgotten.

Workington is also largely a nineteenth-century town, though there are older streets if you know where to look for them. The fells are a long way off and the town lies among the marshy flats at the mouth of the Derwent, which runs black as rotting seaweed into the black shore. The streets are busy with buses and the brisk, noisy, gritty life of a colliery, and there is even a clamorous pit dialect, harsh and croaky, but full of the little turns and appoggiaturas which express the irony and the very resignation of those to whom the world is turned outside-in for half of their waking life. But Workington can never forget that it belongs to Cumberland. For one thing its feet are spliced in the rock; for another, it looks across the Solway. You are aware as soon as you come out of the station of that great trowel of sea and of Scotland, quite near now, no longer just an horizon but a chain of hills, individual and recognisable. Centuries of history flow there with the tides.

Whitehaven is smaller than Workington, but it is un-questionably the capital of industrial Cumberland. Few mining towns have a more exciting history; none have greater character. It lies in a creek, with the rocks of St. Bees Head and Tomlin to the south, and purple sandstone cliffs to the north. Inland are three hills: Hensingham in the centre, and Kells and Bransby joining on to the cliffs, the one south and the other north, and on these three hills the suburbs have developed. Hensingham is the old late nine-teenth-century suburb, the home of retired merchants and mine managers. Here the houses have gardens, and there are even trees, birches black as laurels with coal-dust. There are turrets and pinnacles and spikes, and all the tastelessness of Victorian villas, which, combined, have a queer, almost tart charm, especially when the mists (half coal and half fog) steam among the trees and chimneys, and the sun is not seen but the sky is opalescent above the sea. Kells and Bransty are the modern suburbs, council houses, many of them, box-like and in rows, one above the other against the slope. Taken one by one they are ugly as good intentions, but together, at night, their lights lit, one beside and one above the other, they turn the whole hillside into a distant sky-scraper, every window shining, a dragon of a hundred burning eyes.

The old town lies round the creek at the foot of the three hills. Although there is little room for it to spread, there is a spaciousness in its lay-out, streets running in broad parallels to the sea-front and the docks. Along the wide main street, in the best site in the town, once stood the church of St. Nicholas, not much bigger than a meeting-house, but, to judge from its pictures, a neat and sober building. When this was too small, it was pulled down, and in its place a huge Gothic invention was set up of red sandstone, towering like a nightmare above the quiet gravestones and slabs. As a Victorian church it is unexceptional, but in this town it is the wrong style, the wrong stone, the wrong colour. The Congregational chapel, farther up the same Lowther Street, shows how the Gothic can be used in such a town. It is small, but as spiky as a flowering chestnut tree, and seen at night, in the lamplight, smoke trailing like pennons from its turrets, it has that combination of parody and poetry, of sincerity and sentimentalism which makes John Betjeman's verse so attractive. But on the whole the town wears the eighteenth-century clothes in which it first made its fortune. Not the era of Chippendale and Nash, however, but that of growing trades and empire. There are some large and handsome houses of the period in Irish Street, and one, which is now the Council Offices, in Duke Street, and there are also alleys opening off the main streets into dark, cramped courts which must have swarmed with children and disease at the time of the industrial revolution. Mostly the houses are neither elegant nor squalid, but sturdy and downright, solid as oaks and with walls nearly as thick, ready to stand up to the pneumatic-drill of modern heavy traffic.

It is by the harbour that this plain architecture takes on a beauty which is partly nostalgic. Whitehaven was once an important ship-building centre, and there are shipping offices and chandlers' shops, rope-makers and tallow-merchants, ship's grocers and pubs. Most of these are empty now, eyeless and hollow, but not decrepit. They are of red sandstone, the whitewash still on the stone, some blotched like lepers with stucco and damp; but they have the shape and grammar of simple statements in the right words— doorways, square windows, shutters, chimneys and roofs all related to each other quite naturally, almost unconsciously.

There is no river mouth at Whitehaven, and the shipping has to rely entirely on the tides. For this some fifty acres have been enclosed by piers, and a dredger is continually at work. The two great outer piers hug the harbour like lobster's claws, and inside are smaller piers dividing the water-space into docks and wharves. The piers themselves are quite unexpectedly beautiful—great angular banks of stone, with neither wall nor handrail to prevent the drunks from walking into the water or the mud. The west pier, the outer barrier of the harbour, has a raised parapet for walkers, and at its end, by the lighthouse, it disposes itself in steps and angles and blocks of masonry, as formal as the steps at the entrance to a Wren church. At this point, held out on the bent prong of the pier, you are aware that it is indeed the sea which is beside you. At high tides especially it is no longer a trickle of mud and coal-dust, but the true sea, the Solway, the Irish Sea, the Atlantic. Below you, and for miles farther out, men are digging for coal, but here there is nothing but salt water between you and the Isle of Man. You look back on the town, its roof of smoke lifted between the three hills, the colliery cliffs tacking north in black clefts and scoops and scallops. The chimneys of pit and factory at shore level do not reach as high as the cliffs, but in places terraces of sandstone cottages rise still to the moors above the town. St. James's on the hill is conspicuous, its tower, above the blocks of roofs, looking surprisingly graceful yet not incongruous. The tall buildings of the flour mill on the dockside are, from this distance, almost graceful, and against the steep hill above the castle there is a grey-green fume of trees. It is the cliffs which most hurt the eyes—the scarred sand and sandstone, scabbed with coal and blood: yet they are not without grandeur. Perhaps night spreads like smoke, and the lighthouse shines out, and the sunset stretches from St. Bees Head to Scotland. The sea slaps wet hands against the pier, the seaweed smells, the gulls wheeze and bark, and here for a moment or two you can forget the dirt and the fight of generations.

The Smaller Towns

In the larger towns, as is to be expected, there is growing up a way of life that has much in common with that of all industrial towns. There are the slums, the semi-detached villas, huge picture-houses and dance-halls, multiple shops, advertisements; for the suburban woman there is morning coffee and for the worker's wife fish-and-chip suppers—the cuticle of twentieth-century civilisation is growing up the nail. But the smaller towns are still close to the country, and the old traditions persist, however changed they may seem.

The colliery villages are mostly just a few streets grouped round a pit. They scarcely have the organisation of a town, but live more as outposts of Workington or Whitehaven. As the smaller pits close down and the industry becomes concentrated in the two larger towns, these villages are growing into grim dormitories, very different from those of outer London. When new houses are built the people will no doubt desert many of the smaller places, which will be left in ruins on the hillsides.

Flimby, north of Workington, has a rather different character because it is on a flat dune coast very like that of Allonby farther up the Solway. At intervals there are conical pit-heaps, like Coolins of coal, and cinders are dropped by the tide, but the village has a surprisingly clean and sea-washed look. The cattle roam on the shore to which they have access by the astonishing cattle-creeps, low tunnels made under the railway, where the couples have to do their courting bent like old crones. One seeming cattle-creep is, in fact, a culvert, a walled-in stream, and when little dogs wander along they have to be rescued at manholes high up in the village.

Still farther north, at Maryport, is a town which has probably suffered the greatest depression of any in West Cumberland. Looking down the steps which descend the steep cliff above the harbour, you see perhaps the saddest houses in the county—streets jammed against each other like boxes in the narrow strip between the sea and the cliff. Yet behind you is the square, bare and wide and dignified, very reminiscent of the Scottish Lowlands, say Annan or Ecclefeckan; and nearby are the church and houses of rich red sandstone, giving the town a much more prosperous look than could possibly be expected from the houses by the harbour. In the difficult years much good work was done at Maryport by the local Educational Settlement, and the town may now look forward to better times with the establishment of several new industries. Much needed as they were, however, coal is likely to remain of primary importance on this coast.

But in the case of the iron-ore towns, we are dealing with an industry which is slowly exhausting itself. It is true that the iron mining takes place now mostly in the Egremont and Millom districts, but there is no development, no gathering in of the population from the outer villages. Instead, therefore, of concentration as in the coal trade, we have a number of small towns which (so far as the iron trade goes) are already derelict, and a lesser number where the trade still exists but has been dwindling for years. Not even the war has made much difference to the production of iron-ore in Cumberland, and in Furness no mine has been re-opened. No doubt there is much ore still in the old mines, but if it is not thought worth the getting during the war, it is not likely to be profitable at any other time. The Furness towns had already attached themselves as satellites to Barrow, and I will consider later in the chapter how the rest are facing the new situation. What we must remember is that these towns have been declining for three or four decades. There has been, till recently, next to no building, nor any new industries. They have clung desperately to the shrinking heaps of ore; houses, shops and halls have stood stagnant or rotted to the ground; and children have been born, brought up and schooled, with few hopes beyond that of the dole, the back-street and the old slag-heap. In the fantastic and accidental prosperity of war it is easy to forget all this, but we must never forget it. Yet, for a moment, let us try to dissociate the towns themselves from the generations of hardship and anxiety which they have brought forth.

You expect nineteenth-century industrial towns to be ugly, and these of course *are* ugly. But the ugliness is only in detail; it does not soak into the stones and saturate them, as it does in many larger towns. Here there are no acres of dreary streets, nor a tent of smoke stretched over miles of land. The old working-class streets are squat and drab, but usually they are not long. Often there is only a row on one side and the light gets in at the other. They were built in small blocks as trade grew and new workers needed to be housed, so there is frequent change of pattern, a variety of ugliness, captivating at times in the way gargoyles are. It is not ordinary for a village in Cumberland to be built like Cleator, almost entirely in one long street, with dark sand-stone houses peering at you like gossips on either side. The first houses built for the workmen were small and dark, but they were usually solid. You can't knock a nail through nine inches of slate or sandstone. They are gloomy, stuffy and depressing, but except where there is heavy traffic they have rarely fallen down, and, indeed, seem much more able to endure wear and tear than the new council houses to which many of their former inhabitants have moved. In the towns which suffered most during the depression, towns which relied entirely on mines and blast furnaces, there is much poor property, houses and shops. Shops in particular show the economic health of the town like eyes and mouths. Where shops are empty, or many of them struggle on with dirty stocks, peeling paint-work and broken windows stuffed up with cardboard—then indeed the town is in a poor way, and there are many such graveyards of business in the Cumberland towns.

Often a little part of a town withers for reasons that could not be foreseen. Let me write of the town I know best. When the iron-ore was discovered near the shore, the town natur-ally began to spring up round the old village a mile or so in-land. The main street developed. Shops were built and a post office opened. This was in the first few years. Then came the railway. The station was built quite near the village, but now the town began to grow, and many new houses were built, nearer the mines and the new blast furnaces. The village became less important, but a level-crossing led from the old main street directly to the new town and the new business centre. The railway company was under obligation to build a bridge, so the new town was planned (so far as it was planned at all) to fit itself to this. A broad street of better houses led from the crossing to a green, round which were set an hotel and the first larger shops. This became the business centre; shops, public-houses, chapels, all grew up in this district. Then the railway built the bridge, but they built it not at the expected point, but at the other end of the station, and so threw the whole town out of step. The level-crossing was closed and the streets which opened to it were left like toy soldiers marching into a blank wall. A new square was made at the place to which the bridge led, and the market hall, banks, library and the church were all built nearby. The streets near the old green began to decay. Business crept away from them. Shops failed, were closed down, and new ones were opened around the square and in residential streets. One such 1880 brick terrace, with little plots of land in front, hemmed by low walls with sandstone toppings, is now turned entirely into shops, except for a single house. That one house, with its small bay-window, remains to tell of the time when the town was growing like a nine-weeks-old puppy, and the pebble path still surrounds a patch of soil, no bigger than a table-top, where, in the last dusty-bright years of Victoria, fuchsias, lily-of-the-valley and hydrangeas grew.

So, as the towns prospered, and clerking and trading classes grew in importance, better houses were built: houses of three storeys, faced with khaki sandstone; houses with little front gardens and long back-yards. There were even roads with sycamore trees at the edge of the pavement and seats here and there, and the bank manager grew laburnums in his garden, and the trees in the graveyard and around the railway station became tall enough for the rooks to nest there. The newness was wearing off; the town was finding itself. Now it became clear that each town had its own character, even its own peculiar feature that is at once evident to the visitor. Sometimes this feature belonged to the past, as Egremont's old castle lifted above the town like the Ark in the wilderness. Or perhaps merely to the town's environment, like the lumpy fells menacing Rowrah and Arlecdon, and the sad, damp sands at the back-door of Askam. More often it belonged to happily haphazard planning, like Cleator Moor's totally unexpected square, with the trees and the steps where the children play, or the tower of Millom's market hall, blue and jolly as a pewter pepper-pot, with its four clock faces giving you a choice of times, so that if you miss your train by one you will be too early for the next by another.

In all these towns you are continually aware of the country round the corner or across the other side of the road. The houses are not huddled together in a knot, they are splayed out like the limbs of a starfish. Sometimes the railway cuts them in two, and traffic drips from one half to the other over the railway bridge as through the waist of an hour-glass. Then, along the railway sidings, grasses and air and light blow into the town, and again in the gaps between the outlying streets. Scarcely any spot is more than two hundred yards from open fields or waste land, and most places are very much less. Maryport, Harrington, Parton and St. Bees have the sea beside them, sharing the same ocean as Florida and Iceland. At Askam, in Furness, the sand blows along the back streets, and lady's bedstraw and bird's-foot trefoil grow at the doorstep. The sand silts up the old slag-banks, and children run with bare feet out of the back doors on to the dunes. At Haverigg, in South Cumberland, which looks like a fishing village, the mining company built rows of concrete houses on three sides of a huge square, rather gaunt but not without some feeling for grouping. On the fourth side the square slopes down an embankment, slated like a roof, to the sea. Dogs chase the gulls in the water, and girls loll in bathing suits on the rocks. Two miles away, at Millom, you forget about the sea. This is surely an inland town with Black Combe above it and the Eskdale fells looking down into its streets. Yet the marshes curve round the estuary, and the sea-birds fly over, and at high tide the sea comes in within a few hundred yards of the market hall.

Everywhere, gardens, parks, playing fields and waste ground creep up behind the backs of the streets and peep through their legs. Even at Whitehaven the cricket field and the school sports field help the Pow Beck to drive a green wedge into the centre of the town. There are also allotments, the gardening so typical of the north. Allotments are not show gardens; they are entirely practical, one of the most intensive forms of agriculture. Yet a well-cared-for allotment, especially in spring, is an enchanting place—the little greenhouses painted white, and here and there a toolshed shining like coal in its new coat of tar. It is then you see the soil, almost black, rigged up for potatoes, or dug and raked for greens. Then the currant bushes are brightest, the shoots of the peas and beans begin to swamble up bamboo poles or brushwood, the rhubarb begins to unfold above the grain-and-varnish heaps of manure. And in the late summer evenings, when the time of digging is past, the gardeners walk along the paths between their plots, smoking pipes to kill the green-fly, and pick a basketful of lettuce and runner beans. There is a tangle and smother of fruitfulness then, and there are weeds in the less-tended plots and some of the cabbages have gone to seed. The first marigolds are out and will go on glowing till December, and there are the dark, bitter colours of dahlias, and clumps of green which will soon have the slow coke-smoulder of Michaelmas daisies. Nearby, perhaps, there is a chicken run, where the fowls have scratched the soil bare, and now walk up and down behind wire-netting, pecking at cabbage-stumps or groundsel.

Such are the allotments in a prosperous time, but they had their value too in the time of slump, even when the men had scarcely the strength or the heart to dig, and when vegetables were as often stolen as gathered by those who grew them. There was no white paint on the greenhouses then; the little huts were broken down and the fences rusty. Lots of the plots were untilled, and grew weeds to spread to others, for not all men can fight the apathy of months of idleness. But in the rest the men worked on—digging for self-confidence and self-respect as much as for carrots and potatoes.

The Return of the Celts

During the nineteenth century these Cumberland and Furness towns were almost as remote from the rest of the country as were the dales. They developed, therefore, a self-reliance and even self-sufficiency which is quite remarkable. They learned to produce their own entertainments, to encourage their own talent, and to incubate a passionate, ingrown society which hid and deposited its own riches like ore in veins of rock.

Oddly enough, the main stimulus came not from inside, but from outside. When the mines developed the Celts returned to Cumbria—from Ireland, from Wales and from Cornwall.

The men of Cornwall and of Devon were miners already. They left the dwindling tin mines to seek their fortune in the new iron trade, and at once they began to make their way. Soon they were the foremen, the underground captains, the head joiners and store managers. They had much say in the taking on of new hands and they became influential and respected people in their towns. Young lads, wanting to get a job at the mines, would make a point of being seen at chapel for a few weeks, for the chapel became the centre of the new dominant class—or, rather, many chapels, as the Cornishmen were rigid, sectarian and divided among themselves, but always enthusiastic and fundamentalist. The chapel made a deep impression on the growing towns, influencing the lives of Anglicans as well as Methodists. Sunday was in the grasp of the local preacher; pubs, cards, and all entertainments outside of the Sunday-school were given to the devil. A temperance ground landlord could put a bar against licensed houses over half a town—and the bar is in force today. The Irish, too, brought their distinctive Roman Catholic culture, but this was more segregated, being treated often with suspicion and even fear, so that it made less mark outside its own communion.

The Methodist chapels were in many ways the true temples of nineteenth-century industrialism, belonging much more to the towns than did the older Anglican churches. Because their congregations were not, at that time, prosperous, they are plain and reserved, but they carry on the eighteenth-century style, and have often charming interiors with galleries, hanging gas-brackets and painted texts on the walls. Unlike the Anglican churches, which are sometimes rather aloof from the towns they serve, the nonconformist chapels are to be found among the older and poorer streets. They have iron rails round them, Sunday-schools built separately, with gravel yards where poplars grow, and moss-green foundation stones, laid in the 1880's by wives of town councillors. Children climb over the railings at night and play among the alleys and outhouses; the glass in the round-headed windows reflects the street lamps, and the mist fumes among the poplars and the spouts.

Sunday-schools became important social instruments,

shaping children in a way from which they never escaped however much they might rebel. Every child in the town attended one Sunday-school or another—and there was a competitive spirit, which showed itself at the anniversaries and school treats. On the Sunday the chapels would be packed, floor and gallery, while the children sang special hymns and a choral march, and the brighter scholars said recitations or sang solos. In the afternoon the Infants, the "Primary," had their own matinée—crowds of tiny children sitting on chairs on a platform built above the communion rails. One after another they would totter to the front, say their little piece (quite inaudible to anyone not in the front pews), and then sit frozen out of fidgeting by sheer fright, or else fall asleep and rock on their chairs as perilously as the baby in the tree-tops. The next day, or perhaps on the Wednesday, came the procession. Children, teachers and friends would gather in the school yard—youths in blue serge suits, little girls in satin dresses that crinkled and shone like tinfoil. There would be a band—Sons of Temperance out to earn enough for a night's booze—and off they would go, two or three hundred yards long, the young men carrying the great picture banner of the Good Shepherd, and the smaller children, each with a flag, or a pole bearing a text, "God is Love," or "Suffer little children," or the one which made me shiver like the touch of a ghost, "Remember now thy Creator in the days of thy youth." The people would gather at the doors of the grey streets, while the wind flapped the banners, making the silk sheep gambol round their Shepherd, and the sun skimmed along the cornets and trombones of the band. Half-way round, the tiny children—who by now had lost formation and were being shooed along like hens—were left behind to wait, clutching their mugs and cups, while the others marched round the outskirts and then came back to sing hymns in the market square. I knew of one small village which held its Sunday-school anniversary on Good Friday, with a brave defiance of such Catholic practice as the observance of Holy Week. Methodists from the towns would walk there or go by wagonette, and, later, by bus, would attend the service, and eat their sandwiches in the field nearby. Pace eggs could not be rolled till Easter

Monday, but you could get pots of hot water or cups of tea, and more recently there was usually an ice-cream cart. The procession dwindled as the Sunday-schools decayed in influence, till now few of the chapels have enough scholars to want to display them to the town. With the Sunday-school parades have gone the club walks, "Hearts of Oak," the Buffs and the Blues, which were a regular feature of Whit-Mondays.

Music

Until the 1940's church and chapel were by far the most powerful social units in the town, and each sent a pattern of complicated relationships, like roots of a tree, through all classes. The family adhered to its own sect long after its members had ceased to attend services, and connections formed in childhood and adolescence persisted with great tenacity.

It was around church and chapel that music and drama first developed. Sunday Evening Concerts, Pleasant Sunday Afternoons, Faith Teas with concerts, Band of Hope meetings, tableaux, missionary plays, pageants, revealed an immense amount of native talent. This led to more ambitious efforts—*Messiah* at Christmas, Stainer's *Crucifixion* at Easter, *Elijah* at any time, and then, at the turn of the century, to amateur operatic societies performing Gilbert and Sullivan and Edward German, and to choral societies, dramatic societies and the musical festivals.

The local concerts shone like naphtha lamps on these dark outskirts of culture—and still do, though by now the uniform stucco of cinema and radio is being slapped over the local slate. In their lowest form they might be just penny lantern lectures in the Salvation Army Fortress, run for the elementary school-boys who were so rough that the more respectable lads would not be seen inside with them and had to be satisfied with climbing the wall and looking through a hole in the window. At their highest, they might be 2s. or 2s. 6d. concerts with a carpet on the stage, a pot of ferns on a table, the local landowner as chairman, and refreshments served at the interval by ladies of the congregation. In between were many variations—parochial teas in the Anglican churches; Harvest Festival concerts followed by a sale of fruit and vegetables in the Nonconformist Sunday-schools; sing-songs in the Working Men's Clubs; tatie-pie suppers for a champion cricket or billiard team. There have been men who devoted a life's leisure to the entertainment of their fellow-townsfolk at these concerts, singing in rooms not much bigger than huts, and in Sunday-schools with trestle-board stages and sliding green curtains worked by strings which generally got stuck half-way through the concert. They were often men and women of great talent with fine voices, quite untrained but used instinctively in the right way. They kept mostly to a handful of old favourites, *Yeomen of England*, *The Floral Dance* (particularly popular with the many Cornish people), and duets like *Watchman, What of the Night?* and *Madam, Will You Walk?* They would hurry home from work, perhaps after eight hours down the pit, have a quick wash and a bit of supper, change into their Sunday clothes and go, through a roaring wet night, to a half-empty concert in a mission room, where half the notes on the piano were stuck because of the damp.

It was not to be expected that the musical tastes of these audiences were very advanced. They were confined mostly to popular, tuneful, sentimental or dramatic ballads. Among the choral societies there was naturally a higher degree of appreciation—Handel is not a bad standard to start from— but here again there was a complete lack of response to music which was not associated with words. Pianists were in demand almost entirely as accompanists, and the little orchestras, apart from playing waltzes and tea-time music, existed for operatic and choral concerts. It was not unusual to find an old student or conductor with a comprehensive knowledge of the whole range of choral music who had never even heard a symphony orchestra.

Nevertheless, the general standard of performance was quite surprisingly high, and for this the musical festivals were largely responsible. In our area we have annual festivals at Carlisle, Workington, Cockermouth, Millom and Kendal; with other, more famous meetings at such places as More-cambe, Blackpool, Lytham and Newcastle, fairly accessible to the Cumberland and Westmorland singers.

246

Sand Dunes and marram grass, Haverigg

It is, of course, the competition which makes these festivals so popular. There are not the large entries as at Blackpool and Morecambe, but the audiences will cheerfully sit through a dozen renderings of the same song, backing and applauding the local favourites, and waiting anxiously for the adjudicator to come on the platform. His remarks are always heard with interest, for most of the adjudicators enter into the spirit of the meeting and make themselves partly into entertainers—in fact, I think they enjoy the variety and eagerness of the small festivals as a change from the monotony of a hundred entries in one class. But it is the marks for which the audience is really waiting. When the adjudicator gathers together his papers, there is a buzz and a groping for programmes and pencils. It is this competitive spirit which helps to keep choirs together and to make them practise. Of course, it sometimes deflects the real aim and, as it were, takes the ear off the music. There are indignant mothers who ask why their children only got 83 marks when another adjudicator had given them 85 for the same piece. There are angry competitors who come round and threaten to knock the adjudicator's head off. Such happenings luckily are rare. The choirs, in particular, take the verdict as a team takes that of a referee, and no amount of "slating" will spoil their enjoyment of a glass of beer or a pennorth of chips before they catch the last train or bus—train being preferred, as when they come by bus half the singers are sick.

Let there be no doubt about the standard of performance, however: it is usually high. As for the soloists, it may be remembered that only a few years ago Miss Kathleen Ferrier, now one of the best-known contraltos in England, was a regular and very popular competitor at the small musical festivals of the North-West.

Sport

The isolation which gave rise to this development of local talent resulted also in sport of great virility. Some of the older gambling sports of the miners persisted for quite a while—whippet racing, quoits, brass pitching—till they were superseded by football pools and greyhound or dirt-track racing. Cock-fighting also exists, driven now into old barns,

Millom Ironworks

distant combes in the fells and desolate mosses by the coast. Occasionally, the police swoop on a larger gathering of cock-fighters (as on Foulshaw Moss by Morecambe Bay not so long ago), and then many arrests are made. The true cock-fighters are often old miners, breeding their birds secretly in back gardens and allotments, holding to their sport as the persecuted hold to their religious faith. The rest of the followers are often gentry, gentlemen farmers, magistrates and the like, who feel that the sport contains something of a dying tradition, or who enjoy dodging the law. Certainly the stories you hear of cock-fights are rarely stories of the battles themselves, but of hide-and-seek with the police: men who escape by the back window when the police are at the front; dead birds hidden under straw, live ones carried off in sacks; the followers left to talk to the police, and explain how they had come to buy some bullocks or look at a tractor, while the cock-fighters make off behind the wall, to find shelter in the nearest wood, and then bag a lift in a car which will get them as quickly as possible out of the area.

The miners have a fondness for sport which involves the keeping of a bird or an animal—cock-fighting, whippet and greyhound racing, hound trailing, pigeon flying. During the war a Dalton pigeon owned by Mr. William Brockbank so distinguished itself that it was awarded the Dickin Medal—the Pigeon V.C. In 1942, it was released in a race at Christchurch, Hampshire, and was blown across to Holland where it fell, exhausted, into the hands of a Dutch patriot. The Dutchman took care of the bird, fed it and finally set it free, carrying a message of important military information. The bird returned to Dalton, where the owner found the message and passed it on to the Government.

These, however, are mostly sports for the individualist. More popular and of greater importance were the team games. Towards the end of the last century, when the towns were thriving and the populations growing, when there was still little communication with the rest of England, at any rate for the working classes, and when entertainment had to be made, not bought, there was fierce local rivalry in sport. A young man would give up every Saturday and bank holiday in summer to cricket, and spend the evenings of the rest of the week practising. Holidays, too, were sacrificed for a match, and often he would quarrel with his girl, who would be tired of so little attention.

The footballer lived nearly as exacting a life in winter, for he was expected to give up a good many evenings to physical training, and then, perhaps after working night shift on Friday, he had to catch the train and travel to a game which was as fierce as a heavy-weight boxing match. There were often considerable distances to travel, as in those days of the Northern Union (the game most popular in the small towns) the little Cumberland clubs were ready to meet and beat teams which are now famous in the Rugby League. There is a legendary tale which I had often heard of how the local team was drawn at home against a powerful Yorkshire club. They lost three-nil, but I was told the match should have been at least a draw, for a home player crossed over for a try half a minute before the end, but the referee wrongly ordered him back for a knock-on. That seemed to be the sort of story which may grow more convincing in the memories of fifty years, but last summer I was staying in a Westmorland village and met an old man who, when he heard where I came from, asked about the former footballers. Some of them were dead, but others I knew—men crippled with rheumatism or even half-blind who will nevertheless sit through a cricket match in North Pole weather. He then began to tell me about this very match.

"It should have been a draw," he said. "The referee made a mistake."

"That's what I've been told," I said. "Were you a spectator yourself?"

"No. I was the referee."

Professional Rugby football is now represented in the district by Barrow, Workington and Whitehaven. Barrow and Carlisle have teams in the third division of the Association League, and Workington, a junior team, fought its way into the later rounds of the English Cup some years ago.

Today it is probably cricket which most closely links the towns in sport, and here the framework is the North Lancashire League, which stretches from Carlisle to Morecambe and inland as far as Kendal. Other towns north of

Whitehaven have fine cricket clubs of long tradition, but they lie rather too far away to make frequent travel practicable for the clubs of Furness and South Cumberland, many of which are not wealthy, and whose players, moreover, are unable to leave work before Saturday midday. The North Lancashire League cannot claim the same standard of play to be found in the great leagues of central Lancashire and Yorkshire, nor do the clubs receive anything like the same support. Yet there is good cricket to be found in these matches, and of a fierce, tense type, playing always against weather and time, the spectators sitting round, eyes concentrated on the pitch like the rays of the sun through a burning-glass, every man with his watch in his hand. Let the opposing side try to waste time and a roar will come from the crowd like a wave breaking along the shore. Yet they appreciate the tactics of cricket; they do not clamour for runs all the time. A good stone-waller will get their tongues but he will also get their respect—especially if he's in the home team.

The one thing they will not bear with is the bad sportsman—the man who sulks on the field or disputes a decision. They themselves may call an umpire everything between him and Edinburgh, but the player himself must not argue. I remember an incident at a ground for which I have a particular affection. The field is near the sea, sandy and bumpy, with bits of barbed-wire and tin pushed in among the gorse to keep the sheep out, and a tidal river flowing past, with the smell of scurvy-grass blowing in on a west wind. You sit beneath the wall whitewashed for the sight-board, with the dark houses overlooking you, and away on the skyline are the fells. Here is the home of one of those clubs supported by a small group of hard-working enthusiasts, a club at which the more fashionable teams may look down their noses, but which yet is likely at any time to produce players who will overturn expectations and upset form. This was the club which one year produced a fast bowler of quite extraordinary merit, who knocked the pride out of many of the leading teams in the league. It was while he was playing that one of the visiting team was given out l.b.w. The batsman stood for a while looking at his feet, then

he stared around, obviously very reluctant to go. At last he
took a step or two away from the wicket, then turned and
faced the players again. The umpire signalled once more
that he was out, then put his hands behind his back, swung
round and walked away. The batsman stood where he was.
By now the crowd was beginning to growl, but not angrily,
just with the usual impatient chaff: "Play the game," "Get
yourself off," "Look in the paper on Monday and you'll see
whether you're out." He started to walk in a very surly
manner towards the pavilion, going slowly and slapping his
bat against his pads. There was a repressed buzz among the
spectators, each one turning to the other, discussing, justi-
fying: "'Course he was out. Stepped clean in front." The
batsman was more than half-way to the boundary, but he
stopped, turned again, raised his bat and began to argue
with a fielder. The crowd's patience broke and there was a
rumble of criticism right round the field. He marched on,
now defiant, his head up, chin angry, ready to fight if need
be. A group of young men and youths was near the pavilion
gate and he had to pass near. Suddenly he lost his temper,
put out his hand and pushed one of the lads out of his way.
The crowd did not realise at once what had happened. Some
of them gathered round, and a cry went up: "Put him in the
pool." The tide was out and there was not enough water to
do him any harm, though it would certainly have taken the
crease out of his trousers. By now, however, the rest of the
team had gathered round him, thrust him in the changing-
room and locked the door, and when eventually he came
away it was with the protection of a policeman. Such a hap-
pening may not be approved by Wisden, but it is one of my
most valued memories of cricket.

The Future of West Cumberland

The future of West Cumberland and Furness is no doubt
bound up with the economic life of the whole of England,
and about this I cannot pretend to speak. Whitehaven and
Workington depend on coal; Barrow depends on shipbuilding; and coal and shipbuilding depend on factors outside the area. But there is still the iron-ore trade, and though
it may continue for some time to react to world slump and

boom, this is only the reflex of a dying patient. Those who have lived through the 1920's and 1930's in the mining towns of Cumberland can guess what will be the course of this last illness if help is not brought from outside. In the large industrial cities hardship usually strikes in patches—there are places where it is scarcely felt, there are places where it can be forgotten, but in the small mining towns a terrible decay creeps over every street and house. In some towns, during the worst period of unemployment, eighty per cent. of the insurable population were on the dole. The other twenty per cent. were merely servants of the rest—shopkeepers, council workmen, teachers, policemen. Shops went bankrupt; windows were broken and not replaced; walls fell and were not rebuilt; houses became empty and stood with gaping skylights open to wind and rain, till the plaster peeled away like bark off a rotting tree. Rates fell off and town and county councils struggled against increasing costs and lessening income. Schools were dilapidated, often ill-equipped and unhealthy, and the children themselves were mostly underfed and stunted. Men stood at the street corners, not for weeks or months, but for years. They grew from young men to middle-aged, or from middle-aged to old. They lost their skill; some of them lost their strength. Above all, they felt that the civilisation to which they belonged no longer needed them; that they were redundant; that their towns, their industry, their part of the country was England's abandoned rubbish tip, the slag of a generation. Mines, indeed, were closed down then which have never been reopened, for during that time of stoppage the water broke into the levels, or the workings so decayed that the little ore that is left is not worth the trouble to put them in order again.

During the slump various measures were tried to make things easier. There were social clubs and training centres; there was some attempt to persuade the young to migrate to more prosperous districts; and there was the small-holding scheme. About the economic aspects of the scheme I cannot speak, but psychologically it was a grave error. The men may have enjoyed digging in their allotments and keeping pigs, but they felt they were being given only a hobby. Industry did not want them and tried to fob them off with a bit of harmless gardening. They had lost all thought of the land as a primary source of wealth and life; to them, agriculture was merely the odd-job man of industry. During the war prosperity came to the district, but it was even more obviously artificial than in most parts of England. The coal, steel and shipbuilding industries were working at full pressure, but there was not much difference in the iron-ore trade, and the men of the mining towns found work in munition and ordnance factories. After the war, however, most of these factories closed down and for a time unemployment began rapidly to increase, and it was clear that, if the district was not to decline to an even worse condition than that of the '20's and early '30's, either the population must be transported elsewhere (which would have been deplorable) or new industries must be established. Even before 1939 an attempt had been made by the Cumberland Development Council, under the leadership of Mr. J. J. Adams, to attract these new industries, but it was not until after the war that their work began to show large-scale results. By now many new factories have been opened—tanning, leather goods, clothing, footwear, chemicals and others. A large rayon factory had been promised for Sellafield, with water supply to be drawn from Ennerdale Lake, but this has been superseded by the plan for an atomic power plant. For the most part these factories have been built where labour was available—a plan which I hope will be followed in the future, or else we shall have new towns in the countryside and the old ones will be more derelict than ever.

At the time of writing unemployment has almost disappeared in West Cumberland, but, quite apart from the general uncertainty of English economics and world trade, this prosperity brings new problems. The social and occupational structure of the towns has been greatly changed, and a new governing class has grown up of people who are all strangers and mostly foreigners (many are Jewish refugees). Whether this class can be absorbed eventually into the local society (as were the German miners in the seventeenth century) remains to be seen. For my part I think that they can, but at present it must be admitted that few of them show very much awareness of the value of the local tradition, but remain an alien, unassimilated and apparently affluent minority, and as such they naturally arouse a certain suspicion and jealousy. Tolerance and understanding are necessary on both sides if we are to preserve the native culture of the mining towns.

Finally, one word which will probably be futile, so unintelligible will it be to our technological civilisation. Any honest industry is better than stagnation and decay, yet I do not want to see the people of Cumberland making all the mass-produced goods and gadgets which can just as well be made in the suburbs for which they are intended. The traditional industries of Cumberland have always had a clear relation to the land: slate, lead, coal, iron, from the rock; milk, mutton, wool, timber, from the soil; fish from the sea and the lakes. Can this not continue? There must be many industries for which these are the raw material. Let such be set up among us. It will help the miner, the labourer, the farmer, the clerk, the shopkeeper, the manager, the housewife, the school-boy to remember that in a world where many places are losing their individuality, even their names, Cumberland is still Cumberland and nowhere else. It will help them to remember, or to know without remembering, that they are the descendants of the Celts, the Angles, and above all the Norsemen; of the men who fought the Scots, the men who brought the Herdwick sheep, the men who dug the first mines; the men who hunted with John Peel, wrestled with William Litt, lied with Will Ritson, and drank with everyone; the men who were drowned fathoms below the shore at Whitehaven, or starved to death above it; the men who never did anything much but just happened to be there; to remember, in fact, that they are Cumbrians.

INDEX